SIMPLE & LIGHT

박노준 PATTERN 영어

심플하고 라이트하게 모든 문제를 패턴으로

기승전 노준하프

SEASON 2

이 책의 순서

문제편

해설편

하프모의고사
Season 2

문제편

01-25 회

제 01 회 하프 모의고사

해설편 p.107

제한 시간 15 분 | 소요 시간 분 | 점수 /10

PART Ⅰ 어법

01

다음 글의 밑줄 친 부분 중, 어법상 틀린 것은?

While studying the cosmetics section of a drugstore chain, we watched a woman in her sixties approach a wall rack, study it carefully and then kneel before it so she could find the one item she needed: concealer cream, which, due to its lack of glamour, was ① kept at the very bottom of the display. Similarly, in a department store we watched an overweight man trying to find his size of underwear at a large aisle display — and saw him stooping dangerously low ② to reach them, down near the floor. In both cases, logic should have dictated ③ that the displays be tailored to the shoppers who use them, not to the designers who made them. Move the concealer up, we advised, and put something aimed at younger shoppers down near the floor. Young shoppers will find their products ④ whatever they're stocked.

02

우리말을 영어로 잘못 옮긴 것은?

① 모든 정보는 거짓이었다.
→ All of the information was false.

② 토마스는 더 일찍 사과했어야 했다.
→ Thomas should have apologized earlier.

③ 우리가 도착했을 때 영화는 이미 시작했었다.
→ The movie had already started when we arrived.

④ 바깥 날씨가 추웠기 때문에 나는 차를 마시려 물을 끓였다.
→ Being cold outside, I boiled some water to have tea.

PART Ⅱ 어휘

03

다음 글의 빈칸에 들어갈 말로 가장 적절한 것은?

The inverse relationship between interest rates and inflations is one of the __________ principles of macroeconomics.

① derisive
② augmentative
③ fundamental
④ gregarious

04

밑줄 친 부분과 의미가 가장 가까운 것은?

The introduction of a stream engine needed an ample supply of coal.

① simple
② sufficient
③ proper
④ dissent

PART Ⅲ 생활영어

05

다음 중 두 사람의 대화가 어색한 것은?

① A : How did you do on the math exam?
B : I won't know for certain until the results are announced.

② A : I would like to order a diet coke.
B : I'm sorry. Would you like something else to drink instead?

③ A : Have you made any New Year's resolutions?
B : Christmas is by far my favorite holiday of the year.

④ A : Let's try the new Italian restaurant near the bookstore.
B : Great idea. I'll make reservations for 6:30.

PART Ⅳ 독해

06

다음 글의 빈칸에 들어갈 말로 가장 적절한 것은?

Humans have copied nature for thousands of years, with varying degrees of accuracy and understanding. Our early human ancestors borrowed solutions from the animals and plants they saw around them. Seals swimming below Arctic ice create and maintain holes through which they can surface to breathe; Inuit hunters mimicked the way polar bears lie in wait beside those breathing holes to catch a rich dinner. Polynesian outrigger canoes' design echoed that of floating seed pods. Aboriginal Australians even copied bird wings with their boomerangs. Certain shapes and tools were repeated around the world, created by people who were separated by vast geographical distances yet simultaneously immersed in and observing ________________ ________________.

*outrigger 아우트리거(카누의 뱃전 밖에 나온 안정용 부재)

**seed pot (콩 등의) 꼬투리

① nature's unpredictable changes
② nature's laws of free competition
③ their ancestors' traditional culture
④ nature's problem – solving strategies

07

다음 글의 ① ~ ④ 중에서 주어진 문장이 들어가기에 가장 적절한 곳은?

> When the public hears stories like these, reactions are varied.

Each year about 50,000 species of plants and animals disappear from the planet as a result of human activity. (①) Conservationists and environmental activists have been trying to elevate the priority given to the protection of the environment and its inhabitants for many years, but the public, politicians, and criminologists have largely ignored their efforts. (②) Various media outlets report stories of people tying themselves to trees in order to save spotted owls, or of large-scale construction projects that are halted because an endangered frog's habitat might be in jeopardy. (③) Some see these actions as moral victories while others see them as simply absurd. (④) As more prominent public figures become active in the fight against crimes involving nature, the problem of illegally trading endangered species will gain prominence in society.

08

다음 글의 빈칸 (A), (B)에 들어갈 말로 가장 적절한 것은?

Over the preschool period (roughly ages 3-5 years), friends come to occupy a more important place in children's social world. Spending any amount of time around preschool children quickly leads one to the conclusions that most preschoolers have friends and that their friends are highly valued. Friendship at this age typically centers around play. Preschoolers' expectations for friends are not as mature or complex as older children's. ____(A)____, they focus on enjoying common interests and activities together. Friends are people who are fun to play with and who like to play the same things; thus, both play and similarity are important for choosing friends in the first place and then spending time with them. ____(B)____, friendships provide preschool children someone with whom to "test out" various behaviors and emotions while at play.

	(A)		(B)
①	Rather	···	Last of all
②	Rather	···	As a result
③	Similarly	···	As a result
④	Similarly	···	On the contrary

09

주어진 글 다음에 이어질 글의 순서로 가장 적절한 것은?

It is important to recognize the nature of mathematics and the very radical abstraction that it involves. Galileo, Descartes, Huygens and Newton all produced formulae.

(A) But reason, in its purest form, is seen in logic and mathematics, and it was therefore natural to expect that the world would be, in principle, comprehensible in terms of 'laws of nature' which, with mathematical precision, would determine the movement of all things.

(B) In other words, they were seeking to create a mathematical and abstract way of summing up physical phenomena, using mathematics to express patterns seen in nature. That it should be possible for an abstract formula to correspond to nature was a fundamental assumption made by those involved in the emerging sciences.

(C) Beneath it lay the deeper assumption that the world is a predictable and ordered place. Escaping from the earlier era of crude superstition and magic, they saw themselves emerging into a world where reason and evidence would triumph.

① (B) – (A) – (C)
② (B) – (C) – (A)
③ (C) – (A) – (B)
④ (C) – (B) – (A)

10

Mortimer J. Adler에 관한 다음 글의 내용과 일치하지 <u>않는</u> 것은?

Mortimer J. Adler was an American philosopher, educator, editor, and supporter of adult and general education by study of the great writings of the Western world. While still in public school, Adler was taken on as a copyboy by the New York Sun, where he stayed for two years doing a variety of editorial work full-time. He then attended Columbia University, completed his coursework for a bachelor's degree, but did not receive a diploma because he had refused physical education (swimming). He stayed at Columbia to teach and earn a Ph.D. and then became professor of the philosophy of law at the University of Chicago. There, with Robert M. Hutchins, he became a supporter of the pursuit of liberal education through regular discussions based on reading great books. For his entire life, he remained active in what he called the great-books movement and in educational reform, and continued to lecture and write into his nineties.

① It supported adult education and general education.
② He was in charge of part-time editing for "New York Sun" for two years.
③ Columbia University rejected physical education.
④ He became a professor of law philosophy at the University of Chicago.

제 02 회 하프 모의고사

📖 해설편 p.110

제한 시간 15 분 | 소요 시간 분 | 점수 /10

PART Ⅰ 어법

01

(A), (B), (C)의 각 네모 안에서 어법에 맞는 표현으로 가장 적절한 것은?

Peer mediation programs are a popular example of a restorative program in schools. Peer mediators are usually nominated by peers or teachers because they are respected and trusted by their peers and have demonstrated leadership and communication skills. Students come to mediation voluntarily, and peer mediators guide them through a process (A) [that / in which] moves from blaming each other to developing and committing to solutions that are acceptable to all parties. Peer mediation programs have (B) [found / been found] to be effective in improving student attitudes toward conflict, increasing understanding of nonviolent problem-solving methods, and enhancing communication skills. They have also reduced the number of school suspensions for fighting and (C) [improving / improved] students' ability to manage conflicts.

	(A)		(B)		(C)
①	in which	···	been found	···	improving
②	in which	···	been found	···	improved
③	that	···	been found	···	improved
④	that	···	found	···	improving

02

우리말을 영어로 가장 잘 옮긴 것은?

① 나는 이 집으로 이사 온 지 3년이 되었다.
→ It was three years since I moved to this house.

② 우리는 해가 지기 전에 그 도시에 도착해야 한다.
→ We must arrive in the city before the sun will set.

③ 나는 그녀가 오늘 밤까지 그 일을 끝마칠지 궁금하다.
→ I wonder if she finishes the work by tonight.

④ 그는 실수하기는 했지만, 좋은 선생님으로 존경받을 수 있었다.
→ Although making a mistake, he could be respected as a good teacher.

PART Ⅱ 어휘

03

밑줄 친 부분과 의미가 가장 가까운 것은?

My grandmother is one of the most <u>charitable</u> people I know. She is always doing something kind.

① intense
② notorious
③ benevolent
④ candid

04

밑줄 친 부분과 의미가 가장 가까운 것은?

> There is such <u>an abundance</u> of apples this year that many of them are not picked.

① a disease
② a plenty
③ a deflation
④ a harvest

PART III 생활영어

05

다음 중 두 사람의 대화가 어색한 것은?

① A : How long will this package take to arrive in Japan?
B : Approximately four days by air.
② A : Myong-ja goes to school during the day and works part-time in the evening.
B : It's a wonder how she manages that.
③ A : I left my umbrella on the bus.
B : Well, you must save up for a rainy day.
④ A : Tom claims not to own a television day.
B : I wonder what he does during his free time.

PART IV 독해

06

다음 글의 빈칸에 들어갈 말로 가장 적절한 것은?

> Carbon emissions from fossil-fuel burning (ignoring agriculture, deforestation and cement production), which already total about 32 billion tons of CO_2 per year, on average rose by 676 million tons annually from 2000 to 2010. This is equivalent to almost twice the emissions that Brazil added to the global total during each twelve-month period. Although this massive increase in fossil-fuel burning has caused disastrous pollution and health impacts in China and elsewhere, the dramatic rise in global CO_2 is actually a good thing in one respect, because it shows that developing countries are expanding their energy consumption in order to free themselves from centuries of famine and misery. In other words, ______________________________.

① developed nations typically have high CO_2 emissions for each person
② the earth will face a two-sided problem: air pollution and overpopulation
③ developed countries have to help developing countries with green technology
④ we are losing the war on carbon because we are winning the war on poverty

07

다음 글의 ① ~ ④ 중에서 주어진 문장이 들어가기에 가장 적절한 곳은?

This is shorthand for saying that the weather is a chaotic system.

Computer models have revolutionized weather forecasting. But if you set a computer running on a set of data describing the atmosphere, it would still be foolish to think it will produce a perfect forecast for all time. (①) In practice, even today's forecasts drop fast in reliability when they get more than a week ahead. (②) This is described as the forecast "losing its skill". (③) Part of the difficulty is that the input information for the forecast is imperfect, but a more basic objection is the "butterfly problem". (④) It is not chaotic in the way that the top of my desk is chaotic. In this context, "chaotic" means that it is never possible to allow for every minor immeasurable fluctuation in the input conditions, so that a butterfly flapping its wings over the Amazon could in the end produce a storm in New York.

*shorthand 약칭 **fluctuation 등락, 변동

08

다음 글의 빈칸 (A), (B)에 들어갈 말로 가장 적절한 것은?

In warmer regions, many of us have learned to rely on energy-hungry air-conditioning to keep the inside of our buildings cool. ____(A)____, another approach is simply to let the building itself act as a filter, selectively letting in daylight, warmth, and cool air, depending on the needs of the moment. If this sounds innovative, it's probably worth mentioning that early architects were doing this before anyone had even heard of oil or electricity. The designers of Moorish palaces in Andalucia, ____(B)____, knew all about how to set the slope of a roof so that it would block the burning summer sun, but let in the gentler, more sloping sunlight of winter. Modern buildings can also be designed to do this expertly, but in the meantime any of us can work with what we already have. When the sun is shining directly on the windows, close the shutters or draw the blinds.

*Moorish 무어인(8세기에 스페인을 점령했던 아프리카 북서부의 이슬람 종족) 양식의

	(A)		(B)
①	However	···	as a result
②	However	···	for example
③	Furthermore	···	for example
④	Furthermore	···	on the other hand

09

주어진 글 다음에 이어질 글의 순서로 가장 적절한 것은?

An interesting observation that is pertinent to the idea of an instinctive urge is displacement activity. Displacement activity occurs when two incompatible response tendencies are simultaneously aroused.

(A) At times the activity differs from normal grooming behavior in that it seems hurried and is discontinued before it is completed. But on other occasions the behavior is not distinguishable from normal grooming activity.

(B) For example, a bird might be faced with a rival that elicits both attack and flight. In this situation, behaviors are displayed that appear to be irrelevant to the situation, such as grooming.

(C) Certain species of fish, such as the stickleback, also exhibit such out-of-context displacement activity. When at the boundary between its own territory and that of another stickleback, where both attack and escape behaviors are elicited, inappropriate nest-building behavior is often displayed.

*pertinent 관련 있는 **stickleback 큰가시고기

① (B) – (A) – (C)
② (B) – (C) – (A)
③ (C) – (A) – (B)
④ (C) – (B) – (A)

10

Lakeside Community Kite Fly-In에 관한 다음 안내문의 내용과 일치하지 않는 것은?

The Lakeside Community Kite Fly-In
Saturday 8th September
From 11:00 until 16:00

On the events field at Green Porch Park

The Kent Kite Flyers return to the park to host another fun kite-flying day.

- Whether you're a beginner or an expert, come along and join in!
- FREE kite-making workshop for children
- Food and refreshments will be available in the Parish Hall.
- This event is FREE with no booking necessary! People of all ages and abilities are welcome!

Note

- We request that children be supervised by a responsible adult and that pet dogs be kept on a leash.
- Free parking along Saffron Way, car park closes at 16:30

For more information, visit our website, www.communitykite.com.

① It runs for one day from 11 a.m. to 4 p.m.
② Both beginners and experts can participate.
③ A kite-making workshop for children is held for free.
④ You can participate only if you make a reservation online in advance.

제 03 회 하프 모의고사

해설편 p.113

제한 시간 15 분 | 소요 시간 분 | 점수 /10

PART Ⅰ 어법

01

다음 글의 밑줄 친 부분 중, 어법상 틀린 것은?

Volunteering can help you meet lots of different people. This can be great if you've just moved to an area or are feeling as if you could stand to mix up your social circle. Plus, the people you'll meet while volunteering will probably have different things ① to offer than do most of your peers in school. For instance, if you don't have any grandparents or other senior citizens in your life, residents of a retirement community can help ② fill that void. Or if you've always wanted to see ③ how it would be like to work as a park ranger, volunteering alongside one can be a great opportunity to learn the ropes from a pro. Lots of volunteers say that one of their biggest rewards ④ is getting to know people from different walks of life. Whatever your choice of volunteer work, you're almost sure to meet someone you wouldn't have otherwise met.

02

우리말을 영어로 잘못 옮긴 것은?

① 그녀는 등산은 말할 것도 없고, 야외에 나가는 것을 좋아하지 않는다.
→ She does not like going outdoor, not to mention mountain climbing.

② 그녀는 학급에서 가장 예쁜 소녀이다.
→ She is more beautiful than any other girl in the class.

③ 그 나라는 국토의 3/4이 바다로 둘러싸여 있는 소국이다.
→ The country is a small one with the three quarters of the land surrounding by the sea.

④ 많은 학생들이 졸업 후 취직을 위해 열심히 공부한다.
→ A number of students are studying very hard to get a job after their graduation.

PART Ⅱ 어휘

03

밑줄 친 부분과 의미가 가장 가까운 것은?

His report was organized chronologically.

① in terms of comparisons
② according to a time sequence
③ in a difficult situation
④ not in harmony with each other

04

밑줄 친 부분과 의미가 가장 가까운 것은?

> He felt a deep sense of <u>anguish</u>.

① failure
② dignity
③ pride
④ grief

PART Ⅲ 생활영어

05

다음 중 두 사람의 대화가 어색한 것은?

① A : What a beautiful coat you're wearing!
  B : Thank you. I got it in San Francisco last year.
② A : How about living in Texas?
  B : Yes, we had a great time. We did some shopping.
③ A : I'm so unhappy. Nobody loves me.
  B : I know somebody who loves you. Me.
④ A : Ouch! There's something in my eye!
  B : Let me look. No, I can't see anything.

PART Ⅳ 독해

06

다음 글의 빈칸에 들어갈 말로 가장 적절한 것은?

> Maybe you find yourself asking, "What if I am diagnosed with cancer?" A realistic and studied response to the question might take into account that, for certain types of cancer, the cure rate is 80 percent, and for other types it's 100 percent. A realistic response might also recognize that great strides are being made in research into treating the disease, so that, in fact, this diagnosis is not nearly as catastrophic as it might have been even a few years ago. In other words, the more comprehensive, realistic answer turns out to be manageable, while the indefinite "nonanswer" is so scary as to be debilitating. You can ask the questions, but you must be willing to answer them, as well. If you play the "what if?" game, ______________________.
>
> *debilitating 쇠약하게 하는

① keep away from definite risks
② play it all the way to the answer
③ ignore the previous data from the first
④ try to play the role of the loser seriously

07

다음 글의 ① ~ ④ 중에서 주어진 문장이 들어가기에 가장 적절한 곳은?

However, insiders may be too tightly wedded to a particular mental model of how to do business.

In his latest research, Joseph Bower argues that chief executives may even find highly capable successors at the periphery of their organizations. (①) Bower reconsiders the notion of hiring an insider versus an outsider as the new chief executive. (②) An insider offers the benefit of a wealth of experience in the business and a deep understanding of the firm's culture and values. (③) That cognitive inflexibility might not serve the firm well if it experiences a major shift in the external environment. (④) Outsiders clearly bring a fresh perspective, but they may not always have the adequate experience or fit the firm's culture.

08

다음 글의 빈칸 (A), (B)에 들어갈 말로 가장 적절한 것은?

When I first lived in Saudi Arabia, I tended to answer questions in Arabic about my health (the equivalent of 'How are you?') with the equivalent of my familiar routine responses of 'Okay' or 'Fine.' ____(A)____, I eventually noticed that when I asked a similar question, people generally answered with a phrase that had the literal meaning of 'Praise to God.' I soon learned to use the new expression, wanting to be pragmatically appropriate in that context. My first type of answer wasn't 'wrong' (my vocabulary and pronunciation weren't inaccurate), but it did convey the meaning that I was a social outsider who answered in an unexpected way. ____(B)____, more was being communicated than was being said. Initially I did not know that: I had learned some linguistic forms in the language without learning the pragmatics of how those forms are used in a regular pattern by social insiders.

*pragmatics 화용론

	(A)		(B)
①	However	…	In other words
②	Likewise	…	In other words
③	However	…	On the contrary
④	Likewise	…	On the other hand

09

주어진 글 다음에 이어질 글의 순서로 가장 적절한 것은?

As we trap more heat in the atmosphere, weather patterns become more volatile. A rise in temperature of 1 degree can translate into an increase in the most severe extremes by several degrees.

(A) And indeed, across the United States, while precipitation is up 6 percent, droughts are also up, and the amount of rain that falls in the hardest 1 percent of rainstorms is up 20 percent. There's more rain, concentrated in fewer places, with more left to dry out, and those that do get rain receive more intense rainstorms.

(B) The greater moisture capacity of the air means that water can be sucked out of one area and deposited in another. Moisture becomes more concentrated in a few times and places, leading to droughts in one area or one season, followed by torrential rains in another.

(C) And warmer air can move more moisture around more quickly. For every degree Celsius that the planet warms, the atmosphere can absorb 7 percent more moisture. That 7 percent isn't uniform, though.

*volatile 변동성이 심한 **precipitation 강수량 ***torrential rain 폭우

① (B) – (A) – (C)
② (B) – (C) – (A)
③ (C) – (A) – (B)
④ (C) – (B) – (A)

10

World Championship Hoop Dance Contest에 관한 다음 안내문의 내용과 일치하는 것은?

World Championship Hoop Dance Contest

On February 9 & 10, 2019, top American Indian and Canadian First Nations hoop dancers will compete at the Heard Museum. At the two-day competition, men and women will compete on an equal playing field.

Schedule

- On-site contestant registration will take place in the Encanto Room from 8:00 – 9:00 a.m.
- Competition begins at 10:00 a.m.
- All contestants will be randomly called to dance, regardless of registration order.

Judging Criteria

Contestants will be evaluated on the five categories below.

1. Precision 2. Rhythm 3. Showmanship
4. Creativeness 5. Speed

General Rules

- Dancers will be penalized for going over the time limit of 7 minutes. A large clock will be visible in the arena.
- During the contest, the contestants' number will be called three times. If they are not in the arena after the third call they will be disqualified.

*arena 경연장 **disqualified 실격이 된

① It is impossible to apply on the day of the competition.
② The order of competition will be determined by the order of registration.
③ There are three criteria for judging the competition.
④ Penalties apply if the time limit exceeds 7 minutes.

해설편 p.115

제한 시간 15 분 | 소요 시간 분 | 점수 /10

PART Ⅰ 어법

01

(A), (B), (C)의 각 네모 안에서 어법에 맞는 표현으로 가장 적절한 것은?

Today, we work hard to shield children from life's hardships. But throughout most of our country's history, we (A) [did / were] not. Rather, kids worked. In the earliest days of our nation, they cared for their siblings or spent time in the fields; as the country industrialized, they worked in mines and textile mills, in factories and canneries, in street trades. Over time, reformers managed to outlaw child labor practices. Yet change was slow. It wasn't until our soldiers returned from World War II (B) [that / which] childhood, as we now know it, began. The family economy was no longer built on a system of reciprocity, with parents sheltering and feeding their children, and children, in return, (C) [kick / kicking] something back into the family cashbox. The relationship became asymmetrical. Children stopped working, and parents worked twice as hard. Children went from being our employees to our bosses.

*reciprocity 상호 교환, 호혜(互惠) **asymmetrical 불균형적인

	(A)		(B)		(C)
①	did	…	that	…	kick
②	did	…	which	…	kick
③	did	…	that	…	kicking
④	were	…	which	…	kick

02

우리말을 영어로 잘못 옮긴 것은?

① 그들은 그의 정직하지 못함을 비난했다.
→ They charged him with dishonesty

② 그 사건은 심각한 양상을 띠기 시작했다.
→ The incident began to assume a serious aspect.

③ 언제 당신이 그녀의 어머니를 방문하는 것이 편하시겠습니까?
→ When will you be convenient to visit her mother?

④ 당신의 도움 덕분에 우리는 그 문제를 쉽게 해결할 수 있었습니다.
→ Thanks to your help, we were able to fix the problem with ease.

PART Ⅱ 어휘

03

밑줄 친 부분과 의미가 가장 가까운 것은?

He is such a <u>clumsy</u> idiot that he always messes things up.

① audacious ② awkward
③ fluent ④ uninteresting

04

밑줄 친 부분과 의미가 가장 가까운 것은?

> The Midway Islands were <u>annexed</u> by the United States in 1859.

① obliterated ② coveted

③ merged ④ suppressed

PART Ⅲ 생활영어

05

다음 중 두 사람의 대화가 어색한 것은?

① A : Do you mind if I borrow your book?
B : Of course not. Here you are.

② A : Mary is the winner of the cooking contest.
B : Great! She must be excited.

③ A : What's wrong? You look unhappy.
B : I'm worried about my father. He is very sick.

④ A : It's too hot. Let's dive into the water.
B : Long time no see. How have you been?

PART Ⅳ 독해

06

다음 글의 빈칸에 들어갈 말로 가장 적절한 것은?

> We can tell our dreams to someone else and, if we are lucky, his imaginative response to them may give us the illusion of a shared experience. But if the person we tell a dream to turns out to be a sceptic, we have no means of convincing him that we really did have the dream we have told him. If he asks for proof that we had that precise dream and no other one, that we have remembered it correctly, we cannot give it. We cannot ask the people who appeared in the dream to confirm our story. Unlike the events of everyday life, which can, in principle, be confirmed or otherwise by the laws of evidence, dream experiences have a peculiar ______________ about them, which can only be partially and often only self-deceptively reduced by recounting them to others.
>
> *sceptic 의심 많은 사람

① privacy

② familiarity

③ symbolism

④ consistency

07

다음 글의 ① ~ ④ 중에서 주어진 문장이 들어가기에 가장 적절한 곳은?

> With his helmet off he told of seeing “horses and women.”

Two Greek sponge-fishing boats, on their way home from working the North African coast, were forced by a storm to seek shelter at the Greek island of Antikythera. (①) Not wanting to waste time as he waited for the winds to subside, the captain, Dimitrios Kondos, had his chief diver, Elias Stadiatis, descend in the hope of harvesting additional sponges. (②) After a normal descent, Stadiatis suddenly bobbed up in the water gesticulating wildly. (③) What he had in fact come upon was the sculptural cargo of an ancient wreck positioned precariously at the edge of an undersea cliff. (④) In a follow-up dive Kondos himself brought up an ancient bronze arm and later informed the Greek government of the discovery.

08

다음 글의 빈칸 (A), (B)에 들어갈 말로 가장 적절한 것은?

Americans seldom offer toasts when dining or drinking, except perhaps on New Year’s Eve or if you are the best man at a wedding. In other countries, ____(A)____, it is more common and therefore it is wise to be prepared. At a Chinese meal, for example, the apex of the multi-course meal is in the middle when the shark’s fin soup is served. It is also the customary time to present toasts. Here are some guidelines for toasting wherever you are in the world. The host toasts first. If at a dinner, rise at your place. Keep the toast short. Comment on the graciousness and hospitality of your hosts, the friendship between countries, and the value of good relations both personal and in business. It can be a moment when just the right sentiment can be expressed that will be both memorable and lasting. ____(B)____, a well-delivered toast is worth anticipating, even to the point of developing a small repertoire for different occasions.

*apex 정점

	(A)		(B)
①	that is	…	Therefore
②	moreover	…	Similarly
③	moreover	…	Otherwise
④	however	…	Therefore

09

주어진 글 다음에 이어질 글의 순서로 가장 적절한 것은?

Personal adornment may reflect inner emotional states called mood. It may also reinforce, disguise, or create mood.

(A) Typically, color contrast can be attained by using a number of different colors together, by using bright colors that contrast with a somber background, and by using sharp differences in lightness and darkness of color. Linear contrast occurs if lines suddenly change direction or intersect when proceeding in different directions.

(B) An individual caught up in a certain mood may wish to externalize it so it can be conveyed to and shared with others. Perhaps an individual feels light- hearted and energetic. In America, a culturally recognized way to create this effect is to choose costume with colors and linear arrangements that show contrast rather than sameness.

(C) The culturally encouraged interpretation is that the redirection of eye movements required by line contrasts is symbolic of a dynamic inner state within the wearer. Thus, at least for Americans, contrasting line and color in costume can express exuberant mood to others and also reinforce the same mood in the wearer.

*adornment 치장 **somber 칙칙한 ***exuberant 활기찬

① (A) - (C) - (B)
② (B) - (A) - (C)
③ (B) - (C) - (A)
④ (C) - (A) - (B)

10

Verreaux's sifaka에 관한 다음 글의 내용과 일치하지 않는 것은?

Verreaux's sifaka lives in the forest of south western Madagascar. This species lives in small groups of up to about 12 individuals. Groups contain more or less equal numbers of adult males and females. The group defends a small territory. They use their scent to mark the territory's boundary. Sifakas mate in December, at the height of the dry season. A single young is born five months later and it is weaned after seven months. Sifakas move through the trees by leaping. The distance they can jump is increased slightly by small flaps of skin under the animal's short forearms. On the ground, sifakas move by hopping sideways on both hind feet. The forearms are held out to the side for balance. Verreaux's sifakas eat all types of plant material apart from the roots. In the rainy season they prefer to eat easily digested soft fruits and flowers, but in the dry season they rely on wood, bark and leaves.

* wean 젖을 떼다

① It lives in small groups of up to a dozen.
② Mark your area using smell.
③ Five months after mating, one baby is born.
④ Move on four legs on the ground.

제 05 회 하프 모의고사

해설편 p.118

제한 시간 15 분 | 소요 시간 분 | 점수 /10

PART Ⅰ 어법

01

다음 글의 밑줄 친 부분 중, 어법상 틀린 것은?

James March has been studying slow learners for over a decade. He shows ① that companies will focus more on exploring new possibilities, and less on exploiting old knowledge, when a significant percentage of members don't follow the code. When people don't know or don't believe the code, they draw on their own knowledge and skill, or invent new ideas or methods to get their work ② done. When they do what they think is right, rather than what everyone else does, they produce more variation in ③ which is thought and done. This means ④ it is smart to hire slow learners, to tolerate deviants, eccentrics, and just plain original thinkers, even though they will come up with many ideas that are strange mutations, dead ends, and utter failures. The cost is worthwhile because they also generate a larger pool of ideas — especially novel ideas — than you can get from just hiring and breeding fast learners.

*deviant 비정상적인 사람

02

우리말을 영어로 잘못 옮긴 것은?

① 그 연사는 자기 생각을 청중에게 전달하는 데 능숙하지 않았다.
→ The speaker was not good at getting his ideas across to the audience.

② 서울의 교통 체증은 세계 어느 도시보다 심각하다.
→ The traffic jams in Seoul are more serious than those in any other city in the world.

③ 내가 말하고 있는 사람과 시선을 마주치는 것은 서양 국가에서 중요하다.
→ Making eye contact with the person you are speaking to is important in western countries.

④ 그는 사람들이 생각했던 만큼 인색하지 않았다는 것이 드러났다.
→ It turns out that he was not so stingier as he was thought to be.

PART Ⅱ 어휘

03

밑줄 친 부분과 의미가 가장 가까운 것은?

You must have cogent reasons for opposing this proposal.

① convincing
② inordinate
③ touchy
④ feeble

04

밑줄 친 부분과 의미가 가장 가까운 것은?

My boss ordered me that I <u>annul</u> the contract with the customer.

① deliver
② abolish
③ stimulate
④ strive

PART Ⅲ 생활영어

05

다음 중 두 사람의 대화가 어색한 것은?

① A: Hi, Yusoo. What is your plan for the coming vacation?
B: Well, I have been to New York.
② A: I guess people of this town need a refuge nearby.
B: Exactly. People must have lost their places.
③ A: Where did the accident take place?
B: Over there. I saw the water rise over the bank.
④ A: Help is on the way, sir. Where is the fire?
B: In the kitchen. The curtains caught fire when I cooked.

PART Ⅳ 독해

06

다음 글의 빈칸에 들어갈 말로 가장 적절한 것은?

To understand ____________ of any evaluation, we have to understand the concept of value. Value (or worth) is perceived utility or usefulness. Anything that has value has some perceived usefulness. Thus, value is an opinion of usefulness that is specific to a given mind. Just like beauty, value is in the mind's eye of the beholder. But if value is nothing more than an opinion, if value is fundamentally subjective, then it is also beyond objective proof. As an opinion, value isn't a fact. Since value isn't a fact, it cannot prove anything factual or objective. What is valuable to one mind may be trash to another. To one person, a Beanie Baby is a collector's item; to another, it's something to be thrown away. To some, a thought of approval from somebody else is a gold coin; to others, somebody's approval is Monopoly money.

*Monopoly (놀이판에서 하는) 부동산 취득 게임

① the intrinsic role
② the arbitrary nature
③ the complex process
④ the cultural implications

07

다음 글의 ① ~ ④ 중에서 주어진 문장이 들어가기에 가장 적절한 곳은?

When his acting career reached a dead end and he was nearly broken, with a pregnant wife, he decided to create his own opportunity and to write a screenplay for himself.

A product of a poor broken home, Sylvester Stallone grew up in Hell's Kitchen, then in Silver Springs, Maryland, and in a Philadelphia slum. (①) He spent years at homes of foster parents and was booted out of fourteen schools in eleven years. (②) For a while, Stallone attended the drama department of the University of Miami, where his instructors discouraged him from pursuing a show business career. (③) He subsequently tried his hand at a variety of jobs, including ushering at the Baronet Theater in N.Y. However, determined to become an actor, he managed to get some bit parts in films.(④) The story of Rocky, whose first draft was completed in three days, is very similar to his own life: a poor boxer triumphs against great odds; the rest is film history.

*foster parents 수양부모 **boot 쫓아내다 ***usher 안내하다

08

다음 글의 빈칸 (A), (B)에 들어갈 말로 가장 적절한 것은?

Plato divided the world into an "apparent" world that appears to us through our senses, and a "real" world that we can grasp through the intellect. For Plato, the world we perceive through the senses is not "real" because it is changeable and subject to decay. Plato suggests that there is also an unchanging, permanent "real world" that can be attained with the help of the intellect. This idea comes from Plato's study of mathematics. The form or idea of a triangle, ____(A)____, is eternal and can be grasped by the intellect. We know that a triangle is a three-sided, two-dimensional figure whose angles add up to 180°, and that this will always be true, whether anyone is thinking about it or not and however many triangles exist in the world. ____(B)____, the triangular things that do exist in the world (such as sandwiches, pyramids, and triangular shapes drawn on a chalkboard), are triangular only insofar as they are reflections of this idea or form of the triangle.

	(A)		(B)
①	for example	…	On the other hand
②	for example	…	In addition
③	in contrast	…	In addition
④	as a result	…	In other words

09

주어진 글 다음에 이어질 글의 순서로 가장 적절한 것은?

The philosopher Nelson Goodman argued that we should replace the question "What is art?" with the question "When is art?". The same object can function as a work of art or not, depending on how the object is viewed.

(A) But if this same line is part of a drawing (say, the outline of a mountain), all of the line's physical properties are suddenly important and part of what the artist wants us to attend to — its color, texture, edges, thickness, among other things. And we cannot translate this experience into a set of numbers.

(B) Told that the line is a stock market graph, all we attend to are the peaks and dips. We could get the same information from a set of numbers.

(C) When an object functions as art, it exhibits certain "symptoms" of the aesthetic. For example, an object functioning as art is relatively replete (full), meaning that more of its physical properties are part of its meaning and should be attended to than when that same object is not functioning as a work of art. Goodman asks us to consider a zigzag line.

① (B) - (A) - (C)
② (B) - (C) - (A)
③ (C) - (A) - (B)
④ (C) - (B) - (A)

10

killer whale에 관한 다음 글의 내용과 일치하지 않는 것은?

Killer whales have been observed in all oceans and seas, but are more prevalent in the coastal waters at higher latitudes. Although reported in both tropical and offshore waters, killer whales prefer colder and more productive waters of both hemispheres, and are found in greatest abundances at high latitudes. Along the West Coast of North America, killer whales occur in British Columbia and Washington inland waterways along the entire Alaskan coast. They also occur along the outer coasts of California, Oregon, and Washington. Killer whales are black with white underparts. There is a white spot on each side of the head, just above and in back of the eye. Their dorsal fins are sharply triangular and very tall, reaching up to 6 feet in height. Killer whales can reach up to 31 feet in length. Like sperm whales, killer whales are unusual among cetaceans in that males reach a much larger size than females.

*dorsal (물고기나 동물의) 등에 있는 **cetacean 고래목의 동물

① It lives in coastal waters of high latitude.
② It has been found throughout the coast of Alaska.
③ There is a white dot on the back of both eyes.
④ After growing up, females are larger than males.

제 06 회 하프 모의고사

해설편 p.121

제한 시간 15 분 | 소요 시간 분 | 점수 /10

PART Ⅰ 어법

01

(A), (B), (C)의 각 네모 안에서 어법에 맞는 표현으로 가장 적절한 것은?

We tend to assume that the way to get more time is to speed up. But speeding up can actually slow us down, as anyone who has ever accelerated out of the house only to realize that their keys, wallet, organizer, and baby son (A) [sitting / are sitting] on the kitchen table knows only too well. And it's not just our efficiency that is reduced. The quality of the experience suffers too, as we become less aware or 'mindful'. Ever eaten an entire meal without (B) [taste / tasting] any of it? Hurrying up doesn't just give us less time, it can also drain the pleasure and benefit from the time that we do have. For many of us, hurrying is a way of life. Some of us enjoy the buzz that it gives us while others are driven crazy by the constant pressure and (C) [feel / feels] that their lives are speeding up to an unacceptable degree. Either way, there are almost certainly areas of our life that could be enhanced by a little go-slow behavior.

	(A)		(B)		(C)
①	sitting	…	taste	…	feels
②	sitting	…	tasting	…	feel
③	are sitting	…	taste	…	feel
④	are sitting	…	tasting	…	feel

02

우리말을 영어로 잘못 옮긴 것은?

① 예산은 처음 기대했던 것보다 약 25퍼센트 더 높다.
→ The budget is about 25% higher than originally expecting.

② 시스템 업그레이드를 위해 해야 될 많은 일이 있다.
→ There is a lot of work to be done for the system upgrade.

③ 그 프로젝트를 완성하는 데 최소 한 달, 어쩌면 더 긴 시간이 걸릴 것이다.
→ It will take at least a month, maybe longer to complete the project.

④ 월급을 두 배 받는 그 부서장이 책임을 져야 한다.
→ The head of the department, who receives twice the salary, has to take responsibility.

PART Ⅱ 어휘

03

밑줄 친 부분과 의미가 가장 가까운 것은?

He <u>collaborated</u> with his son on the English translation of a text on food production.

① put together
② went together
③ started together
④ worked together

04

밑줄 친 부분과 의미가 가장 가까운 것은?

> Most traditional folk songs are of anonymous origin.

① insignificant
② inconspicuous
③ unusual
④ unknown

PART Ⅲ 생활영어

05

다음 대화의 빈칸에 들어갈 말로 가장 적절한 것은?

> A : Please help me out. I don't know what's going on with this computer?
> B : It seems there are some errors in the F-drive. I think you should not only check your USB memory but also the computer drive in the lab.
> A : Thanks for your advice! By the way, can I use your computer and printer?
> B : ________________________________

① Be my guest!
② Enough is enough!
③ What a coincidence!
④ It slipped my mind!

PART Ⅳ 독해

06

다음 글의 빈칸에 들어갈 말로 가장 적절한 것은?

> Any time you use another writer's words or even a close paraphrase of his or her words, you must give that writer credit. If you don't, you've committed the crime of plagiarism. Simply out, plagiarism is using somebody else's words and claiming or pretending that the words are your own. A simple rule of thumb for avoiding plagiarism is: When in doubt, give the original writer credit. If you're applying common information, you do not have to worry about plagiarism. If you say the Earth is round, nobody will accuse you of plagiarism. On the other hand, if you write a research paper stating that 16.5 percent of all merchant marines get seasick, chances are some poor researcher spent months of his or her life to determine that fact. In this case, ______________________________.
>
> *credit 이름에 대한 언급, 공로 **plagiarism 표절

① nobody will claim his or her right
② the researcher deserves the credit
③ you don't have to worry about plagiarism
④ you use the information you don't understand

07

다음 글의 ① ~ ④ 중에서 주어진 문장이 들어가기에 가장 적절한 곳은?

> Conversely, the use of "we" generally demonstrates an awareness of other people and offers a way to show that you recognize or even understand their thoughts and feelings.

The use of pronouns such as "I" and "we" tells a lot about strength and warmth, as well as offering clues about gender, education, and status. Some of these clues are obvious, while others are less so. (①) Most of us have learned somewhere along the way, for instance, that the overuse of "I" suggests self-centeredness or egocentrism, which asserts strength but weakens warmth. (②) This behavior may also suggest this person has some major insecurities they are trying to mask. (③) In either reading of the strength signals, overdoing the "I" is not warm. (④) At a fundamental level, this projects warmth by conveying a sense of shared concerns and interests.

08

다음 글의 빈칸 (A), (B)에 들어갈 말로 가장 적절한 것은?

Although the well-being of societies has hitherto been judged according to economic measures, economic indicators alone are not enough to reveal the quality of life within nations. While income has steadily climbed over the past 50 years, and the gross domestic product (GDP) has tripled, happiness has remained virtually flat. ____(A)____, a recent study utilizing the Gallup World Poll found that life satisfaction increased when national wealth increased, but enjoyment of life experienced little change. This discrepancy between happiness and economic growth is important when one considers that people rank happiness ahead of money as a life goal. However, it is even more significant when one examines the large body of research suggesting that high levels of subjective well-being are not only good in and of themselves, but that they actually produce beneficial societal outcomes. ____(B)____, while monetary considerations are currently dominant in policy debates, other goals should be kept in mind.

*hitherto 지금까지 **monetary 금전적인, 화폐의

	(A)		(B)
①	Instead	···	Therefore
②	Furthermore	···	Therefore
③	Furthermore	···	Similarly
④	For instance	···	Similarly

09

주어진 글 다음에 이어질 글의 순서로 가장 적절한 것은?

Because elites in personalist dictatorships do not belong to a unifying institution like military or party, the leader has greater control over elite recruitment in personalist dictatorships than in other types of dictatorships.

(A) Leaders in single-party and military dictatorships, by contrast, cannot handpick their elite support group. Elites must work their way up the party or military hierarchy to attain their positions, and leaders have less control over individual promotions. This means that elites in single-party and military regimes do not share the exact policy preferences of the leader.

(B) Personalist dictators do not have to adhere to party or military guidelines for elite promotions; they can select those elite supporters who are most likely to agree with them. Because of this, elites in personalist dictatorships tend to have policy preferences that mirror those of the dictator.

(C) Governance by a party or military, however, also brings about the difference of elite preferences in these regimes. Elites in military dictatorships tend to be much more united in their policy preferences than elites in single-party dictatorships.

*personalist dictatorship 1인 독재

① (B) - (A) - (C)
② (B) - (C) - (A)
③ (C) - (A) - (B)
④ (C) - (B) - (A)

10

Shooter's Gold Basketball Camp에 관한 다음 안내문의 내용과 일치하지 않는 것은?

Shooter's Gold Basketball Camp

Under the direction of Coach Paul Hogan, the camp will be held at the Maple Middle School gym from July 6 – 10.

- **Session #1, for boys and girls entering grades 1 – 4,** will run from 8:00 AM – 10:00 AM.
- **Session #2, for boys and girls entering grades 5 – 8,** will run from 8:00 AM – 12:00 PM.

The registration fee is $80 for Session #1 and $115 for Session #2. After June 1, the fee is $85 for Session #1 and $130 for Session #2. Each participant will receive a basketball and a camp T-shirt. Special prizes will be presented throughout the week. The camp covers proper shooting form, one-on-one moves, post moves and how to play the game. Call our office at (451) 345 – 4545 for a registration form or further information.

*post 공격의 중심이 되는 선수 위치

① It will be held for five days from July 6 to 10.
② The end times of the two practice classes are different.
③ The registration fee for Practice Class 2 is cheaper than Practice Class 1.
④ Participants will receive a basketball and a T – shirt.

제 07 회 하프 모의고사

해설편 p.124

제한 시간 15 분 | 소요 시간 분 | 점수 /10

PART Ⅰ 어법

01

다음 글의 밑줄 친 부분 중, 어법상 틀린 것은?

Vernor Vinge, one of my favorite science fiction writers, wrote A Fire Upon the Deep, ① in which the planet Tines is populated by animals with a collective intelligence. These doglike creatures travel in packs, whose members are in continuous acoustical communication with one another, ② giving rise to a powerful, distributed consciousness. Individuals leave the pack because of death, illness, or accident, and new, young members are recruited to replace them, so that the pack maintains its identity far beyond ③ those of any single individual. Each individual member of a pack lacks intelligence when all alone: the pack gains its intelligence through the collaboration of the many individuals. As a result, if an individual strays too far from the pack, the communication path ④ is lost — for sound has limited range — and the resulting "singleton" is devoid of intelligence. Singletons rarely survive, and those that do are doomed to a mindless existence — literally mindless.

*acoustical 음향의, 청각의 **singleton (단독) 개체
***devoid of ~이 전혀 없는

02

우리말을 영어로 잘못 옮긴 것은?

① 나는 매달 두세 번 그에게 전화하기로 규칙을 세웠다.
→ I made it a rule to call him two or three times a month.

② 그는 나의 팔을 붙잡고 도움을 요청했다.
→ He grabbed me by the arm and asked for help.

③ 폭우로 인해 그 강은 120cm 상승했다.
→ Owing to the heavy rain, the river has risen by 120cm.

④ 나는 눈 오는 날 밖에 나가는 것보다 집에 있는 것을 더 좋아한다.
→ I prefer to staying home than to going out on a snowy day.

PART Ⅱ 어휘

03

밑줄 친 부분과 의미가 가장 가까운 것은?

> It was predicted that a comet would <u>collide</u> with one of the planets.

① meet briefly
② narrowly miss
③ hit each other
④ take off

04

밑줄 친 부분과 의미가 가장 가까운 것은?

> She is rather <u>antagonistic</u> to the church members.

① in favor of
② ignorant
③ curious
④ opposed

PART Ⅲ 생활영어

05

다음 중 두 사람의 대화가 어색한 것은?

① A: Oh, I am starving!
B: Why don't we go grab a bite?
② A: Did he win any prize in the singing contest?
B: Yes, he won the second prize.
③ A: It's so good to see you here. Can't we sit down somewhere and talk?
B: Sure, I'd love to touch base with you.
④ A: I'm an economist. I've just finished writing a book on international trade.
B: Oh? That's my field, too. I work in entertainment.

06

다음 글의 빈칸에 들어갈 말로 가장 적절한 것은?

Checking a relationship from time to time can help prevent serious difficulties from arising. Too often with a relationship, as with our health, we assume everything is fine until something goes wrong. Just as visiting a doctor for a regular checkup can help maintain the health of our bodies, so an occasional reflective "checkup" can help maintain the well-being of an important relationship. It can be useful to think in general terms about the implicit goal of a relationship and the strategy for reaching that goal. ____________ each element - with the relationship partner, if possible - we can identify areas that require attention. Sitting side by side, recalling recent encounters, and listing specific questions for discussion can stimulate fresh ideas for improving our pattern of interaction.

① Creating
② Quantifying
③ Changing
④ Reviewing

07

다음 글의 ① ~ ④ 중에서 주어진 문장이 들어가기에 가장 적절한 곳은?

He did, however, after his death, have a West Coast university named after him — Berkeley in California.

The philosopher George Berkeley didn't spend every hour of his day defending his immaterialism. (①) There was much more to his life than that. (②) He was a sociable and likeable man, and his friends included the author of Gulliver's Travels, Jonathan Swift. (③) In later life Berkeley hatched an ambitious plan to set up a college on the island of Bermuda and managed to raise quite a lot of money to do this. Unfortunately the plan failed, partly because he hadn't realized how far from the mainland Bermuda was and how difficult it was to get supplies there. (④) That came from a poem he wrote about America which included the line 'Westward the course of empire takes its way', a line that appealed to one of the university's founders.

08

다음 글의 빈칸 (A), (B)에 들어갈 말로 가장 적절한 것은?

Genetic changes always take many generations, even when fairly strong natural selection is involved. Cultural characteristics, ___(A)___ are not only passed from parents to offspring, but may be passed on from any one individual to another by word of mouth or by writing. So some cultural changes may be adopted quite quickly by a whole population. Transmission of culture is rather like transmission of an infection. Flu and cold epidemics spread very quickly, especially with the large amount of contact that people of all countries of the world now have with each other. In the same way, cultural habits such as pop music preferences and clothing fashions may spread very quickly nowadays, especially through the media of radio and television. ___(B)___ other deep-rooted cultural characteristics of races and racial subgroups are much more difficult to change. These are the cultural patterns that are so resistant to alteration that they have the appearance of being innate.

	(A)		(B)
①	on the other hand	···	Similarly
②	on the other hand	···	However
③	in addition	···	Therefore
④	in addition	···	However

09

주어진 글 다음에 이어질 글의 순서로 가장 적절한 것은?

Let us now consider the behaviour of normal people with low intelligence. We tend to call such people stupid – unless, of course, they occupy a higher position than we do!

(A) Thus a person rated as intelligent on account of his eloquence and ingeniousness may not prove to be so clever in dealing with numerical, or perceptual, material, and vice versa. That is why an understanding of typical "unintelligent" behaviour may be of real importance in education and self-education.

(B) They deserve our attention because of the influence they sometimes exert on the course of vital events, and also because one can only fully recognize and appreciate the most valuable qualities of the mind against a background of its deficiencies.

(C) Besides, even a man with a high level of general intelligence will sometimes behave in an unintelligent way under the influence of such factors as fatigue or violent emotion. It is also known that the development of various primary abilities, which make up the intelligence, is largely uneven.

*ingeniousness 재치가 있음, 독창성

① (B) – (A) – (C)
② (B) – (C) – (A)
③ (C) – (A) – (B)
④ (C) – (B) – (A)

10

Scorpions에 관한 다음 글의 내용과 일치하지 않는 것은?

Scorpions were the first predators to crawl out of the sea onto land, and they have evolved very little in the last 430 million years because they are very good at what they do. In their prime, during the oxygen-rich atmosphere of the Carboniferous period, scorpions as big as dogs roamed the land, and in the sea giant water scorpions grew to twice that size. Like their younger arachnid cousins the spiders, scorpions are tough and adaptable, putting up with subzero temperatures and desert heat. They can even survive two days completely submerged in water. They are found on all major land masses except Greenland and Antarctica.

*Carboniferous period 석탄기 **arachnid 거미류(거미, 전갈, 진드기 등)

① Hardly evolved over 400 million years.
② During the Carboniferous Period, it roamed the land the size of a dog.
③ It withstands sub-zero temperatures and desert heat.
④ It is found on all continents, including Antarctica.

제08회 하프 모의고사

해설편 p.127

제한 시간 15 분 | 소요 시간 분 | 점수 /10

PART Ⅰ 어법

01

다음 글의 밑줄 친 부분 중, 어법상 틀린 것은?

The bright red juice that one sees dripping out of uncooked meat and steaks cooked very rare ① is not blood — although it's a close relative. The explanation for this requires that the reader ② endure a quick lesson in high-school biology. Oxygen is conveyed through the body by the bloodstream in a chemical called hemoglobin, an iron-based compound that is responsible for blood ③ being red. Many animals, however, need that oxygen in their muscles much faster than the circulatory system can deliver it. So they store another iron-based compound called myoglobin in their muscles. When a very fast reaction is needed by muscle tissue, the muscles utilize the myoglobin while the "real stuff," the hemoglobin, is en route. It is this myoglobin ④ whose drips out of the meat we eat and not blood. There is actually almost no blood in a very rare steak.

*en route (어디로 가는) 도중에

02

우리말을 영어로 잘못 옮긴 것은?

① 오늘 밤 나는 영화 보러 가기보다는 집에서 쉬고 싶다.
→ I'd rather relax at home than going to the movies tonight.

② 경찰은 집안 문제에 대해서는 개입하기를 무척 꺼린다.
→ The police are very unwilling to interfere in family problems.

③ 네가 통제하지 못하는 과거의 일을 걱정해봐야 소용없다.
→ It's no use worrying about past events over which you have no control.

④ 내가 자주 열쇠를 엉뚱한 곳에 두어서 내 비서가 나를 위해 여분의 열쇠를 갖고 다닌다.
→ I misplace my keys so often that my secretary carries spare ones for me.

PART Ⅱ 어휘

03

밑줄 친 부분과 의미가 가장 가까운 것은?

He let his oars sink into the water and commenced pulling with long strokes.

① swam
② drowned
③ began
④ crawled

04

밑줄 친 부분과 의미가 가장 가까운 것은?

An animal with canine distemper disorder becomes <u>apathetic</u>, refusing food and water.

① abstract
② considerate
③ indifferent
④ steadfast

PART Ⅲ 생활영어

05

다음 중 두 사람의 대화가 어색한 것은?

① A: Seohee, where are you headed?
B: I am off to Gyeongju.
② A: Yusoo, let us ride the roller coaster.
B: It's not my cup of tea.
③ A: It's too expensive. I don't want to get ripped off.
B: It's water under the bridge.
④ A: Sohyun, have you been behind the steering wheel yet?
B: No, but I can't wait to get my feet wet.

PART Ⅳ 독해

06

다음 글의 빈칸에 들어갈 말로 가장 적절한 것은?

Be very careful when writing material based upon someone else's work, since copyright law prohibits you from copying someone else's work without their permission. If you bring a property to a studio or a producer and it's based on a book, play, or someone's life story, our advice is to tell them. It complicates matters, but it's much better to take care of rights issues up front. If you can't deliver clean rights to your work, you'll risk undermining yourself and the people you're trying to do business with. More than one production has been killed by a studio's legal department because the writer of the ____________ didn't secure the necessary rights. Once a project is ready for production, it can become very difficult and expensive to clear these problems up.

*undermine (입지 등을) 서서히 해치다

① classic
② speech
③ criticism
④ adaptation

07

다음 글의 ① ~ ④ 중에서 주어진 문장이 들어가기에 가장 적절한 곳은?

> Most important, the meaning of particular symptoms may change with age.

How one behaves at any point in adulthood is strongly affected by one's past experiences and the issues one is facing. (①) These life-cycle factors must be taken into account in evaluating adults' behaviors. (②) For example, a middle-aged woman who wants to go back to school may not have an adjustment disorder; she may simply want to develop a new aspect of herself. (③) Some might interpret her behavior as an inability to cope with her current life situation when that is not the case at all; rather, she has a rational evaluation of her life and realizes, for example, that she needs a degree to advance in her profession. Likewise, an older man who provides vague answers to personal questions may not be resistant; he may simply be reflecting his generation's reluctance to disclose the inner self to a stranger. (④) For example, problems with early morning awakenings may indicate depression in a young adult but may simply be a result of normal aging in an older adult.

08

다음 글의 빈칸 (A), (B)에 들어갈 말로 가장 적절한 것은?

Consumers' satisfaction evaluations tend to be tied to specific consumption situations — we may be satisfied (or not) with the offering as we are using it at the current time. Even if we are satisfied now, however, we may not be satisfied the next time we use it. ___(A)___, satisfaction differs from an attitude, which is relatively enduring and less dependent on the specific situation. In addition, research shows that feelings tend to have more influence on satisfaction judgments early on, but this influence decreases over time. ___(B)___, thoughts have more influence on satisfaction judgments as time goes on. Note that a post-decision evaluation can differ from a pre-decision evaluation in that after using the product, a consumer may judge different attributes than he or she did before. For example, after trying frozen microwave pizza, you might decide that you like the taste less than you thought you would.

	(A)		(B)
①	Thus	···	Conversely
②	Thus	···	Likewise
③	Nevertheless	···	Conversely
④	Nevertheless	···	Likewise

09

주어진 글 다음에 이어질 글의 순서로 가장 적절한 것은?

The growth of human brains may have been related to increasing tool use. Although humans are not the only animals who use tools, our species has developed this skill to a far greater extent than any other animal.

(A) The upright stride was also very helpful, because it allowed arms and hands to be used for a much wider range of purposes (although it became harder to swing around in trees). As a result, humans learned to perform ever more tasks with their hands, even while walking.

(B) The emergence of tool use was the result of an unprecedented coordination between stereoscopic eyes, brains and limbs, which had first emerged while our human ancestors were still a forest- dwelling species.

(C) Today, by contrast, great apes cannot do this; they have to sit still to execute such tasks. As a result of these developments, early humans slowly became more powerful with respect to other larger animals.

*stereoscopic 입체적으로 보는

① (B) – (A) – (C)
② (B) – (C) – (A)
③ (C) – (A) – (B)
④ (C) – (B) – (A)

10

Sonnet 18에 관한 다음 글의 내용과 일치하지 <u>않는</u> 것은?

William Shakespeare wrote 154 sonnets, many of which are great achievements of English literature. Among them, "Sonnet 18" is the best known and most frequently quoted. In the sonnet, the speaker compares his beloved to the summer season, and argues that his beloved is better and will live on forever. Readers often assume that this sonnet is addressed to a young woman, an object of the speaker's romantic love. But though the sonnet is indeed a love poem, it is actually an expression of love for a male friend – the same nameless young gentleman to whom the first 126 of Shakespeare's sonnets are addressed. Though scholars have long debated the identity of the young man and the nature of his relationship to the narrator, the matter is clouded by uncertainty. It is unclear even whether Shakespeare is narrating.

*sonnet 소네트(14행으로 이루어진 시)

① It is best known among the 154 sonnets written by Shakespeare.
② The narrator of the poem likens a lover to summer and insists that he will live forever.
③ Readers think that the narrator of the poem sent it to the woman they loved.
④ The relationship between a young male friend and the speaker is clearly revealed in the poem.

제 09 회 하프 모의고사

해설편 p.130

제한 시간 15 분 | 소요 시간 분 | 점수 /10

PART Ⅰ 어법

01

(A), (B), (C)의 각 네모 안에서 어법에 맞는 표현으로 가장 적절한 것은?

Checklists are powerful tools, proven to increase the accuracy of behavior and to reduce errors. They are especially important in situations with multiple, complex requirements, and even more so (A) [that / where] there are interruptions. With multiple people involved in a task, it is essential that the lines of responsibility be clearly spelled out. It is always better to have two people (B) [do / done] checklists together as a team: one to read the instruction, the other to execute it. If, instead, a single person executes the checklist and then, later, a second person checks the items, the results are not as robust. The person following the checklist, (C) [feels / feeling] confident that any errors would be caught, might do the steps too quickly. But the same bias affects the checker. Confident in the ability of the first person, the checker often does a quick, less than thorough job.

*robust 탄탄한

	(A)		(B)		(C)
①	that	…	do	…	feels
②	that	…	done	…	feeling
③	where	…	do	…	feeling
④	where	…	done	…	feels

02

우리말을 영어로 잘못 옮긴 것은?

① 그녀가 어리석은 계획을 포기하도록 설득해 줄래요?
→ Can you talk her out of her foolish plan?

② 그녀의 어머니에 대해서는 나도 너만큼 아는 것이 없다.
→ I know no more than you don't about her mother.

③ 그의 군대는 거의 2대 1로 수적 열세였다.
→ His army was outnumbered almost two to one.

④ 같은 나이의 두 소녀라고 해서 반드시 생각이 같은 것은 아니다.
→ Two girls of an age are not always of a mind.

PART Ⅱ 어휘

03

밑줄 친 부분과 의미가 가장 가까운 것은?

The function of a car engine is <u>comparable</u> to that of human heart.

① similar ② contradictory
③ opposite ④ mixed

04

밑줄 친 부분과 의미가 가장 가까운 것은?

The audience <u>applauded</u> enthusiastically after the performance.

① crawled ② clapped
③ craved ④ clamored

PART Ⅲ 생활영어

05

다음 중 두 사람의 대화가 어색한 것은?

① A: What time are we having lunch?
B: It'll be ready before noon.

② A: I called you several times. Why didn't you answer?
B: Oh, I think my cell phone was turned off.

③ A: Are you going to take a vacation this winter?
B: I might. I haven't decided yet.

④ A: Hello. Sorry I missed your call.
B: Would you like to leave a message?

PART Ⅳ 독해

06

다음 글의 빈칸에 들어갈 말로 가장 적절한 것은?

A brief experiment filmed by Soviet director Lev Kuleshov demonstrates a film editing effect. It was a scene consisting of five shots, each taken separately in a different location. When assembled in a particular sequence, they created a ____________ of space that had no existence in reality. The film showed a boy approaching a girl, their meeting, the boy pointing to a building in the distance, the two starting off toward the building, and finally both climbing up flights of steps together. The first three shots were photographed in different sections of Moscow. The fourth was a picture of the White House taken from an old American movie. The fifth shot was photographed at the steps of a church in Leningrad. When the shots were joined, places which in actuality are thousands of miles apart were brought together and made to look as though they were concentrated in a small area that could be covered in a few paces by the actors.

① lack ② unity
③ surplus ④ division

07

다음 글의 ① ~ ④ 중에서 주어진 문장이 들어가기에 가장 적절한 곳은?

> Older adults, on the other hand, are more likely to vary their strategy given the problem-solving context.

One important factor that influences the way we solve everyday problems is the context in which the problem occurs. (①) Do we use the same strategies when solving a family conflict between two siblings as we do when solving a conflict over the leading role in a project at work? (②) The answer is no. (③) Interestingly, however, age differences reveal that younger adults are more likely to use a similar strategy across problem- solving contexts: self-action in order to fix the problem. (④) In interpersonal conflict problems (e.g., family conflict) they use more emotion-regulating strategies (i.e., managing their emotions) whereas in more instrumental situations (e.g., dealing with defective merchandise) they use self-action strategies (return the product).

08

다음 글의 빈칸 (A), (B)에 들어갈 말로 가장 적절한 것은?

Of all the arguments that can persuade us that beasts do not have thought, the chief, in my view, is as follows. Granted that in a single species some are more perfect than others, no differently than among men — as can be seen in horses and dogs, some of whom learn much more quickly than others what they are taught. Granted also that they all easily communicate to us by voice or other bodily movements their natural impulses, like anger, fear, hunger, and the like. ____(A)____, it has never been observed that any brute beast arrived at such perfection that it could use true speech, that is, that it indicated by words or signs something that can be attributed to thought alone, and not to a natural impulse. For speech is the only certain sign of thought concealed in the body, and all men make use of it, but not any brute. ____(B)____, this can be taken to be the true differentia between man and brutes.

*brute 이성이 없는; 동물[짐승]

	(A)		(B)
①	Nevertheless	…	Instead
②	Nevertheless	…	Therefore
③	In other words	…	Therefore
④	In other words	…	Instead

09

주어진 글 다음에 이어질 글의 순서로 가장 적절한 것은?

Just as conditioning processes sometimes make foods aversive, such processes can also make foods more appetitive.

(A) Instead, parents often try to entice their children to eat a disliked food by offering dessert as a reward – a strategy that easily backfires in that the contrast between the disliked food and the subsequent dessert might result in the former becoming even more disliked.

(B) Similarly, in one study, college students developed increased preference for broccoli or cauliflower after eating it a few times with sugar. Unfortunately, few parents use such a method to improve their children's eating habits, possibly because they perceive sugar to be unhealthy and do not realize that the sugar can later be withdrawn.

(C) For example, a powerful way to increase our preference for a disliked food is to mix it with some food item or sweetener that we strongly prefer. This may be how some people grow to like black coffee: They first drink it with cream and sugar and then gradually eliminate the extra ingredients as the taste of the coffee itself becomes pleasurable.

*aversive 싫어하는

① (B) – (A) – (C)
② (B) – (C) – (A)
③ (C) – (A) – (B)
④ (C) – (B) – (A)

10

Aphra Behn에 관한 위 글의 내용과 일치하지 않는 것은?

Aphra Behn was the first professional woman writer in English literature. She was bornnear Canterbury in 1640. In 1664, she married Johan Behn, a merchant of Dutch parentage, but the marriage didn't last very long. Imprisonment for debt in 1666 led her to write for an income. Behn wrote a series of successful plays. Her first novel, The Forced Marriage was produced in 1671. Behn's novel Oroonoko (1688) was the story of an enslaved African prince, now considered a foundation stone in the development of the English novel. As well as plays and prose Behn wrote poetry and translated works from French and Latin. In her time she was a celebrity, unusual for her independence as a professional writer and her concern for equality between the sexes. Behn died on April 16th, 1689 and was buried in Westminster Abbey.

① He was born near Canterbury in 1640.
② He married a Dutch merchant in 1664.
③ Her Oronoko is considered a cornerstone of the development of British fiction.
④ During his lifetime, he was not much recognized as a writer.

해설편 p.133

제한 시간 15 분 | 소요 시간 분 | 점수 /10

PART Ⅰ 어법

01

다음 글의 밑줄 친 부분 중, 어법상 틀린 것은?

Babies frequently drink warm milk or milk substitutes from bottles. Parents and caregivers must be careful ① that the liquid is not so hot that it burns the infant's mouth. Unfortunately, this is an easy mistake ② to make when you microwave a bottle in the middle of the night. Cooling the bottle to the correct temperature is a slow process, and it can be ③ highly frustrating when a hungry baby is screaming in your arms. Recent innovations linking temperature with color have solved this problem. Royal Industries' Pur division has been making baby products for more than twenty years. Its newest baby bottles change color when liquid within them reaches 100.4°F. By alerting tired parents to turn off the microwave and move on to the next step in the procedure – the universal dribble-on-the-wrist routine – Pur bottles ④ helping them feel confident that the liquid's temperature is just right.

*dribble-on-the-wrist (온도를 확인하기 위해) 손목에 액체를 조금 떨어뜨리는 것

02

우리말을 영어로 잘못 옮긴 것은?

① 제인은 보기만큼 젊지 않다.
→ Jane is not as young as she looks.

② 전화하는 것이 편지 쓰는 것보다 더 쉽다.
→ It's easier to make a phone call than to write a letter.

③ 너는 나보다 돈이 많다.
→ You have more money than I.

④ 당신 아들 머리는 당신 머리와 같은 색깔이다.
→ Your son's hair is the same color as you.

PART Ⅱ 어휘

03

밑줄 친 부분과 의미가 가장 가까운 것은?

I don't think he is competent cook.

① lazy ② proficient
③ inefficient ④ turned to one side

04

밑줄 친 부분과 의미가 가장 가까운 것은?

After they had finished painting the house, they were faced with the arduous tasks of cleaning up.

① rewarding ② resolute
③ boring ④ laborious

PART Ⅲ 생활영어

05

다음 중 두 사람의 대화가 어색한 것은?

① A : May I help you, sir?
B : Just looking, thank you.

② A : What time does the movie start?
B : At 4 o'clock.

③ A : I've lost my wallet at the food court.
B : Let's go to the Lost & Found.

④ A : How long have you been away from home?
B : It's about ten miles.

PART Ⅳ 독해

06

다음 글의 빈칸에 들어갈 말로 가장 적절한 것은?

The intellect cannot command the emotions, but it can channel currently existing emotional energy. If, for example, the emotions want X, the intellect might talk them into wanting to do Y by pointing out that doing it will get them X. As soon as the emotions are convinced that doing Y will get them X, the anxiety they felt with respect to X will transfer to Y. The intellect can then point out to the emotions that by doing Z, they can get Y; again, the anxiety will transfer. In this manner, anxiety flows down the chains of desire ____________________. We thereby become motivated to fulfill the instrumental desires in these chains, even though doing so won't itself feel good – indeed, even though doing so will feel bad.

*instrumental desire 도구적 욕구
(자체의 충족이 아니라 다른 욕구의 충족을 위한 도구로서 갖게 되는 욕구)

① altered in comparison
② formed by the intellect
③ strengthened by rewards
④ diminished over the transfer

07

다음 글의 ① ~ ④ 중에서 주어진 문장이 들어가기에 가장 적절한 곳은?

When rare periods of significant rain produce major vegetation growth, everything changes.

The desert locust lives in two remarkably different styles depending on the availability of food sources and the density of the local locust population. (①) When food is scarce, as it usually is in their native desert habitat, locusts are born with coloring designed for camouflage and lead solitary lives. (②) At first, the locusts continue to be loners, just feasting off the abundant food supply. (③) But as the extra vegetation starts to die off, the locusts find themselves crowded together. (④) Suddenly, baby locusts are born with bright colors and a hankering for company.

08

다음 글의 빈칸 (A), (B)에 들어갈 말로 가장 적절한 것은?

The future school would consist of a series of teaching-learning stations that would permit access to anything anyone wanted to learn, which would or could include not only all of the subjects presently included in common school curricula, but a good deal more that are not. ＿＿(A)＿＿, the stations would permit the student to have access to the information wanted whenever he wanted to try to learn it. The schools would be scattered about local neighborhoods and would be open twenty-four hours a day. If, ＿＿(B)＿＿, someone who wanted to learn algebra couldn't sleep at 2:00 a.m. on Thursday, he could go do algebra to his heart's content. Not only could anybody who wanted to learn anything try to learn it whenever he wanted, he could redo lessons as many times as necessary, without failing any tests or being subject to ridicule from teachers or other students.

*algebra 대수

	(A)		(B)
①	Likewise	…	in contrast
②	Likewise	…	in fact
③	Moreover	…	for example
④	Moreover	…	in contrast

09

주어진 글 다음에 이어질 글의 순서로 가장 적절한 것은?

Self-awareness is observed in chimpanzees and the other apes. When chimps are placed in front of a mirror it takes just a few minutes for them to figure out that they are seeing themselves.

(A) Touching the dot on its own forehead shows that the animal understands that it is seeing its own image in the mirror. A chimp will touch the dot on its own forehead. All of the ape species have been found to touch their own forehead while every monkey species touches the dot in the mirror.

(B) They then spend a while examining inside their mouths, the top of their head, and everywhere else they couldn't see before. Monkeys never figure out that they are seeing their own image – or they just don't behave as a human would do as the image is recognized.

(C) One can put a red dot on the forehead of an animal and then place that animal in front of a mirror. We then watch to see whether the animal touches the dot in the mirror or the dot on its own head.

① (B) – (A) – (C)
② (B) – (C) – (A)
③ (C) – (A) – (B)
④ (C) – (B) – (A)

10

Ottoman Empire에 관한 다음 글의 내용과 일치하지 <u>않는</u> 것은?

In the 1300s the Ottoman Turks established another Muslim empire. The Ottoman rulers, called sultans, took Constantinople in 1453 and made it the Ottoman capital. By the 1600s the Ottoman Empire included most of Southwest Asia and stretched into parts of eastern Europe and most of North Africa. However, political struggles, corruption, and rivalries with other countries slowly weakened the empire. Over time, ethnic minorities within the empire's borders also began to push for independence. During World War I the Ottoman Empire fought on the losing side. After the war, a general named Mustafa Kemal took over the government. He created the Republic of Turkey and established its capital at Ankara. Beyond Turkey, the former Ottoman territories including Iraq, Syria, Lebanon, and Palestine became controlled by Great Britain and France. After World War Ⅱ these regions gained independence.

*ethnic 민족의, 인종의

① It was based on Islam and capitalized on Constantinople in 1453.
② By the 17th century, it had expanded to Southwest Asia, parts of Eastern Europe, and North Africa.
③ As their power weakened, minorities began to demand independence.
④ As one of the victors of World War I, it was reborn as the Republic of Turkey after the war.

해설편 p.136

제한 시간 15분	소요 시간 분	점수 /10

PART Ⅰ 어법

01

(A), (B), (C)의 각 네모 안에서 어법에 맞는 표현으로 가장 적절한 것은?

A new, bold experiment called Start-Up Chile is designed in Chile. The Chilean government is literally importing early-stage entrepreneurs from around the world (A) [who / which] are starting new ventures with the goal of infecting the local community with an entrepreneurial spirit. Start-Up Chile offers start-up companies the chance to come to Chile for six months to start their company. Each venture that is selected to participate (B) [gives / is given] $40,000 to pay for their local expenses as well as space in the Start-Up Chile collaborative workspace. The participants share what they are doing and are encouraged to hire local talent to help with their venture. The goal is to inspire people in Chile to consider starting their own companies by exposing them to role models from around the world. Start-Up Chile literally wants to change their minds, making them less fearful of failure and more (C) [open / openly] to opportunities.

*entrepreneur 기업가, 사업가

	(A)		(B)		(C)
①	who	…	gives	…	open
②	who	…	is given	…	open
③	which	…	is given	…	openly
④	which	…	gives	…	openly

02

우리말을 영어로 잘못 옮긴 것은?

① 나이가 들어가면 들어갈수록 그만큼 더 외국어 공부하기가 어려워진다.
→ The older you grow, the more difficult it becomes to learn a foreign language.

② 우리가 가지고 있는 학식이란 기껏해야 우리가 모르고 있는 것과 비교할 때 지극히 작은 것이다.
→ The learning and knowledge that we have is at the least but little compared with that of which we are ignorant.

③ 인생의 비밀은 좋아하는 것을 하는 것이 아니라 해야 할 것을 좋아하도록 시도하는 것이다.
→ The secret of life is not to do what one likes, but to try to like what one has to do.

④ 이 세상에서 당신이 소유하고 있는 것은 당신이 죽을 때 다른 누군가에게 가지만, 당신의 인격은 영원히 당신의 것일 것이다.
→ What you possess in this world will go to someone else when you die, but your personality will be yours forever.

PART Ⅱ 어휘

03

밑줄 친 부분과 의미가 가장 가까운 것은?

Kim proposed Plan A and Lee, Plan B, but these two are <u>complementary</u>.

① opposed to each other
② almost the same, but not related
③ praiseworthy in every respect
④ different but together form a complete whole

04

밑줄 친 부분과 의미가 가장 가까운 것은?

> Most members of the camel family are found in <u>arid</u> habitats.

① dirty
② dry
③ sandy
④ harsh

PART Ⅲ 생활영어

05

다음 중 두 사람의 대화가 어색한 것은?

① A : I don't want to go alone.
B : Do you want me to come along?
② A : I feel a little tired.
B : I think you need to take a break.
③ A : I can't take it anymore.
B : Calm down.
④ A : I'll keep my fingers crossed for you.
B : When did you hurt your fingers?

PART Ⅳ 독해

06

다음 글의 빈칸에 들어갈 말로 가장 적절한 것은?

> Like a muscle, willpower has limited capacity, and when exercised extensively it can become worn out. Also like a muscle, the primary fuel your brain uses to exercise willpower is sugar from your blood. So when your blood sugar is low (i.e., when you're hungry, which when you're dieting is pretty much all the time), your willpower is weaker than ever, and the only way to fix it is to eat. You can see the difficulty this can cause when you're making food decisions. Throwing exercise into the equation − something dieters use to intentionally burn more calories (i.e., use more blood sugar) − only makes things more problematic. Baumeister and Tierney call it a nutritional catch-22: the less you eat and the more you exercise, the less likely you will be to ______________________ in the end and maintain your weight loss.
>
> *catch-22 (소설의 제목에서 유래한 표현) 진퇴양난, 모순

① build muscles fast
② lower blood sugar levels
③ burn calories efficiently
④ make good food decisions

07

다음 글의 ① ~ ④ 중에서 주어진 문장이 들어가기에 가장 적절한 곳은?

However, the Vikings may have had another navigation aid.

No one can say when or where the mariner's compass was invented, but the Vikings seemed to have managed without it, since they seemed to have already crossed the North Atlantic before the compass was known in Scandinavia. (①) Even earlier, other maritime civilizations such as the Minoans and Phoenicians made ocean voyages out of the sight of land without a compass. (②) Early seamen probably knew how to navigate using stars, sunrise and sunset, and prevailing wind patterns. (③) Scandinavian sagas refer to sun stones. (④) Some scientists believe that these were minerals with polarizing properties.

08

다음 글의 빈칸 (A), (B)에 들어갈 말로 가장 적절한 것은?

The types and amount of measurement equipment the researcher takes with him into the field depend largely upon the purpose of his fieldwork, the climate, the nature of the geography, and the nature of the maps and data he can obtain from others. If the proposed study focuses upon agriculture, ____(A)____, essential equipment may include rain gauges, a soil thermometer, and soil color charts. If the climate is tropical, corrosion-resistant implements, silica gel to remove excess moisture, and special tropical packs may be the order of the day. If climbing steep, rough terrain presents special problems, light-weight equipment is necessary. An important step in planning equipment needs, ____(B)____, is to seek the advice of those who have done similar research in nearby areas. Such checking might have spared past researchers the grief of having their too-beautiful rain gauges turn up as the personal adornment of informants.

*corrosion-resistant 잘 부식되지 않는 **adornment 장식

	(A)		(B)
①	for example	…	however
②	for example	…	therefore
③	in contrast	…	however
④	in contrast	…	therefore

09

주어진 글 다음에 이어질 글의 순서로 가장 적절한 것은?

The growing emphasis on 'work readiness' is the subject of much debate. Some believe that work and education are qualitatively different social sites.

(A) Employers report that work experience improves graduates' soft skills, increases confidence and helps relate their studies to employment, making them more rounded and with more realistic expectations of work. The opportunity to make contacts and create networks for future employment is another advantage. In other words, work experience improves work readiness.

(B) While education provides skills and knowledge useful both in the short and long term, it can only provide broad or generic training for work. Specific training for a particular job can only be undertaken after study.

(C) However, the demand for work-ready graduates, who are familiar with organisational practices in the workplace, is increasing. Employers value work experience believing that exposure to the workplace while studying provides students with the opportunity to acquire valuable insights into how the workplace operates and what is expected of them in different workplace settings.

① (B) – (A) – (C)
② (B) – (C) – (A)
③ (C) – (A) – (B)
④ (C) – (B) – (A)

10

Marjorie Kinnan Rawlings에 관한 다음 글의 내용과 일치하지 <u>않는</u> 것은?

Marjorie Kinnan Rawlings, an American author born in Washington, D.C. in 1896, wrote novels with rural themes and settings. While she was young, one of her stories appeared in The Washington Post. After graduating from university, Rawlings worked as a journalist while simultaneously trying to establish herself as a fiction writer. In 1928, she purchased an orange grove in Cross Creek, Florida. This became the source of inspiration for some of her writings which included The Yearling and her autobiographical book, Cross Creek. In 1939, The Yearling, which was about a boy and an orphaned baby deer, won the Pulitzer Prize for Fiction. Later, in 1946, The Yearling was made into a film of the same name. Rawlings passed away in 1953, and the land she owned at Cross Creek has become a Florida State Park honoring her achievements.

*grove 과수원

① Washington, D.C., American writer.
② One of her stories appeared in The Washington Post.
③ After graduating from university, I worked as a journalist.
④ The novel The Yearling was made into a film under a different title.

해설편 p.138

제한 시간 15 분	소요 시간 분	점수 /10

PART Ⅰ 어법

01

다음 글의 밑줄 친 부분 중, 어법상 틀린 것은?

We have a strange belief in the power of signals. If a visitor from a planet without cars ① <u>were</u> to visit Earth, he might be truly puzzled by the strange daubs of paint on the street. Do you remember the children's game Red Light, Green Light? The person ② <u>acts</u> as the stoplight would stand with his back to the other players and announce, "Green light." The players would move forward. Then he would say, "Red light" and spin around. If you didn't stop before he saw you, you were "out." ③ <u>What</u> makes the game work is that children do not always stop in time. ④ <u>Nor</u> do adults in real life, which is even more complicated, because we have things like yellow lights − do I stop or do I go? A line on the street or a light in the air may keep cities from getting sued, but it does nothing to prevent a driver from misbehaving, perhaps even killing someone.

*daub (아무렇게나 발라 놓은 페인트 따위의) 칠, 얼룩

02

우리말을 영어로 잘못 옮긴 것은?

① 그들은 지구상에서 진화한 가장 큰 동물인데, 공룡보다 훨씬 크다.
→ They are the largest animals ever to evolve on Earth, larger by far than the dinosaurs.

② 그녀는 나의 엄마가 그랬던 것만큼이나 아메리카 원주민이라는 용어를 좋아하지 않았다.
→ She didn't like the term Native American any more than my mother did.

③ 우리가 자연에 대해 정보로 받아들이는 것의 4분의 3은 눈을 통해 우리 뇌로 들어온다.
→ Three − quarters of what we absorb in the way of information about nature comes into our brains via our eyes.

④ 많은 의사들이 의학에서의 모든 최신의 발전에 뒤떨어지지 않기 위해서 열심히 공부한다.
→ The number of doctors study hard in order that they can keep abreast of all the latest developments in medicine.

PART Ⅱ 어휘

03

밑줄 친 부분과 의미가 가장 가까운 것은?

My friend sent me a few <u>complimentary</u> tickets for the concert.

① splendid
② enigmatic
③ compatible
④ free

04

밑줄 친 부분과 의미가 가장 가까운 것은?

If I am physically <u>assaulted</u>, it will permit me to retaliate with reasonable violence.

① endorsed
② divulged
③ assailed
④ resented

PART Ⅲ 생활영어

05

다음 중 두 사람의 대화가 어색한 것은?

① A: How did you like the movie you saw yesterday?
  B: Wait, please don't spoil it for me.
② A: James, what's your goal for this year?
  B: Well, I want to learn to play the violin.
③ A: How is your group project going, Peter?
  B: Not very well. It's harder than I thought.
④ A: Your cap looks great. Where did you get it?
  B: I bought it at a flea market last Saturday.

PART Ⅳ 독해

06

다음 글의 빈칸에 들어갈 말로 가장 적절한 것은?

I have found it interesting to compare the electronic equipment sold to consumers with the equipment sold to professionals. Although much more expensive, the professional equipment tends to be simpler and easier to use. Video recorders for the home market have numerous flashing lights, many buttons and settings, and complex menus for setting the time and programming future recordings. The recorders for the professionals just have the essentials and are therefore easier to use while functioning better. This difference arises, in part, because the designers will be ______________________, so they know just what is important and what is not. Tools made by artisans for themselves all have this property. Designers of hiking or mountain climbing equipment may one day find their lives depending upon the quality and behavior of their own designs.

*artisan 장인, 숙련공

① working closely with buyers
② using the products themselves
③ encouraged to create their own work
④ manufacturing various styles of products

07

다음 글의 ① ~ ④ 중에서 주어진 문장이 들어가기에 가장 적절한 곳은?

> Despite such early support, the levels of correlation obtained between measures of simple reaction time and various standard measures of intelligence have been weak.

People who believe that individual differences in intelligence can be traced back to sheer speed of information processing have tended to use simple reaction time and related tasks. In a simple reaction-time paradigm, the individual is required simply to make a single response as quickly as possible following the presentation of a stimulus. (①) For example, we might tell you to press the space bar on your keyboard whenever a picture of a frog showed up. (②) Then we might show you a penguin, a fish, a frog, a giraffe, and a frog. (③) Your reaction time would be measured by how quickly you hit the space bar after the frog was shown each time. This paradigm has been widely used since the days of Francis Galton, the father of psychometrics, as a measure of intelligence. (④) There seems to be much more to intelligence than pure speed.

*psychometrics 심리측정학

08

다음 글의 빈칸 (A), (B)에 들어갈 말로 가장 적절한 것은?

In the past couple of decades, we've seen changes in tax policy, greater overseas competition, ongoing government waste, and Wall Street shenanigans. But when we look at the data and research, we conclude that none of these are the primary driver of growing inequality. ____(A)____, the main driver is exponential, digital, and combinatorial change in the technology that supports our economic system. This conclusion is solidified by the fact that similar trends are apparent in most advanced countries. ____(B)____, in Sweden, Finland, and Germany, income inequality has actually grown more quickly over the past twenty to thirty years than in the United States. Because these countries started with less inequality in their income distributions, they continued to be less unequal than the United States, but the underlying trend is similar worldwide across sometimes markedly different institutions, government policies, and cultures.

*shenanigan 속임수 **exponential 기하급수적인

	(A)		(B)
①	Instead	···	However
②	Instead	···	For instance
③	Nevertheless	···	Consequently
④	Nevertheless	···	Consequently

09

주어진 글 다음에 이어질 글의 순서로 가장 적절한 것은?

Clearly, schematic knowledge helps you – guiding your understanding and enabling you to reconstruct things you cannot remember.

(A) Likewise, if there are things you can't recall, your schemata will fill in the gaps with knowledge about what's typical in that situation. As a result, a reliance on schemata will inevitably make the world seem more "normal" than it really is and will make the past seem more "regular" than it actually was.

(B) Any reliance on schematic knowledge, therefore, will be shaped by this information about what's "normal." Thus, if there are things you don't notice while viewing a situation or event, your schemata will lead you to fill in these "gaps" with knowledge about what's normally in place in that setting.

(C) But schematic knowledge can also hurt you, promoting errors in perception and memory. Moreover, the types of errors produced by schemata are quite predictable: Bear in mind that schemata summarize the broad pattern of your experience, and so they tell you, in essence, what's typical or ordinary in a given situation.

① (B) – (A) – (C)
② (B) – (C) – (A)
③ (C) – (A) – (B)
④ (C) – (B) – (A)

10

pirarucu에 관한 다음 글의 내용과 일치하는 것은?

The pirarucu is one of the largest freshwater fish in the world at up to ten feet long and weighing more than four hundred pounds. That's a true river monster! Because of its size, it is called arapaima, or "dragon fish." All fish can breathe in water, right? Not this one. Unlike most fish, which use their gills to take in oxygen from water, the pirarucu needs to come to the surface about every ten minutes to breathe air. This helps it survive in the muddy lakes of the Amazon, where little oxygen is available. The pirarucu is one of the native fishermen's favorite meals. Every part of the fish is eaten. Even the pirarucu's tough scales are considered valuable and are used as files, like sandpaper. But the pirarucu is endangered. To make sure this gorgeous giant will be around for a long time to come, only certain native people are allowed to catch a limited number of pirarucu each year.

*gill 아가미 **file (금속 같은 거친 표면을 다듬는) 줄

① Gills are used to obtain oxygen.
② It lives in a clear lake on the oxygen-rich Amazon River.
③ There are parts that humans shouldn't eat.
④ Scales are valued and used as strings like sandpaper.

제 13 회 하프 모의고사

해설편 p.140

제한 시간 15 분 | 소요 시간 분 | 점수 /10

PART Ⅰ 어법

01

(A), (B), (C)의 각 네모 안에서 어법에 맞는 표현으로 가장 적절한 것은?

A plant-based diet lets the earth breathe easier. The cultivation of crops for direct human consumption is much more efficient than using grains or beans to fatten up farm animals. Only a small part of the nutrients that cattle or other animals take in are left in their muscles. The rest (A) [are / is] used up to power their movements, metabolism, body warmth, and other life functions. A few decades ago, Scientific American reported that producing a pound of bacon requires ten times as much crop land (in the form of feed grains) (B) [as / than] is used to make the same quantity of artificial bacon from soybeans. The cultivation of those feed crops (C) [requiring / requires] land, water, and pesticides and other chemicals that add to our environmental problems.

*metabolism 신진대사 **pesticide 살충제

	(A)		(B)		(C)
①	are	…	as	…	requiring
②	are	…	as	…	requires
③	is	…	as	…	requiring
④	is	…	than	…	requires

02

우리말을 영어로 잘못 옮긴 것은?

① 그는 빚을 갚고 나니 먹고 살아갈 수가 없게 되었다.
→ The payment of his debts left him nothing to live on.

② 사람의 가치는 재산보다도 오히려 인격에 있다.
→ Aperson's value lies not so much in what he is as in what he has.

③ 나이를 먹음에 따라, 이 속담의 의미를 분명히 알게 될 것이다.
→ As you grow older, you will come to realize the meaning of this saying clearly.

④ 개 짖는 소리에 도둑은 질겁해서 달아났다.
→ They were short of water, so that they drank as little as possible.

PART Ⅱ 어휘

03

밑줄 친 부분과 의미가 가장 가까운 것은?

As shown in the above examples, it's <u>comprehensive</u> term and has more or less four different senses.

① understandable
② broad
③ believable
④ apprehensive

04

밑줄 친 부분과 의미가 가장 가까운 것은?

> They formally <u>assented</u> to the statement.

① resented
② objected
③ pretended
④ agreed

PART Ⅲ 생활영어

05

다음 중 두 사람의 대화가 어색한 것은?

① A : After a long day at work, I'm really tired.
B : That makes two of us!
② A : Do you remember the name of the bar we went to last Friday?
B : Oh man, it's just on the tip of my tongue.
③ A : I am so excited to see this film.
B : Me too. The film got two thumbs up from all the critics.
④ A : I am feeling a little under the weather.
B : It's not actually raining now!

PART Ⅳ 독해

06

다음 글의 빈칸에 들어갈 말로 가장 적절한 것은?

> Traditionally, law schools have tended to keep their distance from other schools at a university – they usually have their own buildings. The law library is separate from other university libraries and contains little other than legal literature, a situation that promotes informational distance between law and other bodies of knowledge. The segregation of students has been nearly total. Undergraduate programs in law are rare. Law courses are peopled nearly exclusively by law students, who in turn take nothing outside of law school. In my own institution at least, law courses are listed in a separate timetable, and the law school even follows a different academic calendar from the rest of the university. Little wonder that lawyers, immersed for three years in this separate world, go forth with the belief that the law ______________________.
>
> *segregation 분리, 구분 **immerse 몰두하게 하다

① is a domain unto itself
② should always be certain
③ requires people to act right
④ is in accordance with justice

07

다음 글의 ① ~ ④ 중에서 주어진 문장이 들어가기에 가장 적절한 곳은?

For example, if you are interested in having a saltwater fish tank or a specific type of tree frog, you may be limited to specialty pet retail stores.

People acquire their pets from a variety of places and under many different circumstances. (①) The type of animal you are interested in bringing into your home may greatly influence where you acquire your pet. (②) For more common companion animal species, the choices may be overwhelming. (③) Some of the most frequently used sources of pets include friends or relatives, animal breeders, animal shelters, newspapers, online sources, and pet stores and superstores, as well as taking in a neighborhood "stray." (④) All resources for finding the right animal are not created equal, however, and there can be both positive and negative aspects to nearly all of these options.

08

다음 글의 빈칸 (A), (B)에 들어갈 말로 가장 적절한 것은?

As a rule, women farmers work longer hours and have lower incomes than do male farmers. This is not because they are less educated or less competent. ____(A)____, it is due to restricting sociocultural factors. Firstly, most women farmers are involved in subsistence farming or food production for the local market that yields little cash return. Secondly, they have less access to credit at bank than men. Government-subsidized rates that would make it possible for them to acquire the 'Green Revolution' technology, such as hybrid seeds and fertilizers are also comparatively inaccessible to women. Thirdly, in some societies women cannot own land and so are excluded from agricultural improvement programs and projects aimed at landowners. ____(B)____, many African agricultural development programs are based on the conversion of communal land to private holdings. This conversion adversely affects women because women have access to communal land while they are excluded from private holdings.

*subsistence farming 자급적 농업 **communal land 공동 토지

	(A)		(B)
①	Rather	···	In short
②	Rather	···	For example
③	In addition	···	For example
④	In addition	···	In contrast

09

주어진 글 다음에 이어질 글의 순서로 가장 적절한 것은?

Worker bees don't "normally" lay eggs. That's because the queen's pheromones suppress the reproductive systems of the workers.

(A) However, since they haven't mated, their unfertilized eggs will yield only male bees. Maybe some of them will get lucky and find a willing queen, passing the hive's genes along in its dying days.

(B) However, if the queen dies and there are no larvae that can be trained to replace her, that can change. Unless a beekeeper intervenes with a new queen, the hive is doomed.

(C) In that case, a dying queenless colony will try to spread its genes before it goes to an end, using an unexpected strategy: some of the workers will start laying eggs.

*pheromone 페로몬 **unfertilized 수정되지 않은 ***larva 유충

① (B) – (A) – (C)
② (B) – (C) – (A)
③ (C) – (A) – (B)
④ (C) – (B) – (A)

10

The Theater at Epidaurus에 관한 다음 글의 내용과 일치하는 것은?

The Theater at Epidaurus was an example of ancient Greek civic architecture meant to be enjoyed by the general public. The art of the theater was an important part of ancient Greek culture and religion, as religious ceremonies were incorporated with music and dance, and performed in public spaces. Greek drama, including tragedies and comedies, was performed in outdoor spaces like the Theater at Epidaurus. At the heart of the theater was the circular orchestra, the central performance area. Fifty-five rows of semicircular tiered seats were carved into a hillside, which allowed as many as fourteen thousand spectators a good view of the orchestra. The design of the Theater at Epidaurus is so effective that it is still in use today, and the acoustics are so perfect that no electrified sound system is needed when performances are held at the site.

*tiered 단으로 배열된

① It was made for the aristocracy in ancient Greece.
② It was an indoor concert hall where Greek plays were performed.
③ There was a square-shaped performance stage in the center.
④ There were seats arranged in semicircular columns.

해설편 p.142

제한 시간 15 분 | 소요 시간 분 | 점수 /10

PART Ⅰ 어법

01

(A), (B), (C)의 각 네모 안에서 어법에 맞는 표현으로 가장 적절한 것은?

According to one traditional definition, aesthetics is the branch of philosophy that deals with beauty, especially beauty in the arts. (A) [Examine / Examining] the pleasing features of the Mona Lisa or a snow-capped mountain, for example, would come under aesthetics. That definition seems too narrow, however, since works of art and natural objects may interest us in other ways than by being beautiful. Instead of evoking admiration of beauty, artists may evoke puzzlement, shock, and even disgust. Consider Picasso's Guernica, a huge (11-ft. x 25.6-ft.) painting in black, white, and grey (B) [that / what] he made in response to the slaughter of Spanish civilians by German and Italian warplanes during the Spanish Civil War. Images of disjointed corpses and people screaming (C) [dominate / dominates] the canvas. This work is widely admired but not for being beautiful. So a better definition of aesthetics would be that it is the branch of philosophy that deals with the ways things please people in being experienced.

*slaughter 대량 학살

	(A)		(B)		(C)
①	Examine	…	that	…	dominates
②	Examine	…	what	…	dominates
③	Examining	…	what	…	dominates
④	Examining	…	that	…	dominate

02

우리말을 영어로 잘못 옮긴 것은?

① 식사가 준비됐을 때, 우리는 식당으로 이동했다.
→ The dinner being ready, we moved to the dining hall.

② 저쪽에 있는 사람이 누구인지 알겠니?
→ Can you tell who that is over there?

③ 이 질병이 목숨을 앗아가는 일은 좀처럼 없다.
→ It rarely happens that this disease proves fatal.

④ 과정을 관리하면서 발전시키는 것이 나의 목표였다.
→ To control the process and making improvement was my objectives.

PART Ⅱ 어휘

03

밑줄 친 부분과 의미가 가장 가까운 것은?

The government <u>conceded</u> defeat as soon as the election results were known.

① compromised ② concealed
③ admitted as true ④ modified

04

밑줄 친 부분과 의미가 가장 가까운 것은?

It is a misconception to <u>assume</u> that the two continents are similar.

① pretend ② suppose
③ assert ④ assemble

PART Ⅲ 생활영어

05

다음 중 두 사람의 대화가 어색한 것은?

① A : This is Carol. How may I help you?
B : Hi, I am calling to inform you that my child is sick and will not be in school today.

② A : Hi, this is Nidia. Is Sherri there?
B : I'm sorry. You have the wrong number.

③ A : I have been working hard lately.
B : Well, I was wondering if you would like to come to the beach with me this weekend.

④ A : Hey, if you are bored you should play basketball with us.
B : I was going to ask them if they wanted to come.

PART Ⅳ 독해

06

다음 글의 빈칸에 들어갈 말로 가장 적절한 것은?

Herbert Spencer, an English sociologist, had a different view of how society works. He believed that a society can be compared to a living organism. Each part of an animal — its heart, lungs, brain, and so on — has its own function to perform, yet all the parts are interdependent; a change in one part affects all the others. Moreover, each part contributes to the survival and health of the animal as a whole. If one organ becomes diseased, the others adapt by working harder to ensure the animal's survival. Similarly, in Spencer's view, each part of a society performs its own function and contributes to the survival and stability of the whole. Family, religion, government, and industry are all seen as ___________________.

*sociologist 사회학자

① means of expressing identity
② parts of one organism: society
③ social devices for ensuring security
④ various forms of human endeavors to survive

07

다음 글의 ①～④ 중에서 주어진 문장이 들어가기에 가장 적절한 곳은?

> But that behavior always comes back to haunt us.

Self-defeating behavior occurs when we fail to learn the lessons that life tries to teach us. It represents the victory of impulse over awareness, immediate gratification over lasting satisfaction, relief over resolution. Self-defeating behavior normally begins as an attempt to make ourselves feel better. (①) It is a coping mechanism. (②) When faced with a crisis, a threat or a potentially upsetting situation, we try to protect ourselves. (③) We grasp for something that will reduce tension or keep us from getting hurt. (④) The action itself seems logical and appropriate at the time, and it might actually succeed in bringing about short-term relief.

08

다음 글의 빈칸 (A), (B)에 들어갈 말로 가장 적절한 것은?

Public policy for consumers is the establishment of laws and regulations that govern business practices in order to protect consumers. Those interested in shaping public policy study consumer behavior to understand the public needs and wants, and at the same time, to protect the public from unfair, unethical, or dangerous business practices. ____(A)____, in the packaged foods industry, the use of chemicals and preservatives has steadily increased as manufacturers have developed longer-lasting and more convenient forms of packaged food. In response, consumers have become increasingly concerned about the ingredients in processed food products because of their potential health risks and the nutritional consequences of synthetic additives. ____(B)____, U.S. Food and Drug Administration regulations now require marketers of food products to supply nutritional information on product packages in the form of "nutrition facts label."

*synthetic additive 합성 첨가물

	(A)		(B)
①	On the contrary	…	As a result
②	On the contrary	…	Nevertheless
③	For example	…	As a result
④	For example	…	Nevertheless

09

주어진 글 다음에 이어질 글의 순서로 가장 적절한 것은?

In the real estate industry, location is all-important in determining the market value of properties. A good house in a slum district will not fetch a high price, no matter how good it is.

(A) These natural advantages are enough that people will seek them out and pay slightly more for them than they would for other properties. When some properties attract elevated prices, they raise the prices of other properties nearby.

(B) In this way, the average prices in one area will drift to become higher than in neighbouring areas. People naturally assume that the area with higher prices must be better to live in. So the process escalates.

(C) But how is it that some locations come to be better than others? Usually, it starts out with a natural advantage. One area may be conveniently placed near to major businesses, or it may be close to the sea or a river, or it may be slightly hilly, allowing good views.

① (B) - (A) - (C)
② (B) - (C) - (A)
③ (C) - (A) - (B)
④ (C) - (B) - (A)

10

Verreaux's sifaka에 관한 다음 글의 내용과 일치하지 <u>않는</u> 것은?

Verreaux's sifaka lives in the forest of south-western Madagascar. This species lives in small groups of up to about 12 individuals. Groups contain more or less equal numbers of adult males and females. The group defends a small territory. They use their scent to mark the territory's boundary. Sifakas mate in December, at the height of the dry season. A single young is born five months later and it is weaned after seven months. Sifakas move through the trees by leaping. The distance they can jump is increased slightly by small flaps of skin under the animal's short forearms. On the ground, sifakas move by hopping sideways on both hind feet. The forearms are held out to the side for balance. Verreaux's sifakas eat all types of plant material apart from the roots. In the rainy season they prefer to eat easily digested soft fruits and flowers, but in the dry season they rely on wood, bark and leaves.

*wean 젖을 떼다

① It lives in small groups of up to a dozen.
② Mark your area using smell.
③ Five months after mating, one baby is born.
④ Move on four legs on the ground.

제 15 회 하프 모의고사

해설편 p.144

제한 시간 15 분 | 소요 시간 분 | 점수 /10

PART Ⅰ 어법

01

(A), (B), (C)의 각 네모 안에서 어법에 맞는 표현으로 가장 적절한 것은?

It's not just in science, of course, (A) [that / what] we use and misuse logic. Logic is the way we order our thoughts and make sense of the world. As we grow up, our eyes learn to interpret things we see, from recognizing particular arrangements of lines and shadows as three-dimensional boxes to (B) [identify / identifying] faces as friendly or hostile. So logic helps us find our way through the world. Logical argument is, also, if our use of logic is good, an invaluable way of checking if our insights are actually correct. And, of course, it can be a very effective way of justifying our ideas to other people. Indeed, logic can seem so (C) [powerful / powerfully] persuasive that all of us bring it into our everyday conversations all the time.

	(A)		(B)		(C)
①	that	···	identify	···	powerful
②	that	···	identifying	···	powerfully
③	what	···	identifying	···	powerful
④	what	···	identify	···	powerfully

02

우리말을 영어로 잘못 옮긴 것은?

① 나의 이모는 파티에서 그녀를 만난 것을 기억하지 못했다.
→ My aunt didn't remember meeting her at the party.

② 나의 첫 책을 쓰는 데 40년이 걸렸다.
→ It took me 40 years to write my first book.

③ 학교에서 집으로 걸어오고 있을 때 강풍에 내 우산이 뒤집혔다.
→ A strong wind blew my umbrella inside out as I was walking home from school.

④ 끝까지 생존하는 생물은 가장 강한 생물도, 가장 지적인 생물도 아니고, 변화에 가장 잘 반응하는 생물이다.
→ It is not the strongest of the species, nor the most intelligent, or the one most responsive to change that survives to the end.

PART Ⅱ 어휘

03

밑줄 친 부분과 의미가 가장 가까운 것은?

A number of our most famous senators are skilled <u>conciliators.</u>

① speakers
② parliamentarians
③ mediators
④ lawyers

04

밑줄 친 부분과 의미가 가장 가까운 것은?

> Mr. Smith will <u>assume</u> the role of Chief Executive with a team of four directors.

① undertake
② presume
③ effuse
④ take down

PART Ⅲ 생활영어

05

다음 중 두 사람의 대화가 어색한 것은?

① A: I'd like to make a reservation for tomorrow, please.
B: Certainly. For what time?
② A: Are you ready to order?
B: Yes, I'd like the soup, please.
③ A: How's your risotto?
B: Yes, we have risotto with mushroom and cheese.
④ A: Would you like a dessert?
B: Not for me, thanks.

PART Ⅳ 독해

06

다음 글의 빈칸에 들어갈 말로 가장 적절한 것은?

> One of the best ways to escape the confines or our worldview is to shirt our peer group and talk to people whose work experiences and daily lives are very different from our own. If you really want to pursue a new career, it might be wise to spend less time with your current colleagues, good company though they may be. More specifically, you can learn an enormous amount by having conversations with people who have made career changes that ____________________. If you really are drawn to teaching at a Steiner school, can you find a Steiner teacher who was once a lawyer or doctor and take them out to lunch? If you are a bored academic hoping to become a garden designer, you should do everything you can to find a fellow scholar who has made this same move, or some other big change.

① inspire your creative mind
② involve more than one step
③ seem to be impossible to attain
④ match where you hope to be heading

07

다음 글의 ① ~ ④ 중에서 주어진 문장이 들어가기에 가장 적절한 곳은?

> To describe this apparent variation in the rate of ageing, scientists like to draw a distinction between 'chronological' and 'biological' age.

'Ageing' is a word that we use all the time, so we have a fair idea of what we mean by it in general terms, but it is when we try to be a little more precise that the trouble starts. (①) For example, within a population there are some individuals who seem to age fast, and others who age more slowly. (②) Chronological age is measured by the simple passage of time − the number of candles on the birthday cake. (③) Biological age tries to express how far we have travelled along the road from birth to death of old age. (④) A woman who is aged 60 years chronologically, but has the appearance and stamina of a typical 50-year-old, may have a slower biological ageing rate than the average.

08

다음 글의 빈칸 (A), (B)에 들어갈 말로 가장 적절한 것은?

To the casual viewer, a film about high school may be nothing more than simple entertainment. When the films are viewed collectively, ___(A)___, the high school film genre reveals patterns that go beyond entertainment and teach deeper lessons about American culture. Motion pictures do not necessarily reflect the high school experience accurately. Hollywood routinely twists and shapes reality to maximize dramatic or comic effects. Films must also frame complicated social relationships within two hours and on a two-dimensional canvas. Nevertheless, even if they are not precise social documents of real high schools and real adolescents, these high school films are still culturally meaningful. ___(B)___, they have something to teach us about how Americans make sense of education, adolescence, and class inequality.

	(A)		(B)
①	however	···	Otherwise
②	however	···	That is
③	for example	···	Likewise
④	therefore	···	That is

09

주어진 글 다음에 이어질 글의 순서로 가장 적절한 것은?

Like all sectors in mature industries, the construction sector is characterized by a relatively few leading thinkers who innovate and monitor trends and a larger group of technical experts who receive and disseminate innovation and new ideas.

(A) However, it gets a great deal of media publicity for innovation and forward thinking, particularly architects. Yet for most construction work, such high levels of technical sophistication are not necessary and are not supported because it is costly.

(B) This dissemination group consists of architects, consultants, designers, and engineers. In the construction sector this dissemination group is very small, relatively conservative, and divided up into groups.

(C) Most buildings are built for functional purposes and not to advance or explore the limits of technology. A practical building with a facade that is interesting or artful is more than sufficient for most purposes.

*disseminate (정보·지식 등을) 전파하다 **facade (건물의) 전면[앞면]

① (B) – (A) – (C)
② (B) – (C) – (A)
③ (C) – (A) – (B)
④ (C) – (B) – (A)

10

Abigail Adams에 관한 다음 글의 내용과 일치하지 않는 것은?

As the matriarch of one of America's first families, Abigail Adams strongly influenced two presidents – her husband, John Adams, and her son John Quincy Adams. She is also recognized as one of the country's greatest and most productive letter writers. Abigail was born on November 11, 1744, in Weymouth, Massachusetts. One of three daughters of a Congregational minister, William Smith, and his wife, Elizabeth, Abigail was a sickly child and was unable to attend school. Small, quiet, and reserved, with piercing dark eyes, she was also strong-willed and had a quick and curious mind. In spite of her lack of formal schooling, Abigail was a voracious reader who took advantage of her father's well-stocked library to study literature, history, and philosophy. She taught herself French and was tutored by her maternal grandmother, whom she adored and who favored a "happy method of mixing instruction and amusement together."

*matriarch 여성 가장 **voracious (새로운 정보·지식을) 열렬히 탐하는

① The husband and son were the presidents of the United States.
② He is recognized as one of the most prolific writers in the United States.
③ I was too weak to attend school.
④ I learned French from my maternal grandmother without self-taught.

제 16 회 하프 모의고사

해설편 p.146

제한 시간 15 분	소요 시간 분	점수 /10

PART Ⅰ 어법

01

다음 글의 밑줄 친 부분 중, 어법상 틀린 것은?

The process of job advancement in the field of sports is often said to ① be shaped like a pyramid: at the wide base are many jobs with youth or high school athletic teams, while at the narrow tip ② is the few, highly coveted jobs with professional organizations. Thus there are many sports jobs altogether, but the competition becomes ③ increasingly tough as one works his or her way up. The salaries of various positions reflect this pyramid model. For example, high school football and basketball coaches are typically teachers who get paid a little extra for their after-class work. But coaches of the same sports at big universities can become national celebrities who earn more than $1 million a year, ④ exceeding the salaries of college presidents. One level higher up are the National Football League and the National Basketball Association, where head coaches can earn many times more than their best-paid campus counterparts.

*covet 탐내다, 갈망하다

02

우리말을 영어로 잘못 옮긴 것은?

① 네가 하는 어떤 것도 나에게는 괜찮아.
→ Whatever you do is fine with me.

② 나는 어떤 일도 결코 우연히 하지 않았으며, 내 발명 중 어느 것도 우연히 이루어진 것은 없었다.
→ I never did anything by accident, nor did any of my inventions come by accident.

③ 사랑은 서로를 응시하는 것에 있지 않고, 같은 방향을 함께 바라보는 것에 있다.
→ Love does not consist in gazing at each other, but looks outward together in the same direction.

④ 자원봉사자들은 그들이 가치가 없기 때문이 아니라, 매우 귀중하기 때문에 보수를 받지 않는다.
→ Volunteers aren't paid, not because they are worthless, but because they are priceless.

PART Ⅱ 어휘

03

다음 글의 빈칸에 들어갈 말로 가장 적절한 것은?

He made a concise statement about the matter.

① terse
② redundant
③ inclusive
④ gorgeous

04

밑줄 친 부분과 의미가 가장 가까운 것은?

> The woman was <u>astounded</u> to learn that her dearest friend had been spreading bad gossip about her.

① surprised
② irrigated
③ disappointed
④ trembled

PART Ⅲ 생활영어

05

다음 중 두 사람의 대화가 어색한 것은?

① A: Did you hear the exam results?
B: They really cut corners when they built an extension.
② A: Tomorrow is the D-day. I am really nervous.
B: Break a leg, Sam. I'm sure your performance will be great.
③ A: Why don't we get this purse? It looks great.
B: We can't afford this purse! It costs an arm and a leg.
④ A: How often do you go to a cinema?
B: I only go to the cinema once in a blue moon.

PART Ⅳ 독해

06

다음 글의 빈칸에 들어갈 말로 가장 적절한 것은?

> It is unfortunate that a lot of people find it extremely difficult to build trust in their created relationships, like in a spouse, and yet find it extremely natural and safe to trust their parents or siblings. Sometimes it is necessary to wonder if this trust stems from some biological connection in the blood or basically has been built over the years of growing up together. But then there are situations when people who may not have grown up together or even met before (as in cases of cousins and distant relatives) still find it easy to trust and depend upon each other as when they say, "Oh, but he is family", as if that is supposed to indicate a certain sense of togetherness to justify ______________________ even in a total stranger.

① pointing out an error
② entrusting one's faith
③ sticking to old customs
④ demanding contribution

07

다음 글의 ① ~ ④ 중에서 주어진 문장이 들어가기에 가장 적절한 곳은?

> Excessive uncontrolled oxidation, however, is the enemy of health and longevity in humans, just as excessive oxidation turns your new car into a junker and your apple slice into compost.

Oxidation is the process by which atoms and molecules lose electrons as they come into contact with other atoms and molecules; it's one of the most basic chemical reactions in the universe. (①) When you cut an apple and it turns brown in contact with air or when your car bumper rusts, you're witnessing oxidation at work. (②) Oxidation happens within our bodies as well. (③) Some of it is natural and good; oxidation facilitates the transfer of energy within the body. Oxidation also gets rid of potentially harmful foreign substances in the body by making them water-soluble (and therefore able to flow out of the body through urine). (④) Oxidation produces something called free radicals, which we know are responsible for encouraging aging and promoting cancer.

08

다음 글의 빈칸 (A), (B)에 들어갈 말로 가장 적절한 것은?

Contrary to some beliefs, you do not need perfect soil to start and grow a productive garden. ____(A)____, it is best to have soil that is fertile, full of organic materials that provide nutrients to the plant roots, and easy to dig and cultivate. Loose, well-drained soil is ideal for growing a good garden. If there is a section of your yard where water does not easily drain after a good, soaking rain, it is best not to plant your garden in that area, as the excess water will most likely drown your garden plants. ____(B)____, soils that are of a clay or sandy consistency are not as effective in growing plants. To make these types of soils more nutrient-rich and fertile, add in organic material such as compost to improve their quality.

*compost 퇴비

	(A)		(B)
①	Similarly	···	Furthermore
②	However	···	Consequently
③	In addition	···	For example
④	However	···	Furthermore

09

주어진 글 다음에 이어질 글의 순서로 가장 적절한 것은?

"Why teach history?" Not, I propose, because it's there. Rather, we should teach history because it is a resource that can shed light on the lives we live today.

(A) It would be equally foolish to ignore our collective history. This is why history should occupy a central place not only in the liberal arts curriculum, but in primary, secondary and post secondary education.

(B) We can learn from history because earlier times and thinkers were confronted with problems, ideas and circumstances which have affinities to those that confront us today.

(C) We can learn from them both when past ages are committed to concepts and views similar to our own, and when they have views that are notable for their differences. Only a fool would ignore his past experience when confronted with a new situation.

*liberal arts 교양과목 **affinity 유사성, 관련(성)

① (B) – (A) – (C)
② (B) – (C) – (A)
③ (C) – (A) – (B)
④ (C) – (B) – (A)

10

Hugh John Lofting에 관한 다음 글의 내용과 일치하지 않는 것은?

Hugh John Lofting was born in England to an Irish father and an English mother. Hugh was an imaginative child and loved to create stories to tell his brothers and sisters. He also loved animals and had many pets as a child. Hugh's concern for animals led to the creation of Doctor Dolittle. Doctor Dolittle began as a cheerful, charming doctor who became more serious as his adventures continued. This was perhaps a parallel to Hugh's life. His adulthood was marked with several sorrows. His first wife died in 1927, only four years after his great success in winning the Newbery Medal. He got remarried, but his second wife died less than a year later. In the twenty-seven years that followed the publication of his first Doctor Dolittle book, Hugh wrote thirteen other books about the kindly doctor, as well as a number of other books for children. The Doctor Dolittle stories are still some of the best loved of all time.

① He liked to tell his siblings the story he created.
② I liked animals and had many pets when I was young.
③ Interest in animals led to the creation of Dr. Dolittle.
④ I didn't write any children's books other than Dr. Dolittle's.

제 17 회 하프 모의고사

해설편 p.148

제한 시간 15 분 | 소요 시간 분 | 점수 /10

PART Ⅰ 어법

01

(A), (B), (C)의 각 네모 안에서 어법에 맞는 표현으로 가장 적절한 것은?

Some of us are pessimists, and some of us are realists, but most of us are optimists. With respect to risk, most of us believe that we are above average, meaning that we think that we are less vulnerable than most people. Odds are that you believe that you are less likely than others (A) [suffer / to suffer] from life's misfortunes, including automobile accidents, heart attacks, and divorce. Though most people are aware (B) [of / that] about 50 percent of marriages end in divorce, brides and grooms typically believe that the chance that they will get divorced is far lower than that. (Even divorce lawyers, who really should know better, greatly underestimate their chances of getting divorced.) Perhaps more (C) [surprised / surprisingly], one study found that smokers do not underestimate the statistical risks faced by the population of smokers, but they nonetheless believe that their personal risk is less than that of the average nonsmoker.

*pessimist 비관론자 **optimist 낙관론자 ***odds 가능성, 가망

	(A)		(B)		(C)
①	suffer	…	that	…	surprised
②	suffer	…	of	…	surprised
③	to suffer	…	of	…	surprisingly
④	to suffer	…	that	…	surprisingly

02

우리말을 영어로 바르게 옮긴 것은?

① 당신이 부자일지라도 당신은 진실한 친구들을 살 수는 없다.
→ Rich as if you may be, you can't buy sincere friends.

② 그것은 너무나 아름다운 유성 폭풍이어서 우리는 밤새 그것을 보았다.
→ It was such a beautiful meteor storm that we watched it all night.

③ 학위가 없는 것이 그녀의 성공을 방해했다.
→ Her lack of a degree kept her advancing.

④ 그는 사형이 폐지되어야 하는지 아닌지에 대한 에세이를 써야 한다.
→ He has to write an essay on if or not the death penalty should be abolished.

PART Ⅱ 어휘

03

밑줄 친 부분과 의미가 가장 가까운 것은?

The school <u>conferred</u> an award on him.

① compromised
② corrupted
③ collaborated
④ gave

04

밑줄 친 부분과 의미가 가장 가까운 것은?

Audiences cheered as Luke Sky walker and Princess Leia made their <u>audacious</u>, death-defying leap to freedom, escaping Darth Vader's troops.

① prudent
② bold
③ hilarious
④ intelligent

PART Ⅲ 생활영어

05

다음 중 두 사람의 대화가 어색한 것은?

① A : Wasn't that last question on the test tough?
B : Yes, it was tricky.
② A : Hi, please transfer me to Ella Jones. This is her husband.
B : I'll put you right through.
③ A : Why is Mina so fed up at her job?
B : She feels overeaten.
④ A : Chanhee? What brings you to London?
B : I just arrived on business.

PART Ⅳ 독해

06

다음 글의 빈칸에 들어갈 말로 가장 적절한 것은?

Resist the temptation of leaning too much towards the use of convergent thinking to the exclusion of divergent thinking. It's easy for us to fall into the trap of telling our children what is right and wrong even when it comes to ideas and suggestions which may be relatively open-ended and highly subjective. We also need to look at the way we phrase our questions, making sure we ask questions which promote divergent thinking. For example, instead of saying 'Let's use some glue to stick the pictures to make a collage,' you may say 'I wonder how we can attach this to this so that we can make it special.' Simply by rephrasing what we say, we are not just suggesting one correct solution, but rather, we can encourage children ______________________.

① to read as many good books as possible
② to put themselves in someone else's shoes
③ to elaborate their thoughts on the same idea
④ to think about different solutions to a problem

07

다음 글의 ①～④ 중에서 주어진 문장이 들어가기에 가장 적절한 곳은?

This is exactly the same phenomenon evident in the three-dimensional image created by interacting laser beams.

To appreciate the relationship between parts and wholes in living systems, we do not need to study nature at the microscopic level. If you gaze up at the nighttime sky, you see all of the sky visible from where you stand. Yet the pupil of your eye, fully open, is less than a centimeter across. (①) Somehow, light from the whole of the sky must be present in the small space of your eye. (②) And if your pupil were only half as large, or only one quarter as large, this would still be so. (③) Light from the entirety of the nighttime sky is present in every space — no matter how small. (④) This holographic image can be cut in half indefinitely, and each piece, no matter how small, will still contain the entire image.

08

다음 글의 빈칸 (A), (B)에 들어갈 말로 가장 적절한 것은?

When two cultures come into contact, they do not exchange every cultural item. If that were the case, there would be no cultural differences in the world today. ____(A)____, only a small number of cultural elements are ever diffused from one culture to another. Which cultural item is accepted depends largely on the item's use and compatibility with already existing cultural traits. For example, it is not likely that men's hair dyes designed to "get out the gray" will diffuse into parts of rural Africa where a person's status is elevated with advancing years. Even when an innovation is consistent with a society's needs, there is still no guarantee that it will be accepted. ____(B)____, most people in the United States using US customary units (e.g., inch, foot, yard, mile, etc.) have resisted adopting the metric system even though making such a change would enable US citizens to interface with the rest of the world more efficiently.

*compatibility 양립 가능성 **metric system 미터법

	(A)		(B)
①	Instead	···	For example
②	Instead	···	Similarly
③	Nevertheless	···	Conversely
④	Nevertheless	···	For example

09

주어진 글 다음에 이어질 글의 순서로 가장 적절한 것은?

When we're depressed, play can seem like a foreign concept. Sometimes when I ask my depressed clients what they envision when I say the word play, they look at me with a blank stare.

(A) I found that many subjects I spoke with had a hard time conceiving what play is for grown-ups, because it's different from child's play, which was the only kind of play they knew.

(B) So I decided to conduct an experiment about play with a number of people I worked with, as well as some family and friends. It was simple: I asked them all what play meant to them.

(C) This finding relates to a common thought of play. In a culture that prizes productivity, adult play seems to be defined as a negative, unproductive, self-indulgent activity — oreven something X-rated. I believe that we need to update our definition of play.

*self-indulgent 방종한, 제멋대로 하는 **X-rated 성인용 등급의

① (B) – (A) – (C)
② (B) – (C) – (A)
③ (C) – (A) – (B)
④ (C) – (B) – (A)

10

Ferdinand Cohn에 관한 다음 글의 내용과 일치하지 않는 것은?

Born in the German-Jewish ghetto of Breslau, Silesia (now Wroclaw, Poland), Ferdinand Cohn was a child prodigy, able to read before the age of two and attending university at age fourteen. However, his first degree was withheld due to his Jewish ancestry and he was unable to obtain a teaching position in Berlin – probably also because of his Jewish roots. Cohn's interest in the microscopic world developed after his father, a successful merchant, gave him an expensive, high-quality microscope. Cohn was nineteen by this time, with a doctorate in botany and a position at the University of Breslau. His new microscope became one of his treasured research tools. He was appointed associate professor of botany in 1859 and by the 1870s was the foremost bacteriologist of his day, attracting many students and young scientists to his lectures. He is now considered to be a founder of the science of bacteriology. *ghetto 집단 거주지 **child prodigy 신동(神童)

① I have not received a degree because of my Jewish ancestry.
② I got an expensive advanced microscope from my father.
③ In his early 20s, he earned a doctorate in botany.
④ His lecture attracted many students and young scientists.

제 18 회 하프 모의고사

해설편 p.150

제한 시간 15 분 | 소요 시간 분 | 점수 /10

PART Ⅰ 어법

01

(A), (B), (C)의 각 네모 안에서 어법에 맞는 표현으로 가장 적절한 것은?

With the rise of an urban middle class in the nineteenth century, many cats no longer had to serve as full-time mousers. Increasingly, they were kept by owners who simply liked having (A) [them / themselves] around for their beauty, grace, and the affection they could offer. A phenomenon called the "cat fancy" followed. The pets of "fanciers" competed for ribbons at cat shows, and breeders began to refine existing breeds and (B) [develop / developing] new ones. The first recorded cat show — with 170 cats on exhibit — was held in 1871 at London's Crystal Palace. Just eighteen years later, more than three times as many cats were shown, and 20,000 cat fanciers attended. American cat lovers soon followed suit with a show of their own, at New York's Madison Square Garden in 1895. Perhaps not surprisingly, a Maine Coon, a breed of Yankee ancestry, (C) [winning / won] that first best-in-show award. Today the cat fancy is alive and well, and hundreds of clubs worldwide sponsor cat shows.

	(A)		(B)		(C)
①	them	…	develop	…	winning
②	them	…	developing	…	winning
③	them	…	develop	…	won
④	themselves	…	developing	…	won

02

우리말을 영어로 잘못 옮긴 것은?

① 당신은 그 영화를 봤어야 했다.
→ You should have watched the movie.

② 당신을 성공으로 이끄는 것은 재능이 아니라 열정이다.
→ It is not talent but passion that leads you to success.

③ 시간을 엄수하는 것은 모든 사람들이 갖추어야 할 미덕이다.
→ Being punctual is the virtue everyone has to have.

④ 사람들은 나이가 들면서 엄해지는 경향이 있다.
→ People tend to be strict as though they got old.

PART Ⅱ 어휘

03

밑줄 친 부분과 의미가 가장 가까운 것은?

The police <u>confiscated</u> the stolen goods.

① reported ② located
③ released ④ seized

04

밑줄 친 부분과 의미가 가장 가까운 것은?

The driver tried to <u>avert</u> the accident by bringing the car to a sudden stop.

① prevent ② yearn
③ minimize ④ spur

PART Ⅲ 생활영어

05

다음 중 두 사람의 대화가 어색한 것은?

① A: Why don't you join us for camping tonight?
B: Sorry, I'm grounded for the time being.

② A: I heard you're making another movie! Can I be in it?
B: Sure thing. Cast and crew meeting Saturday at Kimberly's.

③ A: What would you say if you are asked to be a leader of the team?
B: Not my place to judge.

④ A: What are you doing up so early on Saturday?
B: It's a pity that you cannot work this out.

PART Ⅳ 독해

06

다음 글의 빈칸에 들어갈 말로 가장 적절한 것은?

Our first lessons in empathy begin in infancy, when we are held in our mother's or father's arms. These primary emotional bonds lay the groundwork for learning how to cooperate and be welcomed into a game or group. The extent to which we master this emotional curriculum determines our level of social competence. Take children on the playground who don't pick up the crucial cues for smooth interaction; when they want to join a game, they'll often just wade in and thereby disrupt it. More socially skilled children, on the other hand, wait and watch awhile. They tune in to the game first and then enter seamlessly at a natural opening. It's the same with adults: ______________________ is essential.

*wade in (싸움·토론·게임 등에) 마구 뛰어들다(덤벼들다)
**seamlessly 매끄럽게, 이음매가 없이

① Reading the political and social currents in an organization
② Having a lot of opportunities for self-improvement and growth
③ Picking up the social rhythm and timing of those we work with
④ Anticipating and recognizing the future needs of their community

07

다음 글의 ① ~ ④ 중에서 주어진 문장이 들어가기에 가장 적절한 곳은?

Plants can apparently still absorb much CO_2 when the temperature increases, but less CO_2 is absorbed when plants do not receive as much water.

Although the extent of human influence on climate change is still being debated, our cars, homes, and factories warm the atmosphere, and these human impacts have increased the pace of climate change. (①) Based on today's scientific knowledge, greenhouse gases need to be reduced in order to prevent the planet's temperature from increasing further. (②) Two recent studies that measure for the first time the quantity of carbon dioxide (CO_2) that plants absorb from the atmosphere suggest that global warming does not have as dramatic an effect on the existing ecosystem as previously thought. (③) The availability of water is thus thought to be more important than minimizing changes in temperature. (④) Models to date that focus on CO_2 targets and measures, which largely strive to limit the rise in the global temperature, may thus be wrong.

08

다음 글의 빈칸 (A), (B)에 들어갈 말로 가장 적절한 것은?

Aesthetics is the area of philosophy that concerns our appreciation of things as they affect our senses, and especially as they affect them in a pleasing way. As such, it frequently focuses primarily on the fine arts, the products of which are traditionally designed to please our senses. ____(A)____, much of our aesthetic appreciation is not confined to art, but directed toward the world at large. We appreciate not only art, but also nature: broad horizons, fiery sunsets, and towering mountains. Moreover, our appreciation reaches beyond pristine nature to our more mundane surroundings: the solitude of a neighborhood park on a rainy evening, the chaos of a busy morning marketplace, the view from the road. ____(B)____, there is a need for an aesthetics of the environment, for in such cases our aesthetic appreciation includes our surroundings: our environment.

*pristine 오염되지 않은, 자연 그대로의 **mundane 일상적인

	(A)		(B)
①	Likewise	…	Thus
②	For instance	…	In addition
③	However	…	Thus
④	Likewise	…	In addition

09

주어진 글 다음에 이어질 글의 순서로 가장 적절한 것은?

I had broken my leg skiing last winter – first time down the hill – and had received some money from a school insurance policy designed to reward unfortunate, clumsy children. I purchased a cassette recorder with the proceeds.

(A) Then I let him hear his own voice. That little bird, one-third the size of a sparrow, began to dive-bomb me and my cassette recorder, attacking back and forth, inches from the speaker.

(B) We saw a lot of that sort of behaviour, even in the absence of the tape recorder. If a larger bird ever dared to sit and rest in any of the trees near our birdhouse there was a good chance he would get knocked off his perch by a diving wren.

(C) My dad suggested that I sit on the back lawn, record the wren's song, play it back, and watch what happened. So, I went out into the bright spring sunlight and taped a few minutes of the wren laying furious claim to his territory with song.

*wren 굴뚝새 **perch 앉은 자리, 홰

① (B) – (A) – (C)
② (B) – (C) – (A)
③ (C) – (A) – (B)
④ (C) – (B) – (A)

10

다음 글의 내용과 일치하지 않는 것은?

Victor Borge, born in Copenhagen, Denmark in 1909, was a comedian and pianist. Initially a concert musician, Victor Borge soon developed a performance style that combined comedy with classical music. When the Nazis invaded Denmark in 1940, he was performing in Sweden, and a short time later managed to escape to America. When he arrived in the U.S., he didn't speak a word of English. Learning English by watching movies, he soon managed to translate his jokes for the American audience. In 1948, Victor Borge became an American citizen and a few years later was offered a show of his own, Comedy in Music. The show remains the longest-running one-man show in Broadway history. At the age of 90, he still performed 60 times a year. He died on December 23rd, 2000 at his home in Greenwich, Connecticut, U.S.

① It developed a performance style that combines comedy and classical music.
② When the Nazis invaded Denmark, they were performing in the United States.
③ He became a U.S. citizen in 1948.
④ At age 90, he still performed 60 times a year.

제 19 회 하프 모의고사

해설편 p.152

제한 시간 15 분 | 소요 시간 분 | 점수 /10

PART Ⅰ 어법

01

다음 글의 밑줄 친 부분 중, 어법상 틀린 것은?

Every situation, properly ① perceived, becomes an opportunity. But you have to act on it if you're going to be successful. Distant pastures always look greener than ② those close at hand, but real opportunities are right where you are. You must take advantage of them when they appear. Success is not in your environment, in luck or chance, or in the help of others. Success is in yourself alone. Take a second look at ③ what appears to be someone's "good luck." You'll find not luck but preparation, planning and success-producing thinking. When you're prepared for opportunity, your chance for success is sure to come. The season of failure is the best time for sowing the seeds of success. Decide that this year will be your year for success and prepare for it ④ happens.

*pasture 목초지

02

우리말을 영어로 잘못 옮긴 것은?

① 보증이 만료되어서 수리는 무료가 아니었다.
→ Since the warranty had expired, the repairs were not free of charge.

② 설문지를 완성하는 누구에게나 선물카드가 주어질 예정이다.
→ A gift card will be given to whomever completes the questionnaire.

③ 지난달 내가 휴가를 요청했더라면 지금 하와이에 있을 텐데.
→ If I had asked for a vacation last month, I would be in Hawaii now.

④ 그의 아버지가 갑자기 작년에 돌아가셨고, 설상가상으로 그의 어머니도 병에 걸리셨다.
→ His father suddenly passed away last year, and, what was worse, his mother became sick.

PART Ⅱ 어휘

03

밑줄 친 부분과 의미가 가장 가까운 것은?

The university president's congenial relationship with the city business community resulted in donations to several departments and colleges.

① gracious ② haphazard
③ friendly ④ confidential

04

밑줄 친 부분과 의미가 가장 가까운 것은?

> I am sick and tired of such a <u>barren</u> argument.

① silly ② stubborn
③ aggressive ④ unproductive

PART Ⅲ 생활영어

05

다음 중 두 사람의 대화가 어색한 것은?

① A: Could you deliver this parcel to my office?
B: Consider it done.
② A: Jinmo took an unrelated issue during the conference.
B: He did me a good turn.
③ A: Would you mind opening the door.
B: Of course not.
④ A: Is her business shaping up?
B: Not that I know of. She is having a cash flow problem.

PART Ⅳ 독해

06

다음 글의 빈칸에 들어갈 말로 가장 적절한 것은?

> It is crucial to value __________ in our increasingly interdependent world. Even if you are not operating globally, but just in a workplace in a small town, you will find that there is an increasing level of diversity among the people you work with: old, young, tall, small, black, white, rich or poor. You should not place more value on one over the other, because they are all needed to form the whole. That's called synergy, meaning that the whole is more than the sum of the individual parts. Value that. It may take some initial adjusting for all parties, but it pays off in the long run. Homogeneity is a thing of the past. Heterogeneity has proven its value: More brains, more values, more perspectives, better solutions, greater output, more creativity, and increased understanding. Those are just some of the advantages of embracing the fact that not all herrings in the barrel are the same.
>
> *homogeneity 동질성 **heterogeneity 이질성

① systems
② creativity
③ differences
④ conformity

07

다음 글의 ① ~ ④ 중에서 주어진 문장이 들어가기에 가장 적절한 곳은?

> However, we may be sure that in early times, just like today, maps were created for a variety of purposes and took a variety of forms.

Exactly how, when, why, and where the first maps came to be created is difficult to discover. (①) Much of what was drawn in prehistoric and early historical times has not survived, so what we find today may not be wholly representative of what was once there. (②) There are other problems for the modern observer. (③) Maps made in prehistoric times cannot be accompanied by a title that explains the meaning of the drawing or that describes its content. (④) It may also be clear that, contrary to popular belief, of all the purposes to which maps have been put through the ages, the least important single purpose has been to find the way.

08

다음 글의 빈칸 (A), (B)에 들어갈 말로 가장 적절한 것은?

It is important to recognize that countries are at different stages of economic development, and thus their needs for dams also vary. Also, an industrialized country like the United States has developed nearly all of its best and most economic dam sites. ____(A)____, most potential sites in sub-Saharan Africa (with the exception of South Africa) have yet to be developed. A country like Nepal has a similar amount of hydropower potential to that already developed in the United States. However, Nepal has developed only about 4% of its hydro potential. ____(B)____, What may appear to be a logical and efficient solution for the United States at present is unlikely to be the best and most suitable solution for conditions in Nepal.

	(A)		(B)
①	In contrast	···	However
②	In contrast	···	Thus
③	For example	···	Instead
④	For example	···	Thus

09

주어진 글 다음에 이어질 글의 순서로 가장 적절한 것은?

A very old and typically European method for producing landmarks is a guild symbol. A large key on a store front used to say 'a locksmith works here.'

(A) Featuring binoculars large enough to walk into which cover most of the store frontage, this spectacular building by star architect Frank Gehry says: what is going on behind the main front has to do with insight, far-sightedness and forward thinking.

(B) Guild symbols instantly trigger the brain script of a place, its meaning and the activities expected to happen there. The symbol signals what is going on behind the front.

(C) The principle has survived to this day, in the form of the building's header. The header of an advertising agency in Venice Beach, California in fact became something to be admired and even worshiped in itself.

*frontage (건물의 특히 도로나 강을 향한) 정면

① (B) – (A) – (C)
② (B) – (C) – (A)
③ (C) – (A) – (B)
④ (C) – (B) – (A)

10

Dorothea Lange에 관한 다음 글의 내용과 일치하지 않는 것은?

Dorothea Lange's oeuvre constitutes one of the most moving and committed contributions to the social documentary photography in the 20th century. After studying at Columbia University in New York, she started out as an independent portrait photographer in San Francisco. Shocked by the number of homeless people in search of work during the Great Depression, she decided to take pictures of people in the street to draw attention to their plight. In 1935, she joined the Farm Security Administration (FSA) and reported on living conditions in the rural areas of the USA. In a direct manner, she documented the bitter poverty of migrant workers and their families. One of the most famous photographs of the FSA project is Migrant Mother, the portrait of a Californian migrant worker with her three children. This highly concentrated image has made Dorothea Lange an icon of socially committed photography.

*oeuvre (한 작가·화가 등의) 모든 작품 **plight 곤경, 궁지

① He left works that greatly contributed to social record photography in the 20th century.
② I started my career as a character photographer at San Francisco.
③ I was shocked by the number of homeless people looking for work during the Great Depression.
④ I entered the FSA and reported on the poor living conditions of urban areas in the United States.

제 20 회 하프 모의고사

해설편 p.154

제한 시간 15 분 | 소요 시간 분 | 점수 /10

PART Ⅰ 어법

01

(A), (B), (C)의 각 네모 안에서 어법에 맞는 표현으로 가장 적절한 것은?

An individual driven by companionship is motivated by the opportunity to get things done as a member of a group. The key factor here is not the capability of being a team player, (A) [nor / or] is it the team spirit itself. It is how much somebody is motivated to follow through and achieve a peak result by the fact that he is working together with others to achieve the desired result. Think of exercise bikes, for example. Some people have no problem (B) [being disciplined / disciplining] and riding them in the gym, where there are others doing the same. But if they have one at home, it collects dust and is never used. The reason is not lack of character or missing discipline; the reason is (C) [that / what] the powerful companionship motivator of these individuals is not activated when alone at home.

	(A)		(B)		(C)
①	nor	…	being disciplined	…	that
②	nor	…	disciplining	…	what
③	or	…	being disciplined	…	that
④	or	…	disciplining	…	what

02

우리말을 영어로 잘못 옮긴 것은?

① 이 편지를 받는 대로 곧 본사로 와주십시오.
→ Please come to the headquarters as soon as you receive this letter.

② 나는 소년 시절에 독서하는 버릇을 길러 놓았어야만 했다.
→ I ought to have formed a habit of reading in my boyhood.

③ 그는 10년 동안 외국에 있었기 때문에 영어를 매우 유창하게 말할 수 있다.
→ Having been abroad for ten years, he can speak English very fluently.

④ 내가 그때 그 계획을 포기했었다면 이렇게 훌륭한 성과를 얻지 못했을 것이다.
→ Had I given up the project at that time, I should have achieved such a splendid result.

PART Ⅱ 어휘

03

밑줄 친 부분과 의미가 가장 가까운 것은?

During times of danger, the settlers would <u>congregate</u> in the fort. They felt safe behind its strong log walls.

① live
② coordinate
③ gather
④ hide

04

밑줄 친 부분과 의미가 가장 가까운 것은?

> The pain was almost more than he could <u>bear.</u>

① cure
② tolerate
③ carry
④ produce

PART Ⅲ 생활영어

05

다음 중 두 사람의 대화가 어색한 것은?

① A: Why doesn't this device function properly?
B: You ought to plug in first.

② A: How long does it take from my house to his office?
B: Hopefully, by the end of the week.

③ A: Do you know where I can rent a wheelchair?
B: Try around at the back gate.

④ A: You're going to be present at the staff training session this weekend, aren't you?
B: It's mandatory, isn't it?

PART Ⅳ 독해

06

다음 글의 빈칸에 들어갈 말로 가장 적절한 것은?

> When I was about five years old I found a wild mouse in a field near my house. Obviously it was sick, otherwise it would not have let me pick it up and take it home. My father made it a cage and I fed it grass seeds. The next day, when I returned from school bringing a handful of grasses for my new 'friend', the mouse was dead. I remember to this day how sad I was. This was my first loss. My father, who could not bear my unhappiness, scooped me up. We went to a pet shop and got a new mouse. Without anybody consciously teaching me, I learned that grieving could be avoided by ______________. When, some 14 years later, a much-loved cat died, I was at the cat rescue centre choosing a kitten, also a white male. It has taken me many years of adult life to learn how to grieve.
>
> *scoop up 안아 올리다

① crying
② ignoring
③ replacing
④ observing

07

다음 글의 ① ~ ④ 중에서 주어진 문장이 들어가기에 가장 적절한 곳은?

> Compare this with organisms that do not have the tendency to reciprocate.

Imagine a population of organisms in which each individual, when confronted by strangers, either randomly cooperates or not. If strangers meet and initially cooperate, then it is up, up, and away towards establishing a pattern of behavior in which cooperation becomes increasingly likely. (①) My cooperating with you makes it more likely that you will cooperate with me, which makes it more likely that I will cooperate with you, and so on. (②) This is the behavioral infrastructure that makes social institutions possible. (③) They may experience random incidents of cooperation, but since these will not increase the probability of cooperation, these organisms will not reap the benefits of sustained, mutually reinforcing cooperation. (④) Those who behave only in immediately self-interested ways will do even worse.

08

다음 글의 빈칸 (A), (B)에 들어갈 말로 가장 적절한 것은?

Cultural messages shape many communication behaviors, and listening is no exception. In particular, listening behavior appears to be affected by how people in a given culture think about the importance of time. In individualistic cultures, people often think of time as a resource. Americans, ___(A)___, commonly say that "time is money," and they think of time as a commodity that can be saved, spent, and wasted. People in such cultures typically place a high value on efficiency, and they expect others to do the same. They value direct, straightforward communication, and listeners become impatient with speakers who don't "get to the point." ___(B)___, collectivistic cultures such as Korea emphasize social harmony over efficiency. As part of their listening behavior, people in these cultures often pay close attention to nonverbal behaviors and contextual cues to determine the meaning of a speaker's message.

*collectivistic 집단[집산]주의적인

	(A)		(B)
①	moreover	…	In contrast
②	moreover	…	Consequently
③	therefore	…	In other words
④	for instance	…	In contrast

09

주어진 글 다음에 이어질 글의 순서로 가장 적절한 것은?

In the case of perfume and odours emitted from non-food sources, people believed they were intuitively able to differentiate between 'naturally-occurring' and 'synthetic' odours by the nature of the source.

(A) However, the distinction between naturally-occurring odours and those of synthetic origin is not as straightforward as it might seem; the odour of leather, for example, comes about as a result of tanning, which is itself a chemically-dependent process. Also, synthetic odours of leather are frequently used in product manufacturing processes in order to provide an illusion of leather and an association with quality and newness, as is the case when these odours are sprayed into some new cars.

(B) 'Synthetic' is defined in the Oxford English Dictionary as 'a substance made by chemical synthesis, especially to imitate a natural product'. Perfumes, for example, were generally described as synthetic, whereas leather was considered to have its own natural odour.

(C) Furthermore, some odours of perfume are produced by combinations or extractions of naturally occurring products. The line between natural and unnatural, genuine and synthetic is therefore highly blurred with respect to the perception of smell, with distinctions varying between people.

*tanning 무두질

① (B) – (A) – (C)
② (B) – (C) – (A)
③ (C) – (A) – (B)
④ (C) – (B) – (A)

10

orchid bees에 관한 다음 글의 내용과 일치하지 않는 것은?

As pretty as the orchids they pollinate, orchid bees come in a brightly colored array of brilliant and metallic blues, greens, and purples. These bees are not social like honeybees — they are typically solitary in nesting, with no division of labor and little communal activity. The males leave the nest shortly after birth and never return, spending their lives collecting flower fragrances that they store in special grooves on their hind legs and that may be released to attract females. Females construct nests from mud, resins, and other materials and gather both nectar and pollen from a variety of plants. The two hundred species of orchid bees are native to Central and South America and play an important role in the pollination of many orchids. Only a single species can be found in the United States. This bee, Euglossa vidrissimia, is a recent arrival from either Mexico or Central America and was likely introduced to the United States accidentally.

*orchid 난초 **groove 홈 ***resin 수지, 송진

① It has blue, green, and purple light.
② Create a honeycomb alone and do not divide labor with colleagues.
③ The male spends his life collecting incense in the grooves of his head.
④ Females make honeycombs and collect plant honey and pollen.

제 21 회 하프 모의고사

해설편 p.156

제한 시간 15 분 | 소요 시간 분 | 점수 /10

PART Ⅰ 어법

01

다음 글의 밑줄 친 부분 중, 어법상 틀린 것은?

Some of the skills and abilities that are ① <u>encouraged</u> in video games are useful for many different purposes. Most of all, video games are excellent for developing visual awareness. For example, recent studies show that they can ② <u>significantly</u> improve a surgeon's skill in using her hands when performing operations. Also, playing video games has been shown ③ <u>to increase</u> short-term memory of people in test groups. The reason for this is that most games require players to spread their attention over the screen quickly in order to detect and react to ④ <u>change</u> events. In fact, playing video games may trigger previously inactive genes that are important for developing neural pathways necessary for spatial attention. Research is now suggesting that playing video games could even increase attention spans rather than reduce them.

*surgeon 외과의 **neural pathway 신경 연결 통로

02

우리말을 영어로 가장 잘 옮긴 것은?

① 그는 제인이 제안한 대안이 실효성이 없을 것이라고 굳게 믿고 있다.
→ He strongly believes that the alternatives had been offered by Jane won't work.

② 히틀러가 다른 유럽 국가를 침략하지 않았다면 제2차 세계 대전은 일어나지 않았을 것이다.
→ If Hitler hadn't invaded other European countries, World War II might not take place.

③ 나는 커튼 뒤에 숨어서 그림자가 다시 나타나기를 기다렸다.
→ Hiding behind the curtain, I waited the shadow to reappear.

④ 탐은 자기 생각을 영어보다 러시아어로 표현하는 것이 훨씬 쉽다고 한다.
→ Tom says that it is much easier for him to express his thoughts in Russian than in English.

PART Ⅱ 어휘

03

다음 글의 빈칸에 들어갈 말로 가장 적절한 것은?

This work is <u>congruous</u> to his character.

① avaricious
② industrious
③ harmonious
④ luxurious

04

밑줄 친 부분과 의미가 가장 가까운 것은?

> Bazille, who, as friend, <u>benefactor,</u> and colleague of the Impressionists, played an important role during the movement's formative years.

① critic
② peer
③ master
④ supporter

PART Ⅲ 생활영어

05

다음 중 두 사람의 대화가 어색한 것은?

① A: What's happening? Why the long face this morning?
B: Does it show? I'm feeling a bit under the weather.
② A: Have you decided where you want to travel this summer?
B: Well, actually I am open to suggestions at this point.
③ A: I can't believe the water faucet is leaking badly again.
B: Does it mean that you are going to get a huge bill?
④ A: I'm staying in Room 351. Do you have any messages for me?
B: Let me check.... I'm afraid we're fully booked up tonight.

PART Ⅳ 독해

06

다음 글의 빈칸에 들어갈 말로 가장 적절한 것은?

> Hunting is sometimes used as ______________. In the absence of predators, populations of deer and other prey species sometimes exceed the ability of the habitat to support them, and in unchecked numbers they threaten the health of the ecosystem or human safety. Hunters reduce the number of animals so that the survivors have enough food and shelter to lead healthy lives. For example, limits have been removed for hunting some species of geese, which have become so numerous that they are destroying the Arctic and subarctic breeding grounds of many species. Professional hunters are sometimes hired to control animals in populated areas, such as bears in parks. Modern American hunters support conservation efforts to protect their sport by buying land to set aside or by lobbying governments for game-animal protection.

① a physical training program
② a wildlife management tool
③ a social and competitive event
④ a recreational activity for men

07

다음 글의 ① ~ ④ 중에서 주어진 문장이 들어가기에 가장 적절한 곳은?

> You can eliminate these problems if, for example, you precede your question with, "Let me ask you a question to make sure I understand what you just said."

Whenever you ask a question, say why you're asking it. (①) If a question stands alone, it raises another question in the listener's mind, like, "Why did he ask that question?" (②) The person you're talking to will instantly stop listening to you as they contemplate possible answers in their mind. (③) They can become irritated if they don't know why you're asking the question. They might feel like you are cross-examining them or they may feel anxious because your question is a demand on them to provide you with information. (④) In addition to avoiding jumping to the wrong conclusion about what someone has said, you show an interest in what the person in communicating to you, which in turn sharpens their listening powers in what you have to say.

08

다음 글의 빈칸 (A), (B)에 들어갈 말로 가장 적절한 것은?

> Different media accumulate their audiences in different ways. In print media, such as newspapers and magazines, one measure of success is the actual number of publications distributed, or circulation. ___(A)___, more than one person usually reads each copy of a publication; for example, most newspapers average two readers per copy, while certain magazines, such as People, may have upwards of eight readers per copy. So the total audience is the circulation multiplied by the readers per copy. ___(B)___, in print media, the circulation is the number of copies printed, while the audience is the number of persons who read those copies of the publication. Because you want to attract more than one reader per copy of the publication, the number for the audience will usually be larger than the number for circulation.

	(A)		(B)
①	However	…	Thus
②	However	…	Furthermore
③	As a result	…	Similarly
④	As a result	…	Thus

09

주어진 글 다음에 이어질 글의 순서로 가장 적절한 것은?

The goal of legal socialization is to instill in people a felt obligation or responsibility to follow laws and accept legal authority. The goal of moral socialization is to instill in people a duty to follow societal standards of proper behavior independent of rules and codes.

(A) Criminalizing a behavior does not make it immoral, nor is all immoral behavior necessarily criminalized. Most people can think of an instance where they believe a behavior is immoral, but would not support criminalizing it or using the full force of the law to stop people from doing it.

(B) Given that in normal everyday life those behaviors that society considers immoral are frequently prohibited by law, the two usually work toward the same goal. However, that is not always the case.

(C) At the same time, even if people do abstractly support legal regulation of immoral behavior, they vary in how and the extent to which they want the legal system to intervene. Such views are strongly shaped by the way in which people understand the position and function of the law within society.

*instill (사상·감정 따위를) 심어주다, 주입하다

① (B) – (A) – (C)
② (B) – (C) – (A)
③ (C) – (A) – (B)
④ (C) – (B) – (A)

10

John McCarthy에 관한 다음 글의 내용과 일치하지 않는 것은?

In the 1940s, when he was a student at the California Institute of Technology, John McCarthy attended a lecture by Hungarian-American mathematician John von Neumann about "self-replicating automata," or machines that could make copies of themselves. (No such machines existed. Von Neumann's idea was just a theory.) After the lecture, McCarthy reasoned that a machine that could reproduce itself might be able to attain some form of intelligence. The idea stuck in his mind. In 1964 McCarthy joined the faculty of Stanford University in California and founded the school's AI (Artificial Intelligence) lab. At that time, he was optimistic that scientists could create an AI system within ten years. In later life, McCarthy had a more realistic view. Writing for the Journal of the Association for Computing Machinery in 2003, he set the odds of achieving artificial intelligence at "0.5 probability in the next 49 years, but a 0.25 probability that 49 years from now, the problems will be just as confusing as they are today."

① In the 1940s, he attended a lecture on self-replicating machines.
② It was inferred that a machine that can replicate itself could have intelligence.
③ After the establishment of the AI Research Institute at Stanford University, he became a professor at the university.
④ When the AI research institute was established, it was optimistic that artificial intelligence systems would be developed within 10 years.

해설편 p.159

제한 시간 15 분 | 소요 시간 분 | 점수 /10

PART Ⅰ 어법

01

(A), (B), (C)의 각 네모 안에서 어법에 맞는 표현으로 가장 적절한 것은?

Seasonal weather conditions are always a concern for greenhouse gardeners. Not only can the climate (A) [determine / determines] what type of greenhouse to build, it can play a critical role in determining how a greenhouse will function after it is built from one season to the next. For example, in a cold-weather climate that frequently experiences heavy snowfall, a high-pitched roof might be ideal because it can prevent the build-up of ice and snow by (B) [efficient / efficiently] helping them to slide off. In a location that sees less snowfall but gets cold, strong winds, a sun-heated pit, which is a greenhouse with the majority of the structure (C) [housed / housing] below ground, might be the best choice, because it is naturally insulated and requires less heat to operate. The same type of roof might not be practical for a more temperate area.

*pit (크고 깊은) 구덩이 **insulate 단열하다

	(A)		(B)		(C)
①	determine	…	efficient	…	housing
②	determines	…	efficient	…	housing
③	determines	…	efficiently	…	housing
④	determine	…	efficiently	…	housed

02

우리말을 영어로 잘못 옮긴 것은?

① 그는 마치 자신이 미국 사람인 것처럼 유창하게 영어로 말한다.
→ He speaks English fluently as if he were an American.

② 우리 실패하면 어떻게 하지?
→ What if we should fail?

③ 만일 내일 비가 온다면, 나는 그냥 집에 있겠다.
→ If it rains tomorrow, I'll just stay at home

④ 뉴턴이 없었다면 중력법칙은 발견되지 않았을 것이다.
→ If it was not for Newton, the law of gravitation would not be discovered.

PART Ⅱ 어휘

03

다음 글의 빈칸에 들어갈 말로 가장 적절한 것은?

He was conscious to the last moment.

① severe ② awake
③ eternal ④ courageous

04

밑줄 친 부분과 의미가 가장 가까운 것은?

The individual is helpless even under benevolent control.

① valuable ② plausible
③ obscure ④ generous

PART Ⅲ 생활영어

05

다음 중 두 사람의 대화가 어색한 것은?

① A: How did you find your dinner?
B: I looked in the refrigerator, and there it was.

② A: It's getting colder.
B: Don't worry. I'll get you a blanket.

③ A: I can't decide which of the two to choose.
B: It looks like a jump ball situation.

④ A: Why are you so hot under the collar?
B: I just got in a fight with my boyfriend.

PART Ⅳ 독해

06

다음 글의 빈칸에 들어갈 말로 가장 적절한 것은?

Suppose the chance that a particular stock will go up tomorrow is 50%. Now suppose on Tuesday the stock goes up. What are the chances it will go up on Wednesday? If Tuesday's result and Wednesday's result are independent of each other – that is, if there is no trend – then the chance it will go up on Wednesday is 50%, just like the chance on Tuesday. The fact that the stock went up on Tuesday hasn't changed anything. Whether or not the stock goes up on Wednesday has nothing to do with whether it went up on Tuesday. Most studies and measurements have found that ____________________. When you assess the chances of what will happen tomorrow, it doesn't help you to know what happened yesterday.

① there was no tendency to trend
② chance can be increased by more trials
③ we can predict and prepare for the future
④ people wanted less risk when the stock went up

07

다음 글의 ①～④ 중에서 주어진 문장이 들어가기에 가장 적절한 곳은?

When the forward pass was legalized in 1906, it was suddenly possible to gain more yards with the flick of a wrist.

In 1905, football was a low-scoring sport of running and kicking the ball. (①) A bunch of guys in leather helmets would line up on the football field and see if they could push the other team back for a three- or four-yard again. (②) A four-yard gain was a big deal. (③) During the first season after the rule changed, all but one of the teams still stayed with their conventional running games. (④) Recognizing that football had entered an era of change (i.e., the forward pass), the coaches at St. Louis University quickly adapted to a passing offensive game.

08

다음 글의 빈칸 (A), (B)에 들어갈 말로 가장 적절한 것은?

Since animals lose body heat through surfaces, a higher surface-to-volume ratio would result in greater loss of body heat. This is why smaller animals lose more body heat. ____(A)____, a mouse or a hummingbird must burn a lot of calories to maintain a constant body temperature. This is the main reason that, among warm-blooded animals, metabolic rate declines with increasing body size. Small mammals have evolved to produce relatively more body heat. Their faster metabolic rate means that they do not live as long. Small animals tend to have shorter lives than large animals, and warm-blooded animals shorter lives than cold blooded animals. ____(B)____, large animals can have warm bodies just because they are large. Large dinosaurs, for example, were probably warm-blooded simply because of their low surface-to-volume ratio.

*surface-to-volume ratio 표면적 대 부피의 비율 **metabolic 물질대사의

	(A)		(B)
①	In contrast	···	Conversely
②	In contrast	···	To conclude
③	As a result	···	To conclude
④	As a result	···	Conversely

09

주어진 글 다음에 이어질 글의 순서로 가장 적절한 것은?

For many years the British-French rivalry has extended from rugby matches, politics and trading insults to trading mortality statistics. Since records in France started to be accurately collected, they have reported considerably fewer deaths from heart disease and a longer lifespan than the British.

(A) Even within France itself there is a wide north-south difference, which suggests that most of the variation between UK and France is due to the healthier habits of the southerners.

(B) Others disagree, asserting that misclassification could only explain at most 20 per cent of the difference, and point to a consistent north-south difference across Europe.

(C) The French are proud of this, but many UK colleagues tell me that much of the difference is due to a reluctance to record deaths properly, with the same 'Anglo-Saxon rigour'.

*mortality 사망자 수[사망률] **rigour 엄격함

① (B) - (A) - (C)
② (B) - (C) - (A)
③ (C) - (A) - (B)
④ (C) - (B) - (A)

10

Alexander Lucius Twilight에 관한 다음 글의 내용과 일치하지 않는 것은?

Alexander Lucius Twilight was born in 1795 in Vermont, the son of a farmer. In 1823, he made history by becoming the first black American to graduate from college. He began teaching in school and was licensed as a preacher to preach in Peru, New York, and Vergennes, Vermont. In 1829, he moved to Brownington, Vermont, becoming minister of the Congregational Church and principal of Brownington Academy, a county secondary school. To ensure that the state of Vermont continued to fund his school, he ran and was elected to the Vermont state legislature and became the first black American to be elected to such a position. When Twilight accepted the principalship of Brownington Academy, the school consisted of a two-story wooden building. It had no dormitory, so students stayed with families in the neighborhood. Twilight was determined to change that. He managed to raise enough money to finance the construction of a large, sturdy building made of stone called Athenian Hall. The stone building now is the home of Orleans County (Vermont) Historical Society.

*state legislature 주(州) 의회

① He was the first black American to graduate from college.

② have a background in teaching at school

③ At Brownington, he held the position of minister and principal of a secondary school.

④ I built a dormitory consisting of wooden buildings in my school.

해설편 p.161

제한 시간 15 분 | 소요 시간 분 | 점수 /10

PART Ⅰ 어법

01

다음 글의 밑줄 친 부분 중, 어법상 틀린 것은?

Learn to express what you want rather than putting the emphasis on what you don't want when ① <u>speaking</u> with a child. Children are highly responsive to the messages they receive. If an adult says, "Don't slam the door," the child listening hears the phrase slam the door, with the word don't in front of ② <u>it</u>. The child must figure out ③ <u>what</u> slamming the door is the undesirable thing to do, which is difficult to comprehend, especially for young children. The chances for a successful response from a child ④ <u>increase</u> dramatically when an adult says, "Please close the door gently." Now the child has a visual image to follow. The words spoken fit together well with the request, which makes it much easier to understand.

*slam 쾅[탁] 닫다

02

우리말을 영어로 <u>잘못</u> 옮긴 것은?

① 예산이 빡빡해서 나는 15달러밖에 쓸 수가 없다.
→ I am on a tight budget so that I have only fifteen dollars to spend.

② 그의 최근 영화는 이전 작품들보다 훨씬 더 지루하다.
→ His latest film is far more boring than his previous ones.

③ 우리 회사 모든 구성원의 이름을 기억하다니 그는 생각이 깊군요.
→ It's thoughtful of him to remember the names of every member in our firm.

④ 현관 열쇠를 잃어버려서 안으로 들어가기 위해 나는 벽돌로 유리창을 깼다.
→ I'd lost my front door key, and I had to smash a window by a brick to get in.

PART Ⅱ 어휘

03

밑줄 친 부분과 의미가 가장 가까운 것은?

There was some <u>consensus</u> of opinion.

① approval ② dissent
③ dispute ④ contradiction

04

밑줄 친 부분과 의미가 가장 가까운 것은?

> Although the weather had been <u>benign</u> when Anthony and Robert had sailed out onto the lake in the morning, by noon, conditions changed dramatically.

① steady ② crucial
③ temperate ④ tremendous

PART Ⅲ 생활영어

05

다음 중 두 사람의 대화가 어색한 것은?

① A: I don't think I can finish this project by the deadline.
B: Take your time. I'm sure you can make it.

② A: Mom, what do you want to get for Mother's Day?
B: I don't need anything. I just feel blessed to have a son like you.

③ A: I think something's wrong with this cake. This is not sweet at all!
B: I agree. It just tastes like a chunk of salt.

④ A: Would you carry this for me? I don't have enough hands.
B: Sure, I'll hand it over to you right away.

PART Ⅳ 독해

06

다음 글의 빈칸에 들어갈 말로 가장 적절한 것은?

> Much social comparison research has stressed how people compare themselves to others on objective characteristics that invite evaluation. Typically, such comparisons result in contrast effects, whereby one sees one's own attributes as different from or distinctive relative to others. But people often compare their feelings or reactions with those of others in situations that may yield a sense of __________. For example, if you're on a plane that suddenly begins to rock and lurch rather wildly before settling down, you may well compare your reactions with those of nearby passengers. Your purpose in so doing might be less a desire to evaluate your own response of fear than to experience a sense of belonging and comfort with others who are sharing the experience.

① control
② bonding
③ superiority
④ determination

07

다음 글의 ①~④ 중에서 주어진 문장이 들어가기에 가장 적절한 곳은?

It may be a good idea to take out the extremes when computing the average temperatures for vacation scheduling.

Many scientists in the physical world are subject to foolishness, misreading statistics. (①) One obvious example is in the global warming debate. (②) Many scientists failed to notice it in its early stages as they removed from their sample the spikes in temperature, under the belief that these were not likely to recur. (③) But it does not work when we study the physical properties of the weather – particularly when one cares about a cumulative effect. (④) These scientists initially ignored the fact that these spikes, although rare, had the effect of adding disproportionately to the cumulative melting of the ice cap.

*spike 급등 **cumulative 누적되는

08

다음 글의 빈칸 (A), (B)에 들어갈 말로 가장 적절한 것은?

The scientific value of wildlife results from the role it serves in the advancement of science. Much of what we know about ecology and behavior came from studying wildlife. Some types of wildlife serve as sentinel species and are used to monitor environmental health. ___(A)___, spotted owls are used by environmentalists to monitor whether we have preserved enough old-growth forests in the Pacific Northwest of the U.S. Because spotted owls have large home ranges, they are one of the first species to be affected when old-growth forests become scarce. ___(B)___, we reason that if there are sufficient old-growth forests to support a healthy population of spotted owls, then there should be a sufficient amount of forests to meet the needs of other species.

*ecology 생태(계) **sentinel species 보초 종

	(A)		(B)
①	For instance	···	Instead
②	Therefore	···	In other words
③	Nevertheless	···	In other words
④	For instance	···	Hence

09

주어진 글 다음에 이어질 글의 순서로 가장 적절한 것은?

Once harvested, potatoes, even under ideal conditions, keep for only a few months before they sprout, and they are vulnerable to mould and decay.

(A) After harvest, the potatoes were covered to prevent dew from settling on them and left out overnight in freezing temperatures. The following day, the potatoes were exposed to the sun and farm families – men, women and children alike – trod on the frozen potatoes to express their liquid, a process repeated several times during the following days.

(B) Native South Americans, however, developed a method of preserving them so that they could be stored for years to provide a safeguard against famine. The cold, dry climate of the altiplano (the high Andean plateau) made this possible.

(C) The resulting freeze-dried potato, called chuño, was stored in sealed, permanently frozen underground warehouses where it would keep for years before deteriorating. Chuño was ground into flour and baked into bread, or rehydrated and used for thickening soups and stews, such as chupe, which was made with available meat and vegetables.

*plateau 고원, 대지(臺地) **deteriorate (상태가) 나빠지다
***rehydrate (건조식품 등에) 물을 넣어 원상으로 되돌리다

① (B) – (A) – (C)
② (B) – (C) – (A)
③ (C) – (A) – (B)
④ (C) – (B) – (A)

10

Guatemala에 관한 다음 글의 내용과 일치하는 것은?

Guatemala lies in Central America, or Mesoamerica, between Mexico to the north, Honduras and El Salvador to the south. It is a mountainous country with only small coastal plains along the Pacific Ocean and the Gulf of Mexico. With a tropical climate in the lowlands and cooler temperatures in the highlands, Guatemala is a perfect place to raise bananas. In pre-Hispanic times, Guatemala was within the Mayan culture zone. Today, some of the world's most famous Mayan archaeological sites are found in the northern parts of the country. When that civilization collapsed in the 9th and 10th centuries AD, the people did not disappear. Instead, they remained in villages scattered across the country. Mayan speakers are still there, mainly in the highlands, and represent about 40 percent of the population. Most of the rest are mestizos, or people of mixed European and indigenous heritage.

① Honduras and El Salvador are located in the north.
② Most of the land is plains and away from the Pacific Ocean.
③ World-class Mayan ruins are in the northern part of the country.
④ The Mayan civilization of Guatemala began around the 9th and 10th centuries.

제 24 회 하프 모의고사

해설편 p.163

제한 시간 15 분 | 소요 시간 분 | 점수 /10

PART Ⅰ 어법

01

(A), (B), (C)의 각 네모 안에서 어법에 맞는 표현으로 가장 적절한 것은?

Closely related to the debate over readers' conceptions of fictional characters (A) [are / is] the question of the nature of the emotions that readers experience. Many of the philosophers and literary scholars who allow for the possibility of significant emotional response to fiction do so with qualifications and reservations about the nature of the types of emotions (B) [that / where] fiction can generate. Indeed, this has led some theorists to draw sharp distinctions between readers' responses to fiction and fictional characters, on the one hand, and non-fiction and real-life individuals on the other. Kendall Walton, an American philosopher, calls fiction-induced emotions quasi-emotions, (C) [implies / implying] that they are of an entirely different nature from our experiences in real life. Yet, this division is less obvious than it would appear.

*quasi- 유사~, 준(準) ~

	(A)		(B)		(C)
①	are	…	that	…	implies
②	is	…	that	…	implying
③	are	…	where	…	implies
④	is	…	where	…	implying

02

우리말을 영어로 가장 잘 옮긴 것은?

① 나는 너의 답장을 가능한 한 빨리 받기를 고대한다.
→ I look forward to receive your reply as soon as possible.

② 그는 내가 일을 열심히 했기 때문에 월급을 올려 주겠다고 말했다.
→ He said he would rise my salary because I worked hard.

③ 그의 스마트 도시 계획은 고려할 만했다.
→ His plan for the smart city was worth considered.

④ Cindy는 피아노 치는 것을 매우 좋아했고 그녀의 아들도 그랬다.
→ Cindy loved playing the piano, and so did her son.

PART Ⅱ 어휘

03

밑줄 친 부분과 의미가 가장 가까운 것은?

His description of the accident is <u>consistent</u> with what the police reported.

① effective
② viable
③ compatible
④ venomous

04

밑줄 친 부분과 의미가 가장 가까운 것은?

He was so <u>bewildered</u> that he didn't know what to do.

① greatly confused
② greatly angered
③ greatly amused
④ greatly injured

PART Ⅲ 생활영어

05

다음 중 두 사람의 대화가 어색한 것은?

① A : Would you like to go to dinner with me this week?
B : OK. But what's the occasion?
② A : Why don't we go to a basketball game sometime?
B : Sure. Just tell me when.
③ A : What do you do in your spare time?
B : I just relax at home. Sometimes I watch TV.
④ A : Could I help you with anything?
B : Yes, I would like to. That would be nice.

PART Ⅳ 독해

06

다음 글의 빈칸에 들어갈 말로 가장 적절한 것은?

The plow might be a sacred symbol of agricultural productivity, but it wrecks the soil and, as we've known for a long time, compromises basic agricultural health. In her 1943 book, The Living Soil, Lady Eve Balfour declared that "the criteria for a sustainable agriculture can be summed up in one word — permanence, which means adopting techniques that maintain soil fertility indefinitely." Tilling soil to manage weeds, however, _________________________; it dries soil out, causes chronic erosion, and in so doing renders soil impermanent. It is for this reason that, also writing in 1943, Edward Faulkner noted in Plowman's Folly that "there is nothing wrong with our soil except interference." For Faulkner, as his book's title suggests, interference meant the plow.

*till (땅을) 갈다 *render (어떤 상태가 되게) 만들다

① leads to what is profitable
② does precisely the opposite
③ always wins the weed battle
④ implies a practical alternative

07

다음 글의 ①~④ 중에서 주어진 문장이 들어가기에 가장 적절한 곳은?

For example, a consumer may have reservations about his weight and expresses those concerns while trying on business suits.

Flattery involves excessive compliments or praise designed to make someone feel good about him- or herself. (①) Flattery does not have to be insincere. (②) In fact, effective flattery should be targeted at important attributes where people feel uncertain about their abilities or performance. (③) For example, if a friend expresses anxiety about his performance on an important and recently delivered speech, an earnest comment such as, "I appreciate that you spoke slowly and clearly," is likely to gain favor for the ingratiator. (④) Similarly, when a salesperson flatters a potential customer regarding an important but uncertain attribute, the customer is likely to respond favorably.

08

다음 글의 빈칸 (A), (B)에 들어갈 말로 가장 적절한 것은?

Mentors are persons who have a vast breadth and depth of experience in the field that they train. Mentors have had both experience and professional training in the subject that they have to mentor. ____(A)____, leadership mentors need to have adequate experience as leaders and should have undergone leadership training themselves. What do mentors offer to their students that formal training sessions cannot offer? First of all, mentors can use personal experiences as lessons for their students. ____(B)____, mentors are capable of resolving dynamic issues due to their abundant knowledge and experience in the field. A training program cannot possibly prepare students to face unexpected challenges. Mentors can vary their training depending on the nature of their students and the different levels of complexity faced by the mentees.

	(A)		(B)
①	As a result	···	Nevertheless
②	As a result	···	Therefore
③	For instance	···	Moreover
④	For instance	···	In fact

09

주어진 글 다음에 이어질 글의 순서로 가장 적절한 것은?

When the interactors are communicating about the external world, pointing is sufficient to make minds meet on a referent. However, when they need to share referents in their inner worlds, a different tool is required.

(A) For example, an infant may point to Daddy's chair as a reference to the absent daddy. This type of pointing can be seen as a transition from using pointing as a proto-demonstrative with a temporary meaning to using pointing symbolically with a more permanent meaning.

(B) In a sense, language is a tool for reaching joint attention by "pointing" to places in our inner worlds. This mechanism is bootstrapped by pointing, other forms of gestures, and emotive expressions.

(C) Susan Goldin-Meadow goes beyond this metaphorical assertion and writes that in children, "pointing gestures form the platform on which linguistic communication rests and thus lay the groundwork for later language learning." For example, prelinguistic children at about twelve months can sometimes refer metonymically to an absent object by pointing to a place where that object has recently been or is normally located.

*proto-demonstrative 초기 단계의[원형의] 지시사
**bootstrap (자연스럽게 혹은 최소의 노력으로) 달성하다
**metonymically 환유적으로

① (B) – (A) – (C)
② (B) – (C) – (A)
③ (C) – (A) – (B)
④ (C) – (B) – (A)

10

수영 강사 모집에 관한 다음 글의 내용과 일치하는 것은?

Looking for Swimming Instructors

The Little Swimmers Program is now looking for swimming instructors.

- It is a summer vacation swimming program for children aged 8-10
- It is a 4-week program beginning on August 1.

Requirements

- Over 20 years of age
- Previous experience in teaching children
- Lifeguard and first aid certifications

Applicants should download the application form form the website at www.littleswimmersclub.com. After completing the form, submit it by e-mail at lsp@me.com no later than July 15. For additional inquiries, please contact us at 123-456-7890 or visit our website.

① The program runs for five weeks from August 1.
② There is no age limit for applicants.
③ Applicants must have experience teaching children.
④ You cannot submit your application by email.

제 25 회 하프 모의고사

해설편 p.165

제한 시간 15 분 | 소요 시간 분 | 점수 /10

PART Ⅰ 어법

01

다음 글의 밑줄 친 부분 중, 어법상 틀린 것은?

The Greek philosopher Aristotle cites the archer as his favorite example in ① describing moral wisdom. An archer comprehends his task if firstly he knows what his target is and secondly if he is aware of all circumstances (the means) that determine the situation ② what he has to shoot. He has assessed the strength and direction of the wind, the characteristics of the arrow and the tension of the bow. Aristotle sees the wise person as ③ such an archer, someone with knowledge of the target (the goal) and of the means to reach the goal (the pathways). The archer is more likely to hit the right mark if he has a target ④ to aim at. Aristotle stated that striving for excellence is important but that knowledge of the goal is only useful if there is a striving to attain that goal (agency).

*archer 궁수

02

우리말을 영어로 잘못 옮긴 것은?

① 그녀는 젊었을 때 더 열심히 일하지 않았던 것을 후회한다.
→ She regrets not having worked harder in her youth.

② 그는 경험과 지식을 둘 다 겸비한 사람이다.
→ He is a man of both experience and knowledge.

③ 분노는 정상적이고 건강한 감정이다.
→ Anger is a normal and healthy emotion.

④ 어떤 상황에서도 너는 떠나면 안 된다.
→ Under no circumstances you should not leave here.

PART Ⅱ 어휘

03

밑줄 친 부분과 의미가 가장 가까운 것은?

He was awarded the Military Cross for conspicuous gallantry in combat.

① terse
② rational
③ abortive
④ noticeable

04

밑줄 친 부분과 의미가 가장 가까운 것은?

The expert may not be aware of his bias.

① prejudice
② hobby
③ jeopardy
④ inability

05

다음 중 두 사람의 대화가 어색한 것은?

① M: Could you tell me how to make chocolate chip cookies?
W: Sure, but it's pretty complicated.

② M: Don't you like horror films, Tom?
W: Not really. I prefer action movies.

③ M: Do you think it's possible for us to have a talk sometime today?
W: I'd love to, but I've got a pretty tight schedule today.

④ M: How would you like to pay for this?
W: I'm really happy to pay for it.

06

다음 글의 빈칸에 들어갈 말로 가장 적절한 것은?

Some of us don't know what we are missing. We don't have access to our emotions, and we can't imagine what they feel like or what good could come of them. The difference between acknowledging our emotions and cutting off our ability to experience them can be as big as the difference between what a child at four knows and what a child at seventeen understands, or the difference between dating and falling in love. We ____. Think of two turtles – one from a pond and one from an ocean – sharing stories. The pond turtle cannot comprehend the magnificence of the ocean because his pond environment is limited. The ocean turtle invites the pond turtle to go with him to the ocean because he knows that the pond turtle will only truly understand by seeing for himself.

① tend to hide our real feelings
② can't know until we get there
③ often miss out important events
④ prefer to stand out among the others

07

다음 글의 ① ~ ④ 중에서 주어진 문장이 들어가기에 가장 적절한 곳은?

> The Germans, by contrast, had a much longer and tiring voyage.

Both the English and German settlers in America suffered from nutritional diseases. Nevertheless, the latter experienced far higher mortality rates. The diets of the two groups were similar, but the English arrived in better health. (①) Their journey across the Atlantic was shorter, and they were provided with a satisfactory diet aboard ship. (②) By the time the symptoms of the nutritional diseases appeared, the first crops were being harvested, thus inhibiting a major outbreak among the English settlers. (③) Their diet was inadequate, and conditions aboard ship proved less than satisfactory. (④) Given their more problematic health status upon arrival, it is not surprising that the characteristic symptoms of the nutritional diseases appeared relatively early.

08

다음 글의 빈칸 (A), (B)에 들어갈 말로 가장 적절한 것은?

One of the great strengths of parents of an only child is their supervision of detail. With multiple children, much can escape parental notice. ____(A)____, some parental resolves are not consistently applied, some good intentions are not carried through, and some requirements are not uniformly enforced, because when managing so many children some slippage is bound to occur. Parents just can't keep up with three children as closely as they can with one. Under undistracted parental focus, ____(B)____, the only child can feel constantly under a microscope, sometimes wishing there was another child in the family to direct parental attention elsewhere. "Some only children find the focus of attention almost overwhelming."

*supervision 감독 **slippage 불이행

(A)		(B)
① In addition	…	for example
② In addition	…	however
③ In short	…	for example
④ In contrast	…	however

09

주어진 글 다음에 이어질 글의 순서로 가장 적절한 것은?

The spring migration of birds is ultimately motivated by the physics of the earth's orbit around the sun. Spring happens because the earth's axis of rotation is tilted 23.5 degrees away from vertical with respect to its annual orbit of the sun.

(A) Birds move north to follow this burst of plant and insect life as the sun moves northward with the season. The migrants time their travel to arrive at their breeding habitat at a point of maximum seasonal abundance.

(B) As the earth circles the sun, its poles gradually tilt toward and then away from the sun. As the earth moves from its northern winter solstice to spring equinox, more direct sunlight hits the earth's surface in the Northern Hemisphere and day length increases.

(C) These two physical changes to our north-temperate sector of the planet produce the procession of spring. Longer days and increased daily solar radiation encourage the rapid growth of plant life and the invertebrates that live on plants.

*winter solstice 동지점 **spring equinox 춘분점
***invertebrate 무척추동물

① (B) – (A) – (C)
② (B) – (C) – (A)
③ (C) – (A) – (B)
④ (C) – (B) – (A)

10

Slavoj Žižek에 관한 다음 글의 내용과 일치하지 <u>않는</u> 것은?

Slavoj Žižek was born in 1949 in Ljubljana, Slovenia (then part of communist Yugoslavia). His father was a civil servant economist, his mother an accountant in a state-owned firm. He received a doctor's degree in philosophy from the University of Ljubljana, before going to Paris to study psychoanalysis. Back in Slovenia, Žižek was unable to get a university position, spent several years in national service, and was then unemployed. In the late 1970s he was part of a group of Slovenian intellectuals focused on the work of psychoanalytical philosopher Jacques Lacan, and in the 1980s translated Freud, Lacan, and Althusser into Slovene. In the late 1980s he published a book on film theory, wrote for the alternative magazine Mladina, and was an activist pushing for democracy in Yugoslavia. When Slovenia gained independence in 1990, he became an unsuccessful presidential candidate.

① My father was an economic official and my mother was an accountant for a state-owned enterprise.
② Before studying in Paris, he received a doctorate in philosophy from the University of Ljubljana.
③ I came back to Slovenia and got a job at a university.
④ In the 1980s, he translated Freud, Lacan, and Althusser's writings into Slovenian.

하프모의고사
Season 2

해설편

01-25 회

빠른 정답 보기

제 01 회

01 ④	02 ④	03 ③	04 ②	05 ③
06 ④	07 ③	08 ②	09 ②	10 ②

제 02 회

01 ③	02 ④	03 ③	04 ②	05 ③
06 ④	07 ④	08 ②	09 ①	10 ④

제 03 회

01 ③	02 ③,①	03 ②	04 ④	05 ②
06 ②	07 ③	08 ①	09 ④	10 ④

제 04 회

01 ③	02 ③	03 ②	04 ②	05 ④
06 ①	07 ③	08 ④	09 ①	10 ④

제 05 회

01 ③	02 ④	03 ①	04 ②	05 ①
06 ②	07 ④	08 ①	09 ④	10 ④

제 06 회

01 ④	02 ①	03 ④	04 ④	05 ①
06 ②	07 ④	08 ②	09 ①	10 ③

제 07 회

01 ③	02 ④	03 ③	04 ④	05 ④
06 ④	07 ④	08 ②	09 ②	10 ④

제 08 회

01 ④	02 ①	03 ③	04 ③	05 ③
06 ④	07 ④	08 ①	09 ①	10 ④

제 09 회

01 ③	02 ②	03 ①	04 ②	05 ④
06 ②	07 ④	08 ②	09 ④	10 ④

제 10 회

01 ④	02 ④	03 ②	04 ④	05 ④
06 ②	07 ②	08 ③	09 ②	10 ④

제 11 회

01 ②	02 ②	03 ④	04 ②	05 ④
06 ④	07 ③	08 ②	09 ②	10 ④

제 12 회

01 ②	02 ④	03 ④	04 ③	05 ①
06 ②	07 ④	08 ②	09 ④	10 ④

제 13 회

01 ②	02 ②	03 ②	04 ④	05 ④
06 ①	07 ②	08 ②	09 ②	10 ④

제 14 회

01 ④	02 ④	03 ③	04 ②	05 ④
06 ②	07 ④	08 ③	09 ③	10 ④

제 15 회

01 ②	02 ④	03 ③	04 ①	05 ③
06 ④	07 ②	08 ②	09 ①	10 ④

제 16 회

01 ②	02 ③	03 ①	04 ①	05 ①
06 ②	07 ④	08 ④	09 ②	10 ④

제 17 회

01 ④	02 ②	03 ④	04 ②	05 ③
06 ④	07 ④	08 ①	09 ①	10 ③

제 18 회

01 ③	02 ④	03 ④	04 ①	05 ④
06 ③	07 ③	08 ③	09 ③	10 ②

제 19 회

01 ④	02 ②	03 ③	04 ④	05 ②
06 ③	07 ④	08 ②	09 ②	10 ④

제 20 회

01 ①	02 ④	03 ③	04 ②	05 ②
06 ③	07 ③	08 ④	09 ①	10 ③

제 21 회

01 ④	02 ④	03 ③	04 ④	05 ④
06 ②	07 ④	08 ①	09 ①	10 ③

제 22 회

01 ④	02 ④	03 ②	04 ④	05 ①
06 ①	07 ③	08 ④	09 ④	10 ④

제 23 회

01 ③	02 ④	03 ①	04 ②	05 ④
06 ②	07 ③	08 ④	09 ①	10 ③

제 24 회

01 ②	02 ④	03 ③	04 ①	05 ④
06 ②	07 ④	08 ③	09 ②	10 ③

제 25 회

01 ②	02 ④	03 ④	04 ①	05 ④
06 ②	07 ③	08 ②	09 ②	10 ③

제 01 회 하프 모의고사 해설

문제편 p.004

ANSWER

01 ④	02 ④	03 ③	04 ②	05 ③
06 ④	07 ③	08 ②	09 ②	10 ②

01 ④

해설 ④ they're stocked로 이어지는 절이 주어와 수동태 동사로 이루어진 완전한 절이므로 복합관계대명사 whatever를 복합관계부사 wherever로 바꿔 써야 한다. 그래야 문맥에도 어울린다.

① 관계대명사 which의 선행사인 concealer cream이 관계절에 속한 동사의 주어인데, 주어가 동작의 주체가 아니라 그 동작을 당하는 대상으로 해석되므로 수동태를 이루는 kept는 적절한 표현이다.

② 목적의 의미를 지닌 to부정사로 쓰인 to reach는 적절한 표현이다.

③ dictated의 목적어인 명사절을 이끄는 접속사 that은 적절한 표현이다.

해석 한 약국 체인점의 화장품 매장을 조사하던 중, 우리는 한 60대 여성이 벽에 있는 상품 선반에 다가가서 그것을 조심스럽게 살핀 다음 그녀가 필요로 하는 한 가지 물건인 컨실러 크림을 찾기 위해 그 앞에 무릎을 꿇는 것을 지켜보았는데, 그 컨실러 크림은 화려하지 않아서 진열대의 맨 아래쪽에 진열되어 있었다. 마찬가지로 백화점에서 우리는 한 과체중의 남자가 큰 통로 진열대에서 자신에게 맞는 치수의 속옷을 찾으려고 애쓰고 있는 것을 지켜보다가, 그가 그것들을 집으려고 바닥 근처로 몸을 위태로울 만큼 낮게 구부리는 것을 보았다. 두 경우 모두 논리적으로는 진열대가 그것들을 만든 디자이너에게가 아니라 그것들을 사용하는 쇼핑객에 맞게 조정되어야 한다고 지시되었어야만 했다. 우리는 컨실러를 위쪽으로 옮기고, 더 젊은 쇼핑객을 목표로 하는 어떤 것을 바닥 근처로 내려놓도록 조언했다. 젊은 쇼핑객은 자신들이 찾는 상품이 어디에 놓여 있든지 그것들을 찾아낼 것이다.

어휘 cosmetics 화장품 approach 다가가다, 접근하다
rack (상품) 선반 kneel 무릎을 꿇다 glamour 화려함
display 진열대, 진열 overweight 과체중의, 비만의 aisle 통로
logic 논리 dictate 지시하다, 명령하다
tailor (요구·조건·필요에) 맞게 조정하다 aimed at ~을 목표로 하는
stock (가게에 물품을) 놓다, 채우다

02 ④

해설 ④ Being cold outside → It being cold outside
문맥상 날씨를 나타내는 비인칭주어인 to 분사구문의 주어이다. 이는 주절의 주어와 일치하지 않으므로 주어를 생략할 수 없다. 'Because it was cold outside ~'가 분사구문이 된 것이다.

① All of 뒤에 절대 불가산명사 information이 온 것으로 보아 all 역시 information을 의미하는 것이므로 단수 취급을 해야 한다. was라는 동사의 단수형태가 바르게 쓰였다.

② "should have pp"는 '~했어야 했다(그런데 하지 않았다)'를 의미하는 표현으로 문맥상 바르게 사용되었다.

③ when 부사절보다 이전에 일어난 사건임을 알 수 있으므로 had started 부사 already를 통해 주절의 시제라는 대과거를 사용했다.

어휘 apologize 사과하다 boil 끓이다

03 ③

해석 이자율과 인플레이션의 역의 관계는 거시 경제의 기본적인 원칙들 중의 하나이다.

어휘 cardinal 기본적인, 진홍색의, 추기경 derisive 냉소하는
augmentative 증가하는 fundamental 기본적인
gregarious 군집의, 사교적인

04 ②

해석 증기 엔진의 등장은 충분한 석탄공급을 필요로 했다.

어휘 ample 넓찍한, 충분한 (= abundant) sufficient 충분한
proper 적당한 luxurious 사치스러운

05 ③

해석 ① A: 수학시험 어떻게 봤니?
B: 결과가 나올 때까지는 확실히 알 수 없을 거야.

② A: 다이어트 콜라 주세요.
B: 죄송합니다. 다른 음료수로 주문하실 수 있겠습니까?

③ A: 새해 결심한 것 있니?
B: 크리스마스는 일 년 중 내가 가장 좋아하는 휴일이야.

④ A: 서점 근처에 있는 새로운 이탈리안 레스토랑에 가보자.
B: 그거 좋은 생각이다. 6시 30분으로 예약을 할게.

06 ④

해설 이 글에서는 인간은 자연으로부터 해결책을 차용했다고 하면서 동식물을 모방한 여러 민족의 여러 사례를 들고 있으므로, 동일한 맥락에서 '자연의 문제 해결 전략'을 관찰하여 특정한 모양과 도구를 세계 곳곳에서 만들었다고 하는 것이 가장 적절하다. 그러므로 ④가 정답이다.

① 자연의 예기치 못한 변화

② 자연의 자유경쟁 법칙

③ 조상들의 전통문화

해석 인간은 수천 년 동안 다양한 정도의 정확도와 이해력으로 자연을 모방해왔다. 우리의 초기 인류 조상은 자신이 주변에서 본 동물과 식물로부터 해결책을 차용했다. 북극의 얼음 아래에서 수영하는 물개는 숨을 쉬기 위해 수면으로 올라올 수 있는 구멍을 만들고 유지하는데, 이누이트 족 사냥꾼은 북극곰이 기름진 만찬거리를 잡기 위해 그런 숨구멍 옆에서 잠복하는 방식을 모방했다. 폴리네시아인의 아우트리거 카누의 디자인은 물에 떠 있는 꼬투리의 그것을 그대로 따라 했다. 호주 원주민은 심지어 새 날개를 부메랑으로 모방하기까지 했다. 특정한 모양과 도구는 광대한 지리적 거리에 의해 떨어져 있었지만 동시에 자연의 문제 해결 전략에 몰두하여 그것을 관찰했던 사람들에 의해 만들어지면서 세계 곳곳에서 반복되었다.

어휘 degree 정도, 도, 학위 accuracy 정확도, 정확
solution 해결책, 해결 seal 물개, 바다표범 arctic 북극의
surface 수면으로 올라오다; 표면 mimic 모방하다, 흉내 내다
lie in wait 잠복하다, 숨어서 기다리다 rich 기름진, 영양분이 풍부한

echo 그대로 따라 하다, 메아리치다 aboriginal 호주 원주민의
simultaneously 동시에 immerse 몰두하게 만들다, (액체 속에) 담그다

similarity 유사점 in the first place 우선, 첫째로
test out ~을 시험해보다

07 ③

해설 주어진 문장의 stories like these는 대중매체에서 보도하는 멸종 위기의 동물들을 지켜내려는 사람들의 이야기를 가리킨다. 그리고 reactions are varied는 ③ 다음의 문장에서 설명되고 있다. 따라서 주어진 문장의 적절한 위치는 ③이다.

해석 매년 약 5만 종의 식물과 동물이 인간 활동의 결과로 지구로부터 사라진다. 자연보호론자와 환경운동가는 여러 해 동안 환경과 환경에 서식하는 동물들의 보호에 부여되는 우선순위를 격상시키려고 노력해 왔으나, 일반 대중, 정치가, 그리고 범죄학자는 그들의 노력을 대체로 무시해 왔다. 다양한 대중매체에서는 반점 올빼미를 구하기 위해 나무에 자신의 몸을 묶는 사람들에 관한 이야기 또는 멸종 위기의 개구리 서식지가 위험에 처할 수 있기 때문에 중지되는 대규모 건설 사업에 관한 이야기를 보도하고 있다. 일반 대중이 이와 같은 이야기를 들을 때 반응은 다양하다. 어떤 사람들은 이러한 행동을 도덕적 승리로 보는 반면, 다른 사람들은 그 행동을 그저 터무니없는 것으로 본다. 보다 저명한 공인(公人)들이 자연과 관련된 범죄에 맞서는 싸움에 적극성을 보이게 될 때, 멸종 위기의 종을 불법적으로 거래하는 문제는 사회에서 중요하게 될 것이다.

어휘 conservationist 자연보호론자
environmental activist 환경운동가 elevate 격상시키다, 승격시키다
priority 우선순위, 우선권 inhabitant 서식 동물, 거주자
politician 정치가 largely 대체로 media outlet 대중매체, 매스컴
spotted owl 반점 올빼미 large-scale 대규모의
construction 건설, 공사 halt 중지시키다
endangered 멸종 위기의 habitat 서식지 absurd 터무니없는
prominent 저명한, 두드러진

08 ②

해설 (A) 빈칸을 전후로 나이가 든 아이들의 친구에 대한 기대치와 미취학 아이들의 친구에 대한 기대치가 서로 다르다는 내용이 제시되고 있으므로 빈칸에는 Rather가 적절하다.
(B) 미취학 아이들이 함께 놀고 같은 놀이를 할 사람을 친구로 선택하여 시간을 보낸다는 내용이 제시되고 난 다음, 그 결과로 친구 관계가 미취학 아이들에게 자신의 행동과 감정을 시험해 볼 수 있는 상대를 제공한다는 내용이 뒤따르고 있으므로 빈칸에는 As a result가 적절하다.

해석 미취학 기간 동안(대략 3세에서 5세), 친구는 아이의 친교 세계에서 더 중요한 자리를 차지하게 된다. 취학 전 아이들의 주변에서 조금이라도 시간을 보내면, 대부분의 미취학 아이들에게 친구가 있고, 자신의 친구를 대단히 중요하게 여긴다는 결론에 곧 이르게 된다. 이 연령의 친구 관계는 보통 놀이를 중심으로 한다. 미취학 아이들이 친구에게 거는 기대는 나이가 더 많은 아이들의 기대처럼 성숙하거나 복잡하지 않다. <u>오히려</u>, 그들은 공통의 관심사와 활동을 함께 즐기는 데 초점을 맞춘다. 친구란 함께 놀기에 재미있고, 같은 놀이를 하기를 좋아하는 사람이다. 그러므로 (좋아하는) 놀이와 유사점 둘 다, 먼저 친구를 선택하고 이후 함께 시간을 보내는 데 중요하다. <u>결과적으로</u>, 친구 관계는 미취학 아이들에게, 놀면서 다양한 행동과 감정을 '시험해' 볼 수 있는 상대를 제공한다.

어휘 preschool 유치원 roughly 대략, 거칠게
typically 보통, 일반적으로 mature 성숙한, 원숙한

09 ②

해설 수학의 본질과 수학이 수반하는 바로 그 근본적인 추상 관념을 인식하는 것이 매우 중요하다는 취지의 글이다. (B)의 첫 문장에 있는 they는 주어진 글에 있는 Galileo, Descartes, Huygens and Newton을 가리키므로 주어진 글 다음에는 (B)가 이어져야 한다. (C)는 (B)에 언급된 근본적인 가정 다음에 이어지는 더 깊은 가정의 내용을 소개하고 있으므로 (B) 다음에는 (C)가 이어져야 하고, 논리와 수학에서 찾아볼 수 있는 가장 순수한 형태로 존재하는 이성을 언급한 (A)는 (C)에 언급된 이성과 증명이 승리할 세계에 대한 부연 설명이므로 (C) 다음에는 (A)가 이어져야 한다. 그러므로 주어진 글 다음에 이어질 글의 순서로 가장 적절한 것은 ②이다.

해석 수학의 본질과 수학이 수반하는 바로 그 근본적인 추상 관념을 인식하는 것은 중요하다. Galileo, Descartes, Huygens, 그리고 Newton 모두 수학 공식을 만들어 냈다. (B) 다시 말해, 그들은 자연에서 보이는 패턴을 표현하기 위해 수학을 이용하여 물리적 현상을 압축해 주는 수학적이고 추상적인 방법을 창조하고자 했던 것이다. 추상적인 공식이 자연과 부합할 수 있어야 한다는 것은 신생 과학에 관련된 사람들에 의해 만들어진 근본적인 가정이었다. (C) 그런 생각의 저변에는 세상이 예측 가능하고 질서 정연한 곳이라는 더 깊은 가정이 깔려 있었다. 조잡한 미신과 마법의 초기 시대에서 벗어나, 그들은 이성과 증명이 승리할 세계 속으로 자신들이 모습을 드러내는 것을 보았다. (A) 그런데 가장 순수한 형태의 이성은 논리와 수학에서 발견되며, 따라서 원론적으로 세상은 수학적 정확성을 가지고 만물의 움직임을 결정지을 '자연법칙'이라는 관점에서 이해될 수 있으리라 기대하는 것은 당연한 일이었다.

어휘 recognize 인식하다, 깨닫다 radical 근본적인, 기초적인
abstraction 추상 관념, 추출 involve 수반하다, 관련시키다
formula (수학) 공식, 화학식 (pl. formulae) in principle 원론적으로
comprehensible 이해될 수 있는 precision 정확성, 정확도
phenomenon 현상(pl. phenomena)
correspond to ~와 부합하다, ~와 상응하다
fundamental 근본적인 assumption 가정 emerging 신생의
ordered 질서 정연한, 정돈된 crude 조잡한 superstition 미신
emerge (모습을) 드러내다, 나타나다 evidence 증명, 증거
triumph 승리하다

10 ②

해설 'New York Sun'에서 정규직으로 다양한 편집 작업을 하면서 2년 동안 머물렀다고 했으므로 일치하지 않는 것은 ②이다.

해석 Mortimer J. Adler는 미국의 철학자, 교육자, 편집자이자 서구 세계의 위대한 저서 연구를 통한 성인 및 일반 교육의 지지자였다. 아직 공립학교에 다니는 동안, Adler는 'New York Sun'에 원고 담당 사환으로 고용되었는데, 그 곳에서 정규직으로 다양한 편집 작업을 하면서 2년 동안 머물렀다. 이후 Columbia University에 다니며 학사 학위를 위한 수업들을 모두 들었지만 체육(수영)을 거부해 졸업장을 받지 못했다. 그는 가르치면서 박사 학위를 따기 위해 Columbia에 머물렀고 이후 University of Chicago에서 법철학 교수가 되었다. 그곳에서 그는 Robert M. Hutchins와 함께, 위대한 책 읽기에 기반을 둔 정기적인 토론을 통하여 일반교양 교육을 추구하는 지지자가 되었다. 평생 동안 그는 자신이 위대한 책[고전] 운동이라고 부르는 것과 교육 개혁에 적극적이었으며 90대의 나이가 될 때까지 계속해서 강의를 하고

글을 썼다.

구문 • [While still in public school], Adler was taken on as a copyboy by the New York Sun, [where he stayed for two years {doing a variety of editorial work full-time }].

→ 첫 번째 [ ]는 시간을 나타내는 분사구이다. 두 번째 [ ]는 관계절로 the New York Sun을 부연 설명하며, 그 안의 { }는 부수적 상황을 나타내는 분사구이다.

• For his entire life, he [remained active {in what he called the great-books movement} and {in educational reform}], and [continued to lecture and write into his nineties].

→ 두 개의 [ ]가 and로 연결되어 주어 he의 술어 역할을 한다. 첫 번째 [ ] 안에 { }로 표시된 두 개의 전치사구가 and로 연결되어 있다.

제 02 회 하프 모의고사 해설

문제편 p.008

ANSWER

01 ③	02 ④	03 ③	04 ②	05 ③
06 ④	07 ④	08 ②	09 ①	10 ④

01 ③

해설 (A) 선행사인 a process를 수식하고 관계절 안에서 동사 moves의 주어 역할을 해야 하므로 주격 관계대명사인 that이 와야 적절하다. in which 다음에는 완결된 형태의 절이 이어진다.
(B) 주어인 Peer mediation programs가 find의 동작을 행하는 주체가 아니라 그 동작을 당하는 의미가 되어야 하므로 수동태의 문장을 만드는 been found가 와야 적절하다.
(C) 문장의 주어인 They에 이어지는 첫 번째 동사인 have reduced와 병렬 관계로 이어져야 문맥이 자연스러우므로 improved가 와야 한다. fighting과 병렬로 연결되는 improving을 택하게 되면 문장의 의미가 통하지 않는다. 그러므로 정답은 ③이다.

해석 또래 중재 프로그램은 학교에서 (관계) 회복 프로그램으로 자주 쓰이는 한 예이다. 또래 중재자는 일반적으로 또래 친구들이나 선생님들에 의해 후보로 추천되는데, 그 이유는 그들이 또래 친구들에 의해 존중과 신뢰를 받으며, 리더십과 의사소통 기술을 발휘해왔기 때문이다. 학생들은 자발적으로 중재를 받으러 오고, 또래 중재자는 그들이 서로를 비방하는 단계에서 모든 당사자가 받아들일 수 있는 해결책을 만들어내고 그것을 지키는 단계로 나아가는 과정을 거치도록 그들을 인도한다. 또래 중재 프로그램은 갈등에 대한 학생의 태도를 개선하고, 비폭력적인 문제 해결 방법에 대한 이해를 높이고, 의사소통 기술을 향상하는 데 효과적인 것으로 알려져 왔다. 그 프로그램은 또한 싸움으로 인한 정학 횟수를 줄여왔고, 학생들의 갈등 조정 능력을 향상해왔다.

어휘 mediation 중재, 조정 restorative 회복시키는
nominate 후보로 추천하다, 지명하다
demonstrate 발휘하다, (행동으로) 보여주다 voluntarily 자발적으로
commit to ~을 지키다, ~에 전념하다 conflict 갈등, 대립
nonviolent 비폭력적인 enhance 향상하다
suspension 정학, 유예

02 ④

해설 ④ Although he made a mistake의 문장에서 주절과 주어가 같으므로 주어를 생략하고 동사에 ~ing를 붙여 분사구문이 된 것이다. 접속사는 의미를 명확하게 하기 위해 분사구문 앞에 쓸 수 있다.
① 뒤에는 시점의 의미를 나타내는 과거시제가 바르게 사용되었으나, 그 시점으로부터 3년이 계속하여 흘렀다는 의미이므로 주절에는 계속의 의미를 표현하는 현재완료가 와야 한다.
② 접속사 before로 시작하는 시간의 부사절에서는 미래를 표현하는 조동사 will을 현재 시제로 대체하여 사용한다. 따라서 will set을 sets로 고쳐야 한다.
③ if '만약 ~라면'이라는 의미로, 조건의 부사절을 이끌 경우 미래 시제 대신 현재 시제를 사용한다. 그러나 접속사 if '~인지 아닌지'의 의미로 명사절을 이끌 경우 미래를 나타낼 때는 미래 시제를 그대로 사용한다. 이 문장에서 if는 동사 wonder의 목적어 역할을 명사절을 이끌고 있다. 또한 by tonight이라는 미래의 부사구가 있으므로 미래 시제를 써야 한다.

어휘 respect 존경하다 make a mistake 실수하다

03 ③

해석 나의 할머니는 내가 아는 가장 자비로운 사람 중 한 명이다. 그녀는 항상 친절한 행동을 하신다.

어휘 charitable 자비로운 intense 강렬한 notorious 악명 높은
benevolent 자비로운 candid 솔직한

04 ②

해석 올해는 사과가 너무 많아서 많은 사과들이 수확되지 않았다.

어휘 disease 질병, 질환 plenty 풍부함
deflation 물가 하락, 바람 빠짐 harvest 수확, 이익, 보수

05 ③

해설 ③에서 우산을 두고 온 것과 저축하는 것은 전혀 관련이 없다. ④에서 a television day는 'TV 보는 시간, TV 방영 시간'의 뜻이다.
ex You should have a television day, a computer day or a reading day so that you don't get bogged down with different activities confusing one another. (여러 가지 일이 서로 혼란을 일으켜 궁지에 빠지지 않도록 TV를 보든, 컴퓨터를 하든, 독서를 하든, 셋 중 하나를 해야 한다.)

해석 ① A: 이 소포가 일본에 도착하는데 얼마나 걸릴까요?
B: 항공으로 대략 4일이요.
② A: 명자는 낮 동안에 학교에 가고 저녁에는 시간제로 일해요.
B: 그녀가 어떻게 그걸 다 해내는지 놀라워요.
③ A: 내가 버스에 우산을 두고 내렸어.
B: 글쎄, 너는 만약의 경우를 위해 저축해야 해.
④ A: 톰은 텔레비전을 안 본대.
B: 그가 한가한 시간에 무슨 일을 하는지 궁금해.

06 ④

해설 화석 연료 연소로 인한 이산화탄소의 대량 배출과 관련하여, 오염과 건강상의 문제를 심각하게 일으키지만, 개발도상국들이 기아와 고통에서 해방되어가느라 그런 문제가 생기는 측면이 있다고 빈칸의 바로 앞 문장에서 기술하고 있다. 빈칸의 바로 앞에 In other words(즉, 다시 말하면)가 있으므로, 앞 문장의 내용을 다른 말로 표현한 ④ '우리는 가난에 대한 전쟁에서 이기고 있으므로 탄소에 대한 전쟁에서 지고 있다'가 정답이다.
① 선진국은 일반적으로 한 사람당 이산화탄소 배출물이 많다.
② 지구는 공기 오염과 인구과잉이라는 양면의 문제에 직면할 것이다.
③ 선진국은 개발도상국의 환경친화적 기술을 도와야 한다.

해석 (농업, 삼림 파괴와 시멘트 생산을 무시하고도) 화석 연료 연소에서 생기는 탄소 배출물은 이미 해마다 대략 총 320억 톤의 이산화탄소가 되는데,

2000년부터 2010년까지 매년 평균적으로 6억 7,600만 톤 씩 증가했다. 이것은 브라질이 매 열두 달 동안 전 세계적 총량에 보탠 배출물의 거의 두 배와 맞먹는다. 화석 연료 연소에서의 이런 대량 증가가 중국과 다른 곳에서 오염과 건강에 파멸적인 영향을 끼쳤음에도 불구하고, 개발도상국들이 수 세기에 걸친 기아와 고통으로부터 벗어나기 위하여 에너지 소비를 확대하고 있다는 것을 보여주기 때문에, 전 세계의 이산화탄소의 급격한 증가는 실제로 한 가지 측면에서는 좋은 일이다. 즉, 우리는 가난에 대한 전쟁에서 이기고 있으므로 탄소에 대한 전쟁에서 지고 있다.

어휘 emission 배출물, 배기가스, 배출
fossil-fuel burning 화석 연료 연소　agriculture 농업
deforestation 삼림 파괴　total 총 ~이 되다; 총량, 총계
annually 매년　equivalent 맞먹는, 동등한
massive 대량의, (규모, 양, 정도 등이) 큰
disastrous 파멸적인, 피해가 막심한　impact 영향, 충격
respect 측면, 점, 존경　expand 확대하다, 확장하다
consumption 소비　famine 기아
misery (가난, 질병 등으로 인한 심한) 고통, 불행

07 ④

해설 주어진 문장의 This는 흐름상 ④ 바로 앞의 the "butterfly problem"을 가리키며, a chaotic system의 개념은 ④ 바로 뒤의 문장에서 설명되고 있다. 따라서 주어진 문장은 ④에 위치해야 한다.

해석 컴퓨터 모형은 기상 예보에 있어 혁명을 가져왔다. 하지만 컴퓨터가 대기를 기술하는 한 세트의 자료로 가동되도록 하면 모든 시간에 대한 완벽한 예보가 산출될 거라고 생각하는 것은 여전히 어리석은 일일 것이다. 실제로는 일주일 넘게 앞을 내다볼 때 오늘의 예보조차도 신뢰성이 빠르게 떨어진다. 이는 예보가 '자신의 기능을 잃어버리는 것'이라고 기술된다. 그러한 어려움 중의 일부는 예보를 위한입력 정보가 불완전하다는 것이지만, 보다 근본적인 장애는 '나비 문제'이다. 이는 날씨가 무질서한 체계임을 말하는 것에 대한 약칭이다. 그것은 내 책상 위가 무질서하다는 방식으로 무질서한 것이 아니다. 이런 상황에서 '무질서한'이라는 말은 입력 조건에 있어서 모든 사소한 측정할 수 없는 등락을 감안하는 것이 결코 가능하지 않아서 나비가 아마존의 상공에서 날개를 펄럭이는 것이 결국 뉴욕에서 폭풍우를 생기게 할 수 있음을 의미한다. 컴퓨터 기술의 발달에도 불구하고 정확한 기상 예보가 여전히 어려운 이유를 설명하는 글이다.

어휘 chaotic 무질서한, 혼란한
revolutionize ~에 있어 혁명을 가져오다　forecasting 예보
atmosphere 대기, 분위기　in practice 실제로
reliability 신뢰성, 확실성　objection 장애, 지장, 반대
allow for ~을 감안하다　immeasurable 측정할 수 없는
flap 펄럭이다, 퍼덕거리다　in the end 결국, 마침내

08 ②

해설 (A) 더운 지역에서는 냉방을 위해 에너지 소비가 많은 냉방 장치에 의존하고 있다는 내용이 (A) 앞에 나오고, 그 뒤에는 상반되는 내용, 즉 냉난방을 위해 건물 자체를 필터의 역할을 하게 하는 접근법에 관한 내용이 나오고 있으므로 However가 적절하다.
(B) 초기 건축가들이 건물 자체를 필터로 활용한 사례를 이어서 제시하고 있으므로 for example이 적절하다.

해석 더 더운 지역에서, 우리 중 많은 사람들은 건물 내부를 시원하게 유지하기 위해 에너지 소비가 많은 냉방 장치에 의존하는 법을 배워 왔다. 그러나, 또 하나의 접근법은 단순히 건물 그 자체가 필터의 역할을 하게 하여 그 순간의 필요에 따라 선별적으로 일광, 온기, 그리고 시원한 공기가 들어오게 하는 것이다. 이것이 획기적으로 들린다면, 어느 누구라도 석유나 전기에 대해 들어보기도 전에 초기의 건축가들이 이런 일을 하고 있었다는 것은 언급할 만한 가치가 있을 것이다. Andaluda에 있는 무어식 궁전의 설계자는, 예를 들면, 타오르는 여름의 태양은 막지만 겨울의 더 부드럽고 비스듬한 햇빛은 들어올 수 있도록 하는 지붕의 경사도를 정하는 방법에 관한 모든 것을 알고 있었다. 현대식 건물도 이를 훌륭하게 하도록 설계할 수 있지만, 그 사이에 우리 누구나 이미 가지고 있는 것으로 해낼 수 있다. 태양이 창문 위를 직접 비추면, 덧문을 닫거나 블라인드를 쳐라.

어휘 energy-hungry 에너지 소비가 많은
selectively 선별적으로, 선택적으로　innovative 획기적인
architect 건축가　sloping 경사진, 비탈진
in the meantime 그 사이[동안]에

09 ①

해설 양립할 수 없는 두 가지 대응 경향이 동시에 자극받을 때 발생하는 것이 전위행동이라는 내용의 주어진 글에 이어 적수와 마주칠 때 새가 보이는 털 손질과 같은 전위행동의 사례를 제시한 (B)가 이어져야 한다. (A)의 첫 문장에 제시된 the activity는 (B)에 언급된 털 손질 행위를 가리키므로 (B) 다음에는 (A)가 이어져야 한다. 또한 새의 전위행동에 이은 물고기의 전위행동을 큰가시고기의 사례로 설명한 (C)가 (A) 다음에 이어져야 한다. 그러므로 주어진 글 다음에 이어질 글의 순서로 가장 적절한 것은 ①이다.

해석 본능적인 충동이라는 개념과 관련 있는 흥미로운 관찰 결과는 '전위행동'이다. 전위행동은 양립할 수 없는 두 가지 대응 경향이 동시에 자극받을 때 발생한다. (B) 예를 들어, 새는 공격과 도망을 둘 다 이끌어 내는 적수와 마주칠 수도 있다. 이 상황에서 털 손질과 같은 그 상황과 무관한 것처럼 보이는 행동이 나타난다. (A) 때때로 그 활동은 서두르는 것처럼 보이고 완료되기 전에 중단된다는 점에서 보통의 털 손질 행동과는 다르다. 그러나 다른 경우에는 그 행동이 정상적인 털 손질 활동과 구별되지 않는다. (C) 큰가시고기와 같은 특정 종의 물고기도 이와 같은 상황에 어울리지 않는 전위행동을 보인다. 공격 행동과 도망 행동을 둘 다 이끌어 내는, 자신의 영역과 또 다른 큰 가시고기의 영역 사이의 경계에 있을 때 집을 짓는 부적절한 행동이 자주 나타난다.

어휘 observation 관찰 (결과)　instinctive 본능적인, 본능의
urge 충동; 권고하다　incompatible 양립할 수 없는
simultaneously 동시에　arouse 자극하다, 깨우다
differ from ~와 다르다　grooming 털 손질, 몸단장
hurried 서두르는　discontinue 중단하다
distinguishable 구별할 수 있는　elicit 이끌어 내다, 유도하다
attack 공격; 공격하다　irrelevant 무관한　exhibit 보이다, 전시하다
territory 영역, 영토　inappropriate 부적절한
displacement activity 전위행동(두 가지의 모순된 자극이 주어졌을 때 두 가지 중 어느 행동도 아닌 제3의 행동을 하는 것)

10 ④

해설 이 이벤트는 예약이 필요 없다고 하였으므로, 안내문의 내용과 일치하지 않는 것은 ④이다.

해석 Lakeside 지역 사회 연날리기
9월 8일 토요일

11시부터 16시까지
Green Porch Park의 이벤트 행사장에서
Kent Kite Flyers가 또 하나의 재미있는 연날리기 행사를 개최하기 위해 공원에 돌아옵니다.

- 여러분이 초보자이든 또는 전문가이든 와서 함께하세요!
- 아이들을 위한 '무료' 연 만들기 워크숍
- 음식과 다과는 Parish Hall에서 이용 가능할 것입니다.
- 이 이벤트는 예약이 필요 없고 '무료'입니다! 모든 연령과 능력을 갖춘 사람들을 환영합니다!

주의 사항
- 아이들은 책임 있는 어른에 의해 감독되고 반려견은 줄에 묶여 다녀야 합니다.
- Saffron Way의 길을 따라 무료 주차, 주차장은 16시 30분에 닫음

더 많은 정보를 원하시면, 우리의 웹사이트인 www. communitykite.com에 방문하세요.

구문 • We request [that children be supervised by a responsible adult] and [that pet dogs be kept on a leash].
→ 두 개의 [ ]로 표시된 부분은 모두 request의 목적어 역할을 한다. 주절 동사가 요구를 나타내는 request나 ask일 때, that절의 동사는 기본 형태인 be가 된다.

제 03 회 하프 모의고사 해설

문제편 p.012

ANSWER

01 ③	02 ③, ①	03 ②	04 ④	05 ②
06 ②	07 ③	08 ①	09 ④	10 ④

01 ③

해설 ③ how it would be like to work ~에서 전치사 like의 목적어 역할을 할 수 있는 의문사가 와야 하므로 how를 what으로 고쳐야 한다. how는 부사 역할을 하는 의문사이므로 전치사 like의 목적어로 사용될 수 없다.
① to offer는 앞의 명사를 수식하는 형용사적 용법의 to부정사이다.
② '~하는 것을 돕다, ~하는 데 도움이 되다'의 의미를 나타내는 <help + (to) + 동사원형> 구문으로 맞게 쓰였다.
④ 주어인 one of their biggest rewards의 핵이 단수인 one이므로 is는 맞게 쓰였다.

해석 자원봉사는 많은 다양한 사람을 만나는 데 도움을 줄 수 있다. 어떤 지역으로 이사한 지 얼마 되지 않았다거나 사교 집단을 섞을(사교 범위를 넓힐) 수 있을 것 같은 느낌이 든다면 이는 근사한 일이 될 수 있다. 게다가, 자원봉사를 하는 동안 만날 사람들은 아마도 학교에 있는 대부분의 또래 친구들과는 다른 제공할 것들을 가지고 있을 것이다. 예를 들어 살아가는 동안에 조부모나 그 외의 어르신들이 없다면 퇴직자 주택 지구에 사는 주민들이 그러한 공백을 채우는 데 도움이 될 것이다. 또는 공원 관리원으로 일하는 것이 어떤 것일지 항상 알고 싶어 했다면 공원 관리원 한 분 곁에서 자원봉사하는 것은 전문가로부터 요령을 터득할 수 있는 대단한 기회가 될 수 있다. 많은 자원봉사자들이 그들이 얻게 되는 가장 큰 보상 중 하나가 다양한 직업의 사람들을 알게 되는 것이라고 말한다. 어떤 자원봉사 일을 선택하더라도 그렇지 않았다면 만나지 못했을 사람을 거의 확실히 만나게 된다.

어휘 stand to do ~할 것 같다, ~할 것이다 circle 집단, 범위
senior citizen 어르신, 노인 resident 거주자
retirement 퇴직, 퇴직 생활 ranger (공원의) 관리원, 순찰대원
alongside ~의 곁에서 walk of life 직업, 신분

02 ③, ①

해설 처음에는 정답이 ③이었으나 ①도 복수 정답으로 인정된 문제이다.
③ 전치사 with로 시작되는 with 분사구문의 목적격보어의 형태를 선택하는 문제이다. with 뒤 목적어인 the three quarters of the land의 뒤 목적격보어인 surround는 목적어와의 관계가 수동이다. 즉 '육지는 바다에 의해 둘러싸여 있는'의 의미가 적합하므로 수동의 의미를 전달하는 과거분사인 surrounded가 적합하다.
① outdoor는 '야외의'를 의미하는 형용사이고, outdoors는 '야외로'를 의미하는 부사이다. 위 문장에서는 야외에 나가는 것을 의미하므로 부사인 outdoors라고 써야 한다. not to mention은 '~은 말할 것도 없고'를 의미하는 표현이다.
② 비교급을 구성하는 more than의 뒤에 <any other + 단수 명사>의 형태를 취하면 최상급의 의미를 가지게 된다.
④ 'a number of ~'는 '많은 ~'을 의미하는 표현으로, 뒤에 복수 명사와 동사의 복수형을 취하게 되므로 are라는 복수가 올바르게 사용되었다.

03 ②

해석 그의 보고서는 시간 순서대로 구성되어 있다.

어휘 chronologically 시간 순서에 따라
in terms of ~의 관점에서 comparison 비교
time sequence 시간 순서

04 ④

해석 그는 깊은 괴로움의 감정을 느꼈다.

어휘 anguish (극심한) 괴로움 failure 실패 dignity 위엄, 존엄
pride 자부심 grief 슬픔

05 ②

해설 'How about ~'으로 질문하면 Yes나 No로 대답할 수 없다. ②의 답변은 "Did you enjoy staying in Texas?" 같은 질문에 적절하다.

해석 ① A: 네가 입고 있는 코트 정말 예쁘다!
B: 고마워. 이거 작년에 샌프란시스코에서 산거야.
② A: 텍사스에서 사는 게 어때?
B: 그래, 우리는 좋은 시간을 보냈어. 쇼핑도 좀 했어.
③ A: 나 너무 비참해. 아무도 나를 사랑하지 않아.
B: 너를 사랑하는 사람을 알아. 바로 나야.
④ A: 아야! 내 눈에 뭐가 있어.
B: 어디 보자. 아니야, 아무것도 안 보여.

06 ②

해설 두려울 수 있는 막연한 질문을 스스로에게 할 수는 있지만, 그 질문을 명확한 대답 없이 그냥 내버려둘 것이 아니라, 여러 조사 자료 등을 통해 그 질문에 대한 현실적인 대답을 찾는 것이 중요하다는 내용의 글이다. 따라서 빈칸에는 ② '대답을 찾을 때까지 놀이를 계속 하라'가 가장 적절하다.
① 명확한 위험을 멀리하라.
③ 처음부터 이전 자료를 무시하라.
④ 진지하게 패자의 역할을 하도록 노력하라.

해석 "내가 암에 걸렸다고 진단받으면 어떻게 될까?"라고 아마 당신은 자기도 모르게 물을지 모른다. 그 질문에 대한 현실적이고 신중한 반응은 어떤 유형의 암은 치료율이 80퍼센트이고, 또 다른 유형은 100퍼센트라는 것을 고려하는 것일지도 모른다. 현실적인 반응은 또한, 그 병을 치료하는 연구에 상당한 진전이 이루어지고 있고, 그래서 사실 이 진단이 불과 몇 년 전에 그랬었을 것보다 훨씬 덜 비극적이라는 것을 인지하는 것일지도 모른다. 다시 말해서, 명확하지 않은 '대답 없음'은 (심신을) 쇠약하게 할 만큼 무섭지만 더 포괄적인, 현실적인 대답은 감당할 수 있는 것으로 드러난다. 그 질문들을 할 수는 있지만, 또한 그것들에 기꺼이 대답할 수 있어야 한다. '~라면 어떻게 될까?' 놀이를 한다면, 대답을 찾을 때까지 놀이를 계속 하라.

어휘 diagnose 진단하다 realistic 현실적인
studied 신중한, 세심하게 계획된 take into account ~을 고려하다
cure rate 치료율 stride 진전, 진보 catastrophic 비극적인

comprehensive 포괄적인 manageable 감당할 수 있는
indefinite 명확하지 않은, 애매한

07 ③

해설 주어진 문장은 내부자의 한계(단점)에 대해 이야기하고, ③ 바로 뒤의 '그 인지적 경직성'은 주어진 문장의 내용을 가리키므로 주어진 문장이 들어갈 가장 적절한 위치는 ③이다.

해석 Joseph Bower는 자신의 가장 최근 연구에서 최고 책임자들은 심지어 그들 조직의 주변부에서 매우 유능한 후임자를 찾을 수 있다고 주장한다. Bower는 새로운 최고 책임자로 내부자를 고용하는 것과 외부자를 고용하는 것에 대한 개념을 재고한다. 내부자는 (자기 기업이 하는) 사업에서의 풍부한 경험의 이점과 그 기업의 문화와 가치에 대한 깊은 이해의 이점을 제공한다. 그러나 내부자는 사업하는 방식의 특정한 정신적 모델에 지나치게 단단히 얽힐 수 있다. 만일 기업이 외부 환경에서 주요 변화를 겪는다면 그 인지적 경직성은 그 기업에 그다지 도움이 되지 않을 수도 있다. 외부자는 분명히 신선한 관점을 가져오지만, 그들이 적절한 경험을 언제나 가지고 있는 건 아닐 수도 있고, 그 기업의 문화에 언제나 적합한 건 아닐 수도 있다.

어휘 chief executive (회사나 조직의) 최고 책임자
capable 유능한 successor 후임자, 계승자 cognitive 인지의
inflexibility 경직성 perspective 관점 adequate 적절한
succession 계승 extensive 아주 많은 venture 모험적 사업

08 ①

해설 (A) 건강을 묻는 질문에 대한 필자의 대답은 'Okay'나 'Fine'과 같은 의미였지만, 이와 달리 사우디아라비아 사람들의 대답은 'Praise to God'와 같은 의미였다는 내용이 나오고 있으므로 However가 적절하다.
(B) 예상 밖의 방식으로 대답하는 것이 사회적 국외자라는 의미를 전달했다는 말이 나오고, 뒤에 실제로 말한 것보다 더 많은 의미가 전달되었다고 앞 내용을 풀어서 설명하는 내용이 이어지므로 In other words가 적절하다.

해석 내가 처음 사우디아라비아에 살았을 때, 나는 내 건강에 관한 ('How are you?'에 해당하는) 아랍어 질문에 'Okay'나 'Fine'처럼 나에게 친숙하고 틀에 박힌 응답에 해당하는 말로 답 하는 경향이 있었다. 그러나, 내가 비슷한 질문을 했을 때 사람들이 일반적으로 문자 그대로 'Praise to God(신을 찬양하라)' 이라는 의미를 지닌 말로 답한다는 것을 결국 알아챘다. 나는 화용론적인 입장에서 언어 사용이 그 맥락에 적절하기를 바라면서 이내 그 새로운 표현을 쓰는 것을 배웠다. 내가 처음 사용한 유형의 대답이 '틀린' 것은 아니었지만(내 어휘와 발음은 부정확하지 않았다), 내가 예상 밖의 방식으로 대답하는 사회적 국외자라는 의미를 전달했던 것이다. 다시 말해서, 실제로 말한 것보다 더 많은 것이 전달되고 있었다. 처음에는 그것을 알지 못했다. 나는 그러한 언어의 형식들이 사회적 내부자에 의해 어떻게 규칙적인 패턴으로 사용되는가에 관한 화용론을 알지 못한 채, 몇 가지 언어 형식을 배웠던 것이다.

어휘 equivalent 상당하는 것; 동등한 phrase 말, 구절
literal 문자 그대로의 pronunciation 발음 inaccurate 부정확한
convey 전달하다, 운반하다 initially 처음에 linguistic 언어의

09 ④

해설 기온 상승이 날씨 패턴의 변동성을 더 심화한다고 언급한 주어진 글 다음에, 주어진 글의 기온 상승을 가리키는 표현인 warmer air로 시작하는 (C)가 이어져, 지구가 더워지는 섭씨 1도마다 대기는 7퍼센트 더 많은 수분을 흡수할 수 있지만, 그 7퍼센트는 균일하지 않다는 내용이 언급되어야 한다. 이어서 공기의 수분 용량에 관한 표현인 The greater moisture capacity of the air로 시작하는 (B)가 이어져, 공기의 수분 용량이 더 커지면 지역이나 계절에 따라 가뭄과 폭우가 다르게 발생하게 된다는 내용 다음에, 미국을 예로 들어 가뭄과 폭풍우가 극심한 경우를 상술하는 내용의 (A)가 마지막으로 이어지는 것이 자연스럽다. 그러므로 주어진 글 다음에 이어질 글의 순서로 가장 적절한 것은 ④이다.

해석 우리가 대기 중에 더 많은 열을 가둘 때, 날씨 패턴은 변동성이 더 심해진다. 1도의 기온 상승은 가장 심한 극단적인 상태에서는 몇 도의 상승을 초래할 수 있다. (C) 그리고 더 따뜻한 공기는 더 많은 수분을 여기저기로 더 빠르게 이동시킬 수 있다. 지구가 더워지는 섭씨 1도마다 대기는 7퍼센트 더 많은 수분을 흡수할 수 있다. 하지만 그 7퍼센트는 균일하지 않다. (B) 공기의 수분 용량이 더 커진다는 것은 물이 한 지역에서 흡수되어 다른 지역에 축적될 수 있다는 것을 의미한다. 수분이 몇 번, 몇 군데 더 집중되어 어떤 지역이나 계절에는 가뭄을 초래하고, 뒤이어 또 다른 지역이나 계절에는 폭우를 내리게 한다. (A) 그리고 실제로 미국 전역에서 강수량이 6퍼센트 증가하는 동안, 가뭄도 또한 증가하고, 가장 극심한 1퍼센트의 폭풍우에서 내리는 비의 양이 20퍼센트 증가한다. 더 많은 비가 더 적은 곳에 집중되며, 더 많은 곳은 가뭄이 들게 되고, 실로 비가 내리는 곳들은 더 심한 폭풍우를 겪는다.

어휘 trap 가두다 translate into ~을 초래하다 drought 가뭄
concentrated 집중된 intense 심한 suck 흡수하다, 빨아들이다
celsius 섭씨 absorb 흡수하다 uniform 균일한

10 ④

해설 제한 시간인 7분을 초과하면 벌칙이 적용될 것이라고 했으므로 안내문의 내용과 일치하는 것은 ④이다.

해석 후프 댄스 세계 선수권 대회
2019년 2월 9일과 10일, 최고의 아메리칸 인디언과 캐나다 원주민 후프 댄서들이 Heard Museum에서 겨룰 것입니다. 이틀 동안의 경연 대회에서 남녀는 동등한 자격으로 겨룰 것입니다.
일정
- 현장 참가자 등록은 오전 8시부터 9시까지 Encanto Room에서 있을 것입니다.
- 경연 대회는 오전 10시에 시작합니다.
- 모든 참가자는 등록 순서와 관계없이 무작위로 호명되어 춤을 출 것입니다.

심사 기준
참가자는 아래 5가지 범주로 평가될 것입니다.
1. 정확성
2. 리듬
3. 쇼맨십
4. 창의력
5. 속도

일반 규칙
- 댄서들은 제한 시간인 7분을 초과하면 벌칙이 적용될 것입니다. 경연장에서는 큰 시계가 보일 것입니다.
- 경기 중에 경연자의 번호가 세 번 불릴 것입니다. 세 번째 불린 후에도 경기장에 있지 않으면 실격이 될 것입니다.

구문 • All contestants will be randomly called to dance, [regardless of registration order].
→ [ ]는 전치사구로 '~과 관계없이'라는 뜻이다

제04회 하프 모의고사 해설

문제편 p.016

ANSWER

01 ③	02 ③	03 ②	04 ②	05 ④
06 ①	07 ③	08 ④	09 ①	10 ④

01 ③

해설 (A) 앞에 나온 work hard ~ life's hardships의 의미를 받는 대동사이므로, 일반동사를 대체하는 do를 시제에 맞게 쓴 did가 적절하다.
(B) <It wasn't until ~ that ...>의 강조 구문이므로 that이 적절하다.
(C) 특정 명사의 동작이나 상태를 표현하는 <with + 명사 + 분사구> 구조로 '명사+현재분사'가 with에 공통으로 연결된 표현이므로 kicking이 적절하다. 그러므로 정답은 ③이다.

해석 오늘날 우리는 아이들을 인생의 고난으로부터 보호하기 위해 열심히 일을 한다. 그러나 우리나라 역사의 대부분 동안 우리는 그렇게 하지 않았다. 오히려 아이들이 일을 했다. 우리나라의 가장 초창기에 그들(아이들)은 자신의 형제자매를 돌보거나 논밭에서 시간을 보냈다. 나라가 산업화됨에 따라 그들은 광산과 방직 공장, 공장과 통조림 공장, 노점에서 일했다. 시간이 흐르면서 개혁가들은 미성년 노동 관행을 가까스로 불법화했다. 그러나 변화는 느렸다. 우리의 병사들이 2차 세계대전에서 돌아온 후에야 비로소 지금 우리가 알고 있는 유년 시절이 시작되었다. 가족 경제는 더 이상 부모가 아이들에게 거처를 제공하고 아이들을 먹이고, 아이들은 보답으로 가족 금고에 뭔가를 되갚아 넣어주는 상호 교환 체제를 기반으로 하지 않았다. 관계는 불균형적이게 되었다. 아이들은 일하는 것을 그만두었고, 부모들은 전보다 두 배나 더 열심히 일했다. 아이들은 우리의 피고 용인에서 우리의 상사가 되었다.

어휘 shield 보호하다 hardship 고난, 어려움 sibling 형제자매
mine 광산 textile mill 방직 공장 cannery 통조림 공장
street trade 노점 reformer 개혁가
manage to do 가까스로 ~을 해내다 outlaw 불법화하다, 금지시키다
shelter 거처를 제공하다, 막아주다 kick ~ back ~을 되갚다

02 ③

해설 ③ convenient는 사람을 주어로 취하지 않는 형용사이다. 따라서 가주어인 it을 사용하고, 진주어인 to visit her mother의 의미상의 주어를 표현하는 <for + 목적격>의 형태로 나타내야 한다.
① 'charge A with B'는 'A를 B라는 이유로 비난하다'를 의미한다.
② 완전타동사 begin은 to부정사와 동명사를 목적어로 취할 수 있다. 이때 의미의 차이는 없다.
④ thanks to는 전치사로서 뒤에 목적어를 취하므로 명사구인 your help가 목적어로 사용된 것은 적절하다.

어휘 dishonesty 부정직, 불성실 incident 사건
aspect 양상, 국면 assume 양상을 띠다, 추정하다
with ease 쉽게(= easily)

03 ②

해석 그는 너무 서투른 바보다. 그래서 그는 항상 일을 망친다.

어휘 clumsy 서투른(= all thumbs) audacious 용감한
awkward 서투른 fluent 유창한

04 ②

해석 Midway 섬들은 1859년에 미국에 합병되었다.

어휘 annex 합병하다 obliterate 지우다 covet 욕심 내다
merge 합병하다 suppress 억압하다

05 ④

해설 ④ 날씨가 더워 물로 뛰어들자는 A의 말에 오랜만에 만나 안부를 묻는 답변은 어색하다.

해석 ① A: 내가 네 책을 빌려도 되겠니?
B: 물론이지. 여기 있어.
② A: Mary가 요리대회 우승자야.
B: 대단해! 그녀는 정말 신이 나겠다.
③ A: 무슨 일이야? 너 슬퍼 보여.
B: 난 아버지가 걱정돼. 그는 매우 편찮으셔.
④ A: 너무 더워. 물 속으로 뛰어들자.
B: 오랜만이야. 어떻게 지냈어?

어휘 mind 꺼리다, 싫어하다, 신경을 쓰다
do you mind ~해도 될까요? dive into ~으로 뛰어들다
long time no see 오랜만입니다

06 ①

해설 꿈은 개인적인 것이어서 다른 사람들과 완전하게 공유할 수 없으며 꿈의 존재를 증명할 수도 없고 남에게 털어놓는다고 해도 사적 영역이 그다지 크게 감소되지 않는다는 내용의 글이므로 빈칸에 들어갈 말로 ① '사적 영역'이 가장 적절하다.
② 익숙함
③ 상징성
④ 일관성

해석 우리는 다른 누군가에게 우리의 꿈에 대해 말해 줄 수 있으며, 운이 좋으면 그 꿈에 대한 상상력을 동원한 그의 반응이 우리에게 공유된 경험이라는 착각을 줄 수도 있다. 하지만 우리가 꿈에 대해 말해 주는 그 사람이 의심 많은 사람이라고 판명되면, 우리는 그에게 말해준 꿈을 우리가 정말로 꾸었다는 것을 그에게 납득시킬 수단이 없다. 우리가 다른 꿈이 아니라 정확하게 그 꿈을 꾸었으며 우리가 그것을 올바르게 기억했다는 증거를 그가 요청하면, 우리는 그것을 제시할 수 없다. 우리는 그 꿈에 나타난 사람들에게 우리의 이야기를 확증해 달라고 부탁할 수 없다. 원칙적으로 증거의 법칙에 의해서 확증되거나 혹은 그 반대로 될 수 있는 일상생활에서의 사건과는 달리, 꿈속에서의 경험은 그것들에 관한 특유의 사적 영역을 지니는데, 그것(사적 영역)은 다른 사람들에게 그것들(꿈속에서의 경험들)에 대해 이야기해주는 것에 의해 오직 부분적

으로만 혹은 흔히 오직 자기기만적으로만 감소될 수 있다.

어휘 imaginative 상상력을 동원한, 상상력이 풍부한
illusion 착각, 오해 turn out to be ~임이 판명되다
confirm 확증하다, 확인해 주다 peculiar 특유의, 특이한
partially 부분적으로 self-deceptively 자기기만적으로
recount 이야기하다, 상술하다 symbolism 상징성, 상징주의
consistency 일관성, 한결같음 abstractness 추상성

07 ③

해설 주어진 문장은 Stadiatis가 헬멧을 벗고 말들과 여자들을 봤다고 말하는 내용이다. 이 문장 뒤에는 그가 본 것들에 대해 정확한 정보를 처음으로 제공해주는 내용이 와야 자연스러우므로 주어진 문장이 들어가기에 가장 적절한 곳은 ③이다.

해석 북아프리카 해안에서 작업하고 귀가 중이던 해면 잡이용 그리스 배 두 척이 폭풍 때문에 그리스의 Antikythera 섬에 대피해야 했다. 바람이 가라앉기를 기다리는 동안 시간을 허비하고 싶지 않았기 때문에, 선장인 Dimitrios Kondos는 해면을 추가로 거두어들이기를 바라면서 그의 수석 잠수부인 Elias Stadiatis를 내려가게 했다. 정상적으로 내려간 후에 Stadiatis는 거칠게 몸짓을 하면서 갑자기 물에서 불쑥 모습을 드러냈다. 헬멧을 벗고 그는 '말들과 여자들을' 본 것에 대해 말했다. 사실 그가 우연히 발견한 것은 해저 절벽 가장자리에 불안정하게 놓여 있는 고대 난파선의 조각품 화물이었다. 이어진 잠수에서는 Kondos 자신이 직접 고대의 청동으로 된 팔을 건져냈고 후에 그리스 정부에 그 발견에 대해 신고했다.

어휘 sponge 해면, 스펀지 work (~에서) 작업하다[일하다]
seek shelter at ~에 대피[피신]하다 subside 가라앉다, 잔잔해지다
chief 수석의, 최고의, 주된 descend 내려가다, 하강하다
harvest 거두어들이다, 추수하다 descent 내려감, 하강
come upon ~을 우연히 발견하다[만나다] sculptural 조각의
wreck 난파선 position (특정한 위치에) 두다
precariously 불안정하게 edge 가장자리 cliff 절벽 vessel 선박
navy 해군 exhausted 지친 rage 휘몰아치다
overhead 머리 위에(서)

08 ④

해설 (A) 앞 문장의 내용은 미국인들이 건배를 제안하는 경우가 드물다는 것인데 (A)를 포함하는 문장에서는 건배가 다른 나라들에서는 더 일반적이며 잘 준비해야 한다는 내용이 이어지므로 역접의 연결사인 however를 쓰는 것이 적절하다.
(B) 앞 문장의 내용은 건배의 순간이 기억할 만하고 오래 갈 감정을 표현하는 때라는 것이고 (B)를 포함하는 문장의 내용은 건배를 잘 준비하는 것이 중요하다는 것이므로 빈칸에 들어갈 연결사는 '그러므로'에 해당하는 Therefore가 적절하다. 그러므로 ④가 정답이다.

해석 미국인들은 아마도 새해 전야(파티)나 결혼식에서 (신랑의) 들러리인 경우를 제외하면 식사를 하거나 술을 마실 때 거의 건배를 제안하지 않는다. 그러나 다른 나라들에서는 그것이 더 일반적이므로 준비하는 것이 현명하다. 예를 들어, 중국의 식사에서 여러 코스로 구성된 식사의 정점은 상어의 지느러미 수프가 나오는 코스의 중간에 있다. 또한 그때가 건배사를 할 관례적인 시간이다. 여기 여러분이 세계어디에 있든 건배의 몇 가지 지침이 있다. 주인이 먼저 건배한다. 만찬 자리라면, 자리에서 일어나라. 건배사는 짧게 하라. 주인의 친절함과 환대, 국가 간의 우정과 개인적인 관계와 사업상 관계가 둘 다 좋은 것의 가치에 관해 언급하라. 그것은 기억할 만하고도 오래 갈 바로 그 적절한 감정이 표현될 수 있는 순간이 될 수 있다. 그러므로 심지어 다양한 경우를 위해 작은 레퍼토리를 개발할 정도까지 말을 잘한 건배사는 기대할 가치가 있다.

어휘 toast 건배, 건배사 best man (신랑의) 들러리 fin 지느러미
customary 관례적인 graciousness 친절함, 상냥함
hospitality 환대, 후대 sentiment 감정, 정서
repertoire 레퍼토리, (한 연주자·가수의 모든) 연주[노래·공연] 곡목

09 ①

해설 개인의 치장은 기분(mood)을 반영하거나 기분에 영향을 미칠 수 있다는 주어진 글 다음에, 주어진 글의 mood에 관한 내용을 전개하는 (B)가 이어져, 유쾌하고 활기 넘치는 기분을 보여 주는 방법은 색 대비와 선 대비가 있는 의상을 선택하는 것이라는 내용이 와야 한다. 이어서 (B)의 색 대비와 선 대비(colors and linear arrangements that show contrast)를 하는 구체적인 방법을 설명하는 내용의 (A)가 와야 한다. 마지막으로, (A) 하단부에서 언급된 선 대비(Linear contrast)가 문화적으로 어떻게 해석되는지에 관한 내용과 미국 문화에서 의상에서의 선과 색 대비가 어떤 효과가 있는지에 관한 맺음말을 하는 내용의 (C)로 이어지는 것이 자연스럽다. 그러므로 주어진 글 다음에 이어질 글의 순서로 가장 적절한 것은 ①이다.

해석 개인의 치장은 기분이라고 불리는 내적 감정 상태를 반영할 수도 있다. 그것은 또한 기분을 강화하거나, 감추거나, 형성할 수도 있다. (B) 특정 기분에 사로잡힌 사람은 그 기분이 다른 사람에게 전달되고 공유될 수 있도록 그 기분을 표현하고 싶을 수도 있다. 아마도 어떤 이는 유쾌하고 활기 넘친다고 느낄 것이다. 미국에서, 이 효과를 내는 문화적으로 인정받은 방법은 유사성보다는 대비를 보여 주는 색과 선을 배열한 의상을 선택하는 것이다. (A) 일반적으로 색 대비는 여러 가지 다른 색을 함께 사용하고, 칙칙한 배경과 대비되는 밝은 색을 사용하고, 그리고 색의 명암에서의 극명한 차이를 사용함으로써 이뤄질 수 있다. 선 대비는 선이 갑자기 방향을 바꾸거나 각기 다른 방향으로 나아가다 교차하면 생긴다. (C) 문화적으로 권장되는 해석은 선 대비에 의해 요구되는 시선 변화가 그 옷을 입은 사람 안에 있는 역동적인 내적 상태를 상징한다는 것이다. 그러므로 적어도 미국인에게, 의상에서 대비를 이루는 선과 색은 다른 사람들에게 활기찬 기분을 표현할 뿐만 아니라, 그 옷을 입은 사람에게도 똑같은 기분을 강화할 수 있다.

어휘 disguise 감추다, 위장하다 contrast 대비, 대조; 대비되다
attain 이루다, 달성하다 linear 선의 intersect 교차하다
externalize (내면의 감정을) 표현하다, 외부화하다 costume 의상
arrangement 배열 redirection 방향 수정

10 ④

해설 땅에서는 두 개의 뒷발을 이용하여 옆으로 깡충깡충 뛰어 이동한다고 했으므로 ④가 글의 내용과 일치하지 않는다.

해석 Verreaux's sifaka는 Madagascar 남서쪽 숲에 산다. 이 종은 대략 12마리까지의 개체 수로 구성되는 작은 무리를 지어 산다. 무리는 거의 동등한 수의 다 자란 수컷과 암컷을 포함한다. 무리는 작은 영역을 방어한다. 그들은 영역의 경계를 표시하기 위해 자신의 냄새를 이용한다. sifaka는 건기가 한창인 12월에 짝짓기를 한다. 단 한 마리의 새끼가 5개월 후에 태어나며 7개월 후에 젖을 뗀다. sifaka는 뛰어 올라서 나무들 사이를 헤집고 이동한다. 그들이 점프할 수 있는 거리는 그 동물의 짧은 팔뚝 아래의 작은 날개 모양의 피부에 의해 약간 증대된다. 땅 위에서, sifaka는 두 개의 뒷발로 옆쪽으로 깡충깡충 뛰어 이동한다. 팔뚝은 균형을 위해 옆쪽으로 내민다. Verreaux's sifaka는 뿌리를 제외하고 온갖 종류의 식물성 물질을 먹는다. 우기에는 쉽게 소화되는 부드러운 과일과 꽃을 먹기를 선호하지만 건기에는 나무, 나무 껍질과 잎에 의존한다.

구문 • The distance [they can jump] is increased slightly by small flaps of skin under the animal's short forearms.
→ [ ]로 표시된 부분은 관계절로 The distance를 수식한다.
• [In the rainy season they prefer to eat easily digested soft fruits and flowers], but [in the dry season they rely on wood, bark and leaves].
→ 두 개의 [ ]로 표시된 독립된 절이 but에 의해 연결되어 전체 문장을 구성하고 있다.

어휘 sifaka 여우원숭이의 일종 more or less 거의 territory 영역
scent 냄새 mark 표시하다 boundary 경계 mate 짝짓기하다
at the height of ~이 한창일 때에 dry season 건기
flap 날개, 덮개 forearm 팔뚝 hop 깡충깡충 뛰다
sideways 옆으로 hind foot 뒷발 apart from ~을 제외하고
rainy season 우기 digest 소화하다 rely on ~에 의존하다
bark 나무껍질

제 05 회 하프 모의고사 해설

문제편 p.020

ANSWER

01 ③	02 ④	03 ①	04 ②	05 ①
06 ②	07 ④	08 ①	09 ④	10 ④

01 ③

해설 ③ which 뒤에 완결된 절이 온 것이 아니므로 앞에 있는 전치사 in과 연결되는 in which는 올 수 없다. 구조상 is thought and done의 주어 역할을 하면서 전치사 in의 목적절을 유도해야 하므로 which를 선행사를 포함하는 관계대명사 what으로 고쳐야 한다.

① shows의 목적어로 완전한 문장 구조를 가진 명사절이 온 형태이므로 접속사 that은 맞게 쓰였다.

② '~가 …한 상태가 되게 하다'의 의미를 나타낼 때 쓰이는 <get + 목적어 + 과거분사> 구조이다. 목적어인 their work가 do의 동작을 당하는 수동의 관계이므로 done은 맞게 쓰였다.

④ 이 문장에서 it은 형식상의 주어로 쓰인 것이고, to hire ~ thinkers가 내용상의 주어로 맞게 쓰였다.

해석 James March는 더디게 배우는 사람들을 십 년 넘게 연구해왔다. 그는 상당한 비율의 사원이 규정을 따르지 않을 때, 회사는 새로운 가능성을 탐색하는 데 더 중점을 두고, 오래된 지식을 이용하는 데는 덜 중점을 두게 되리라는 것을 보여준다. 규정을 모르거나 믿지 않을 때 사람들은 자신의 일을 완수하기 위해 자기 자신만의 지식과 기술에 의지하거나 새로운 아이디어나 방법을 고안해 낸다. 다른 사람 모두가 옳다고 생각하는 것보다 자신들이 옳다고 생각하는 것을 할 때, 그들은 생각과 행동에 더 많은 변화를 일으킨다. 이것은 그들이 이상한 변종, 막다른 골목(발전의 여지가 없는 아이디어), 그리고 완전한 실패작에 해당하는 많은 아이디어를 생각해내더라도, 더디게 배우는 사람을 고용하는 것, 비정상적인 사람, 별난 사람, 그리고 그저 전적으로 독창적인 사고를 하는 사람을 너그럽게 보아주는 것이 '현명하다'는 것을 의미한다. 그들은 단순히 배우는 속도가 빠른 사람을 고용하여 키워서 얻을 수 있는 것보다 이용 가능한 더 많은 아이디어, 특히 참신한 아이디어를 또한 만들어내기 때문에 그 비용은 들일 만한 가치가 있다.

어휘 exploit 이용하다 significant 상당한 code 규정
draw on ~에 의지하다, ~을 이용하다 variation 변화, 변형, 차이
hire 고용하다 tolerate 너그럽게 보아주다, 견디다
eccentric 별난 사람, 괴짜 plain 전적으로; 평범한, 단순한
mutation 변종 dead end 막다른 골목 utter 완전한
novel 참신한, 새로운 breed 키우다

02 ④

해설 ④ 'A는 B만큼 ~하지 않다'라는 의미의 <A + not + as/so + 형용사/부사 원급 + as + B>는 원급 비교의 구문으로, as so와 as 사이에는 형용사나 부사의 원급이 와야 한다. 따라서 비교급 stingier는 원급인 stingy로 써야 한다.

① 동명사는 전치사의 목적어 역할을 할 수 있다. be good at 다음에 동명사 getting이 바르게 쓰였다. 'be시키다'의 뜻으로 사용된다. good at은 '~을 잘하다, 능숙하다'의 뜻이며, get ~ across는 '~을 전달하다, 이해시키다'의 뜻으로 사용된다.

② <주어 + 비교급 + than any other + 단수 명사>는 비교급을 이용한 최상급의 표현이다. 비교급 more serious와 than ~ any other city가 나와 바르게 쓰였다. 그리고 비교 대상인 The traffic jams가 복수로 쓰였으므로 복수인 those로 바르게 비교하고 있다.

③ 동명사가 주어로 쓰일 때는 3인칭 단수로 취급한다. Making eye contact ~이 주어이므로 동사 is가 바르게 쓰였다. with the person (whom) you are speaking to에서 the person은 선행사이며 목적격 관계대명사 whom이 생략된 형태이다. 이때, 전치사의 목적어 역할을 하는 목적격 관계대명사가 생략되는 경우 전치사는 관계대명사 앞으로 가지 않으며 문장 내에 그대로 위치해야 한다.

어휘 get across 전달하다 audience 청중 traffic jam 교통체증
eye contact 시선 마주침 stingy 인색한

03 ①

해석 이 제안을 반대하기 위해서는 당신에게 설득력 있는 논거가 있어야 한다.

어휘 cogent 설득력 있는 convincing 확신시키는
inordinate 지나친 touchy 민감한 feeble 연약한

04 ②

해석 사장은 나에게 그 고객과의 계약을 파기하라고 명령했다.

어휘 annul 폐지하다 deliver 배달하다 abolish 폐지하다
stimulate 자극하다 strive 애쓰다

05 ①

해설 ①에서 have been to + 장소(~에 가본 적 있다)의 표현으로 다가오는 휴가 계획에 대한 미래 지향적인 질문에 맞지 않는 대답이다.

해석 ① A: 안녕, Yusoo. 다가오는 휴가 계획이 무엇이야?
B: 음, 나는 뉴욕에 가본 적이 있어.
② A: 이 마을 사람들은 근처에 피난처가 필요하다고 생각합니다.
B: 맞아요. 사람들이 자신의 집들을 잃었음이 분명해.
③ A: 그 사건은 어디에서 일어났지?
B: 바로 저기. 나는 물이 강둑을 넘어 올라가는 것을 봤어.
④ A: 구조대가 거기로 가는 중입니다, 선생님. 불이 어디에서 발생했죠?
B: 주방에서요. 제가 요리할 때 커튼에 불이 붙었어요.

06 ②

해설 어떤 것이 지니는 가치는 사람에 따라 다르므로 그에 대한 평가는 임의적인 특성을 지닐 것이다. 그러므로 빈칸에 들어갈 말로 ② '임의적인 특성'이 가장 적절하다.

① 고유한 역할
③ 복잡한 과정

④ 문화적 함축 의미

해석 어떤 평가의 임의적인 특성을 이해하기 위해서 우리는 가치의 개념을 이해해야 한다. '가치'(혹은 값어치)란 인지된 용도 혹은 유용성이다. 무엇이든 가치를 지닌 것은 어떤 인지된 유용성을 갖고 있다. 따라서 가치란 특정한 사람과 관련이 있는 유용성에 대한 '의견'이다. 아름다움과 마찬가지로 가치는 보는 사람의 마음의 눈에 달려 있다. 하지만 가치가 의견에 불과하다면, 그리고 가치가 근본적으로 주관적인 것이라면, 그것은 또한 객관적인 증거의 범위를 벗어난다. 하나의 의견으로서, 가치는 사실이 아니다. 가치가 사실이 아니므로, 그것은 사실적이거나 객관적인 것을 어떤 것도 증명할 수 없다. 어떤 사람에게 소중한 것이 다른 사람에게는 쓰레기일 수 있다. 한 사람에게는 Beanie Baby 인형이 진귀한 물건이며, 다른 사람에게 그것은 버릴 물건이다. 어떤 사람들에게는 다른 누군가로부터 인정을 받는다는 생각이 금화(와 같이 소중한 것)이지만, 다른 사람들에게는 누군가의 인정이 Monopoly 게임의 돈(처럼 무가치한 것)이다.

어휘 **concept** 개념 **perceive** 인지하다, 인식하다
beholder 보는 사람 **fundamentally** 근본적으로, 본질적으로
subjective 주관적인 **objective** 객관적인
factual 사실적인, 사실에 기반을 둔
collector's item 진귀한 물건, 수집 대상 물품 **approval** 인정, 승인
intrinsic 고유한, 본질적인 **arbitrary** 임의의, 제멋대로의
implication 함축, 암시

07 ④

해설 주어진 문장은 Sylvester Stallone이 자신의 연기 이력이 막다른 골목에 다다르자 자기 자신의 기회를 만들어 직접 시나리오를 쓰기로 했다는 내용이다. 자연스러운 문맥이 되기 위해서는 이 문장의 앞에는 힘들게 영화에서 단역을 얻어냈다는 내용이, 뒤에는 시나리오에 대한 내용이 이어져야 한다. 그러므로 주어진 문장이 들어가기에 가장 적절한 곳은 ④이다.

해석 가난한 결손 가정 출신인 Sylvester Stallone은 Hell's Kitchen에서, 그 다음에는 Maryland 주의 Silver Springs에서, 그리고는 Philadelphia의 빈민가에서 성장했다. 그는 수양부모 가정에서 여러 해를 보냈으며 11년 동안 14개 학교로부터 쫓겨났다. 한동안 Stallone은 University of Miami의 연극학과에 다녔는데, 그곳에서 그를 가르치던 강사들은 그에게 연예계의 이력을 추구하지 말라고 말렸다. 그 후 그는 뉴욕의 Baronet Theater에서의 안내 일을 포함해서 다양한 직업을 시도해보았다. 그러나 배우가 되기로 마음을 굳힌 그는 영화에서 몇몇 단역을 어렵사리 얻어냈다. 아내는 임신한 채 그의 연기 이력이 막다른 골목에 다다르고 그가 거의 낙심해 있었을 때 그는 자기 자신의 기회를 만들어 직접 시나리오를 쓰기로 했다. 3일 만에 초고가 완성된 'Rocky'의 이야기는 그 자신의 삶과 아주 비슷하다. 가난한 권투선수가 커다란 역경에 맞서 승리한다는 것이다. 나머지 이야기는 영화 역사에 있는 그대로이다.

어휘 **dead end** 막다른 골목 **pregnant** 임신한
screenplay 시나리오 **pursue** 추구하다 **subsequently** 그 후
try one's hand at ~을 해보다 **bit part** (영화의) 단역
draft 초고, 초안 **complete** 완성하다, 끝내다
triumph 승리를 거두다 **odds** 역경

08 ①

해설 (A) 플라톤은 지성의 도움으로 인식될 수 있는 '실제 세계'가 있다고 생각했고, 이런 생각은 그의 수학 연구에서 나온 것이라는 문장이 앞서 오고, (A)가 있는 문장에서 삼각형의 사례가 이어지므로 빈칸에 들어갈 말로는 예시를 나타내는 for example이 가장 적절하다.
(B) 삼각형이라는 불변하는 수학적 개념이나 형태를 반영하는 현실 속의 삼각형 물체에 관한 인식이 (B)가 있는 문장에 제시되므로 빈칸에 들어갈 말로는 대조를 나타내는 On the other hand가 가장 적절하다.
그러므로 ①이 정답이다.

해석 플라톤은 세계를 우리의 감각을 통해 우리에게 나타나는 '현상의' 세계와 지성을 통해 우리가 완전히 이해할 수 있는 '실제' 세계로 나누었다. 플라톤에게 있어서, 우리가 감각을 통해 인지하는 세계는 바뀔 수 있고 쇠퇴할 수 있으므로 '실제'가 아니다. 플라톤은 지성의 도움을 받아 얻을 수 있는 변하지 않는 영구적인 '실제 세계'가 또한 있다는 것을 보여준다. 이 개념은 플라톤의 수학 연구에서 온다. 예를 들어, 삼각형의 형태나 개념은 영원하며 지성을 통해 완전히 이해될 수 있다. 우리는 삼각형이 내각의 합이 180도인 세 변이 있는 2차원의 도형이라는 것을 알고, 누군가 그것에 관해 생각하고 있든 하고 있지 않든, 그리고 세상에 아무리 많은 삼각형이 존재한다 하더라도 이것은 항상 옳으리라는 것을 안다. 반면에, (샌드위치, 피라미드와 칠판에 그려진 삼각형 모양들과 같이) 세상에 정말로 존재하는 삼각형 물체들은 그것들이 삼각형에 대한 이러한 개념이나 형태의 반영인 한에서만 삼각형이다.

어휘 **apparent** 현상적인, 외관상의
grasp 완전히 이해하다, 파악하다 **intellect** 지성, 지적 능력
perceive 인지[감지]하다 **changeable** 바뀔 수 있는, 변덕이 심한
subject to ~될[당할·걸릴] 수 있는 **decay** 쇠퇴, 부패, 부식
permanent 영구[영속]적인 **attain** 얻다, 이루다 **eternal** 영원한
two-dimensional 2차원의 **figure** 도형
insofar as ~하는 한에서(는) **reflection** 반영

09 ④

해설 동일한 사물은 상황에 따라 예술작품일 수도 있고 아닐 수도 있으며, 예술로 기능할 때 미학적 특징을 드러낸다는 주어진 문장 다음에는 (C)에서 그에 대한 부연 설명과 지그재그 선의 예시가 등장하고, 다음으로 (B)에서 그 선이 예술작품이 아닌 경우를 설명하며 마지막으로 (A)에서 이 선이 예술작품으로 기능할 때에 관해 서술하고 있으므로 가장 자연스러운 것은 ④ '(C) - (B) - (A)'이다.

해석 철학자 Nelson Goodman은 ''무엇'이 예술인가?'라는 질문을 ''언제'가 예술인가?'라는 질문으로 대체해야 한다고 주장했다. 동일한 사물은 그 사물을 어떻게 보느냐에 따라 예술작품으로 기능할 수도 있고, 그렇지 않을 수도 있다. 사물이 예술로 기능할 때, 그것은 미학적 특질의 특정한 '징후'를 드러낸다. (C) 예를 들어 예술로 기능하는 사물은 상대적으로 '풍부한'(가득 찬)데, 이는 그 동일한 사물이 예술작품으로 기능하지 않을 때보다 그것의 물리적 특성 중 더 많은 것이 그것의 의미의 일부이며 주목받아야 한다는 것을 의미한다. Goodman은 우리에게 지그재그 선을 생각해 보라고 요청한다. (B) 그 선이 주식시장 그래프라고 들으면, 우리가 주목하는 것은 최고점들과 하락들뿐이다. 우리는 일련의 숫자에서 같은 정보를 얻을 수 있을 것이다. (A) 그러나 만약 이 동일한 선이 그림의 일부(가령, 산의 윤곽)라면, 그 선의 모든 물리적 특성이 갑자기 중요해지고 예술가가 우리가 주목하기를 원하는 것의 일부가 되는데 특히 그것의 색깔, 질감, 가장자리, 굵기가 이에 해당한다. 그리고 우리는 이 경험을 일련의 숫자로 변환할 수 없다.

어휘 **outline** 윤곽 **texture** 질감 **edge** 가장자리
thickness 굵기 **stock market** 주식시장 **peak** 최고점 **dip** 하락
exhibit 드러내다, 보이다 **symptom** 징후, 증상
aesthetic 미학(적 특질), 미적 특질; 미적인 **replete** 풍부한, 가득 찬

property 특성, 속성

10 ④

해설 고래목의 동물들 중 특이하게 수컷이 암컷보다 더 크게 자란다(killer whales are unusual among cetaceans in that males reach a much larger size than females)는 내용이 있으므로, ④가 이 글의 내용과 일치하지 않는다.

해석 범고래는 모든 대양과 바다에서 관찰되어 왔지만, 더 높은 위도의 연안 바다에서 더욱 널리 분포한다. 열대와 연안 바다 모두에서 보고되고 있지만, 범고래는 지구의 두 반구 모두에서 더 차갑고 더 풍요로운 바다를 선호하고, 높은 위도에서 가장 많이 발견된다. 북아메리카의 서부 해안을 따라, 범고래는 알래스카 연안 전체에 걸쳐 British Columbia와 Washington의 내륙 수로에서 발견된다. 그들은 또한 California, Oregon, 그리고 Washington의 외곽 연안을 따라 발견된다. 범고래는 검은색인데 배 부분은 하얗다. 머리 양쪽으로 눈의 바로 위쪽 뒤에 하얀 점이 있다. 그들의 등지느러미는 날카로운 삼각형 모양이고 매우 긴데, 그 높이가 6피트까지 이른다. 범고래는 몸길이가 31피트에 이를 수 있다. 향유고래처럼, 범고래는 수컷이 암컷보다 훨씬 더 크게 자란다는 점에서 고래목의 동물들 중 특이하다.

구문 • [Although reported in both tropical and offshore waters], killer whales [prefer colder and more productive waters of both hemispheres], and [are found in greatest abundances at high latitudes].
→ 첫 번째 [ ]로 표시된 부분은 Although they are reported in ~으로 풀어 쓸 수 있다. 두 번째와 세 번째 [ ]로 표시된 부분은 and에 의해 연결되어 주어 killer whales의 술어를 이룬다.
• Like sperm whales, killer whales are unusual among cetaceans in that males reach a much larger size than females.
→ 「in that ~」은 '~이라는 점에서' 또는 '~이니까'라는 의미이다.

어휘 **killer whale** 범고래
prevalent (특정 시기·장소에) 널리 퍼져 있는[일반적인]
coastal 해안[연안]의 **latitude** 위도 **offshore** 연안의, 앞바다의
hemisphere 반구 **abundance** 풍부 **occur** 존재하다, 발견되다
sperm whale 향유고래

제06회 하프 모의고사 해설

문제편 p.024

ANSWER

01 ④	02 ①	03 ④	04 ④	05 ①
06 ②	07 ④	08 ②	09 ①	10 ③

01 ④

해설 (A) realize의 목적어로 쓰인 that절에서 their keys, wallet, organizer, and baby son을 주어로 하는 동사가 필요한 자리이므로 are sitting이 적절하다.

(B) 전치사(without) 다음에는 명사(taste)와 동명사(tasting)가 모두 올 수 있지만, 뒤에 목적어인 any of it이 있으므로 동명사인 tasting이 적절하다.

(C) 문맥상 접속사 while이 유도하는 부사절에서 복수 명사인 others를 공통의 주어로 are driven과 병렬을 이루는 동사가 필요한 위치이므로 feel이 적절하다.

그러므로 정답은 ④이다.

해석 우리는 더 많은 시간을 얻는 방법은 속도를 내는 것이라고 추정하는 경향이 있다. 하지만 속도를 높여 집을 나가다가 결국 열쇠, 지갑, 수첩, 그리고 어린 아들을 식탁에 두고 온 것을 깨닫게 된 적이 있는 사람이라면 누구나 아주 잘 알고 있듯이 속도를 내는 것이 실제로는 우리의 속도를 늦출 수 있다. 그리고 줄어드는 것은 비단 효율성만이 아니다. 우리가 의식을 덜하거나 '유념을' 덜 하게 되어 경험의 질도 또한 악화된다. 아무 것도 맛을 느끼지 못한 채 식사 전체를 끝내 본 적이 있는가? 서두르는 것은 우리에게 더 적은 시간을 제공할 뿐만 아니라 우리가 진짜로 가지고 있는 그 시간으로부터 즐거움과 혜택을 빼내 간다. 우리 중 많은 사람에게 서두름은 삶의 한 방식이다. 우리 중 몇몇은 그것(서두름)이 우리에게 제공하는 쾌감을 즐기지만, 반면 다른 사람들은 끊임없는 압박으로 미칠 지경이 되고 받아들일 수 없는 정도까지 자신의 삶의 속도를 높이고 있다고 느낀다. 어느 쪽이든, 약간 천천히 가는 행동에 의해 향상될 수 있는 삶의 영역이 거의 틀림없이 있다.

어휘 **assume** 추정하다, (책임, 역할 등을) 맡다
accelerate 속도를 높이다, 가속하다
organizer 수첩, 서류 분류철, 조직자
suffer 악화되다, 고통을 겪다 **aware** 의식하는 **mindful** 유념하는
drain 빼내 가다, 소모시키다; 배수관 **buzz** 쾌감, 신바람, 웅성거림

02 ①

해설 ① 비교되는 것은 처음 기대되었던 과거의 예산과 그에 비해 25%가 더 높은 현재의 예산이다. 주어가 The budget이며 than 뒤에는 역시 동일한 주어인 the budget이 생략된 것이다. 과거에 원래 기대되었던 예산보다 현재의 예산이 더 높다는 의미인데, the budget이 주어일 경우 expect와의 관계는 '기대었던'이라는 수동의 관계가 되므로 expecting이라는 현재분사가 아니라 expected라는 과거분사가 와야 한다.

② to부정사의 형용사 역할 수동형 부정사인 to be done이 앞의 명사 work를 수식하는 형용사적 용법으로 사용되었다. '행해져야 할 일들'의 의미로 바르게 쓰였다.

③ '~하는 데 시간이 걸리다'는 <it + take + 시간 + (for + 사람 + to부정사>의 구문으로 쓸 수 있다. <for + 사람>이라는 행위자는 생략되고 나머지 구문도 바르게 쓰였다. '최소한, 적어도'를 의미하는 at least도 옳게 쓰였다.

④ 'who receives twice the salary'는 the head를 선행사로 하는 관계대명사절이다. head가 여기서는 '머리'의 의미가 아니라 '대표, 책임자'의 의미이므로 선행사가 사람일 때 사용되는 관계대명사 who가 바르게 쓰였다. receives라는 동사가 바로 왔으므로 주격도 바르다. 또한 <배수사 + 명사>의 구문으로 '~의 몇 배'의 어순이 맞다. 문장 전체의 주어가 head이므로 문장 전체의 동사인 has to 역시 단수로 바르게 쓰였다.

어휘 **originally** 처음에, 원래 **department** 부서
take responsibility 책임을 지다

03 ④

해석 그는 식량 생산에 관한 지문의 영어 번역에 대해 아들과 협력했다.

어휘 **collaborate** 협력하다(= cooperate) **put together** 결합하다

04 ④

해석 대부분의 민속노래는 익명의 기원이다.

어휘 **anonymous** 익명의(= incognito) **insignificant** 의미 없는
inconspicuous 현저하지 않은 **unusual** 비범한

05 ①

해설 'Be my guest.'는 '내 손님이 되세요.'의 의미로, 상대방으로 하여금, '편하게 행동하세요.', '당신 뜻대로 하세요.', '먼저 하세요.' 등의 의미로 사용된다.

해석 A: 좀 도와주세요. 컴퓨터가 어떻게 됐는지 모르겠어요.
B: F-드라이브에 뭐가 잘못된 것이 있나 봐. USB 뿐만 아니라, 컴퓨터도 살펴봐야겠는데.
A: 조언 고마워. 그런데 네 컴퓨터와 프린터 좀 이용해도 될까?
B: 얼마든지.
② 참을 만큼 참았다.
③ 우연의 일치이다.
④ 깜빡 잊어버렸다.

06 ②

해설 빈칸이 있는 문장에 나오는 In this case라는 표현은 바로 앞의 내용인 '전체 상선의 선원 중 16.5퍼센트가 뱃멀미를 한다고 언급하는 연구 논문을 쓰는' 경우이다. 이러한 구체적인 정보를 알아내기 위해 노력한 연구자에 대한 언급이 없으면 표절이 되는 것이므로, 빈칸에는 ② '그 연구자가 공로를 인정받을 자격이 있다'가 가장 적절하다.
① 아무도 자신의 권리를 주장하지 않을 것이다
③ 표절에 대해 걱정할 필요가 없다
④ 독자는 원저자를 비난할 것이다

해석 다른 저자의 말 혹은 심지어 그 저자의 말을 비슷하게 바꾼 표현을 사용할 때마다, 그 저자의 이름을 언급해야 한다. 그러지 않으면, 표절이라는 범

죄를 저지른 것이다. 간단히 말해서, '표절'은 누군가 다른 사람의 말을 사용하면서 그 말이 자기 자신의 것이라고 주장하거나 그런 척하는 것이다. 표절을 피하는, 경험에 의거한 간단한 방법은 의심스러울 때는 원저자를 언급하는 것이다. 흔한 정보를 쓸 때는 표절에 대해 걱정할 필요가 없다. 만약 지구가 둥글다고 말한다면 아무도 표절로 비난하지 않을 것이다. 반면, 모든 상선 선원 중 16.5퍼센트가 뱃멀미를 한다고 언급하는 연구 논문을 쓴다면, 아마 어떤 가련한 연구자가 그 사실을 알아내기 위해 자기 인생의 몇 달을 소비하였을 것이다. 이런 경우는 그 연구자가 공로를 인정받을 자격이 있다.

어휘 paraphrase 다른 말로 바꾸어 표현한 것 commit 저지르다
pretend ~인 척하다, 가장하다
rule of thumb 경험에 의거한 간단한 방법, 어림 감정
in doubt 의심스러운 apply 쓰다, 적용하다 accuse 비난하다
state 언급하다 merchant marine 상선의 선원
seasick 뱃멀미하는 deserve ~을 받을 자격이 있다

07 ④

해설 주어진 문장은 대명사 '우리'를 사용하면 다른 사람들을 의식한다는 것을 보여주고 그들의 생각과 감정을 인정하거나 이해하는 방법을 알게 된다는 의미인데, 이 문장이 Conversely로 시작하므로 앞 문장과 반대 관계를 갖는다. ④의 앞 문장은 '나'를 너무 많이 쓰는 것에 대한 부정적 견해를 나타내고 ④의 뒷 문장은 이것이 따뜻함을 보여준다고 말하고 있어서 글의 흐름이 어색한데, 주어진 문장을 ④에 넣으면 앞뒤의 연결이 자연스러워진다. 따라서 주어진 문장이 들어가기에 가장 적절한 곳은 ④이다.

해석 '나'와 '우리' 같은 대명사의 사용은 성별, 교육, 그리고 지위에 관한 실마리를 제공해줄 뿐만 아니라 힘과 따뜻함에 대해서도 많은 것을 알려준다. 이 실마리들 중 몇몇은 명백한 반면에 다른 것들은 덜 그렇다. 예를 들어 우리들 대부분은 '나'의 과다한 사용이 자기 본위 또는 자기 중심성을 보여준다는 것을 살아오면서 어디선가 배웠는데, 그것(자기 본위 또는 자기 중심성)은 힘을 확고히 하지만 따뜻함을 약화시킨다. 이런 행동은 또한 이 사람에게는 그가 숨기려 하고 있는 몇 가지 주요한 불안감이 있다는 것을 보여주는 것일지도 모른다. 그 힘의 신호들을 둘 중 어느 쪽으로 해석할 때든지, '나'를 지나치게 많이 쓰는 것은 따뜻하지 않다. 역으로, '우리'의 사용은 일반적으로 다른 사람들을 의식한다는 것을 보여주고, 여러분이 그들의 생각과 감정을 인정하거나 심지어 이해한다는 것을 보여주는 방법을 제공한다. 근본적인 수준에서 이것은 관심과 흥미를 공유하고 있다는 느낌을 전달함으로써 따뜻함을 보여준다. '우리'가 이러한 방식으로 사용될 때, 우리는 그것을 '동그라미 언어'로 생각한다. 그것은 여러분과 청중 양자의 둘레에 동그라미를 그려서 여러분을 청중과 함께 그 동그라미 안에 들어가게 한다.

어휘 conversely 역으로, 정반대로
demonstrate 보여주다, 입증하다 obvious 명백한
self-centeredness 자기 본위 insecurity 불안감
overdo 지나치게 많이 쓰다 fundamental 근본적인
project 보여주다, 투사하다 convey 전달하다 concern 관심, 배려

08 ②

해설 (A) 경제적 지표는 삶의 질을 나타내는 데 충분하지 않다는 것을 보여주는 한 가지 사례가 (A) 앞에 기술된 다음, 또 다른 사례가 덧붙여 제시되고 있으므로 첨가를 나타내는 연결사 Furthermore가 와야 적절하다.
(B) 높은 수준의 주관적인 안녕과 행복은 그 자체로도 좋고 사회에도 이롭다는 연구를 검토해 보면, 행복과 경제 성장 간의 괴리는 훨씬 더 중요하다는 내용이 (B) 앞에 기술된 다음, 정책 토론에서 금전적 고려사항보다는 다른 목표들을 염두에 두어야 한다는 결론이 이어지므로 Therefore가 와야 적절하다. 그러므로 ②가 정답이다.

해석 지금까지 사회의 안녕과 행복이 경제적 척도에 따라 판단되었을지라도, 경제적 지표로만 국가 내의 삶의 질을 나타내는 것은 충분하지 않다. 지난 50년 동안 소득이 꾸준히 상승했고, 국내 총생산(GDP)이 세 배가 되었지만, 행복은 거의 그대로였다. 게다가 Gallup World Poll을 활용한 최근의 한 연구에서 국가의 부가 증가했을 때 삶의 만족은 증가했으나, 삶의 즐거움은 거의 변화를 겪지 않았다고 밝혀졌다. 행복과 경제 성장 간의 이러한 괴리는 사람들이 삶의 목표로 행복을 돈 앞에 위치시킨다(돈보다 우선시한다)는 것을 고려해 보면 중요하다. 그러나 높은 수준의 주관적인 안녕과 행복은 그 자체로도 좋을 뿐만 아니라, 그것(높은 수준의 주관적인 안녕과 행복)이 실제로 이로운 사회적 결과물을 산출한다는 것을 보여주는 광범위한 연구를 검토해 보면, 그것(행복과 경제 성장 간의 괴리)은 훨씬 더 중요하다. 따라서 금전적 고려사항이 정책 토론에서 현재 지배적이지만, 다른 목표들을 염두에 두어야 한다.

어휘 well-being 안녕과 행복(을 추구함) measure 척도, 조치, 표시
indicator 지표, 척도, 표지 steadily 꾸준히
gross domestic product 국내 총생산(gdp)
triple 세 배가 되다; 세 배의
virtually 거의, 사실상 utilize 활용[이용]하다
discrepancy 괴리, 불일치, 차이
rank 위치시키다, 위치를 정하다, 매기다
in and of oneself ~ 자체로는, ~ 자체는
societal 사회적인, 사회의[에 관한] dominant 지배적인, 우세한

09 ①

해설 1인 독재에서 지도자는 엘리트에 대한 통제력을 가진다는 주어진 글 다음에는, 왜 그런지에 대한 이유를 설명하는 (B)로 이어져 지도자가 엘리트를 선택할 수 있기 때문이라고 한 다음, (A)에서 그와 다르게 일당 독재와 군부 독재는 둘 다 엘리트를 선택할 수 없다는 반대 진술로 이어진 후, 마지막으로 그렇지만 군부 독재와 일당 독재는 엘리트 선호에 차이점이 있다고 설명하는 (C)로 연결되는 것이 자연스럽다. 따라서 글의 전개로 가장 적절한 것은 ① (B) - (A) - (C)이다.

해석 1인 독재에서의 엘리트들은 군이나 당과 같은 통일된 기관에 속하지 않기 때문에 지도자는 다른 유형의 독재에서보다 1인 독재에서 엘리트 채용에 더 큰 통제력을 가지고 있다. (B) 1인 독재자들은 엘리트의 진급을 위해 당이나 군 지침을 준수할 필요가 없는데, 그들은 그들과 가장 동의할 것 같은 엘리트 지지자들을 선택할 수 있다. 이 때문에, 1인 독재 하의 엘리트들은 독재자의 것을 반영하는 정책에 대한 선호를 갖는 경향이 있다. (A) 그와 다르게, 일당 독재와 군부 독재의 지도자들은 그들의 엘리트 지지 집단을 손수 고를 수 없다. 엘리트들은 그들의 지위를 얻기 위해 정당이나 군부의 위계에서 진급하여야만 하고, 지도자들은 개인의 진급에 대해 통제력을 덜 갖는다. 이는 단일 정당이나 군부 정권에서 엘리트들이 지도자와 꼭 들어맞는 정책 선호를 공유하지는 않음을 의미한다. (C) 그러나 군부에 의한 통치 또는 정당에 의한 통치가 이들 정권에서 엘리트의 선호의 차이점을 가져오기도 한다. 군부 독재의 엘리트들은 일당 독재 하의 엘리트들에 비해 정책 선호에 있어서 더 통일되는 경향이 있다.

어휘 dictatorship 독재(정권) recruitment 채용, 모집
adhere to 준수하다, 고수하다 promotion 진급, 승진
mirror 반영하다, 비추다 handpick 손수 고르다, 골라내다
work one's way up 승진하다 hierarchy 위계, 계층

regime 정권, 체제　governance 통치, 지배

10 ③

해설 Shooter's Gold 농구 캠프
6월 1일 이전이든 그 이후든, 연습반 1의 등록비가 연습반 2의 등록비보다 더 싸므로(The registration fee is $80 for Session #1 and $115 for Session #2. After June 1, the fee is $85 for Session #1 and $130 for Session #2.) ③이 안내문의 내용과 일치하지 않는다.

해석 Paul Hogan 코치의 지도 아래, (농구) 캠프가 7월 6일부터 10일까지 Maple 중학교 체육관에서 개최될 예정입니다.

- 1~4학년 남녀 아이들을 위한 연습반 1은 오전 8시부터 10시까지 운영될 것입니다.
- 5~8학년 남녀 아이들을 위한 연습반 2는 오전 8시부터 정오까지 운영될 것입니다.

등록비는 연습반 1의 경우 80달러이고 연습반 2는 115달러입니다. 6월 1일 이후에는, 등록비가 연습반 1의 경우 85달러이고 연습반 2는 130달러입니다. 참가자 각각은 농구공과 캠프 티셔츠를 받게 될 것입니다. 특별 상품이 그 주 내내 제공될 것입니다. 캠프에서는 제대로 된 슛 자세, 일대일 움직임, 공격의 중심이 되는 선수의 위치의 움직임과 경기를 하는 방법을 다룹니다. 등록 양식과 추가적인 정보를 얻기 원하시면 우리 사무실 전화번호인 (451) 345-4545로 전화해 주십시오.

구문 • The camp covers [proper shooting form], [one-on-one moves], [post moves] and [how to play the game].
→ [ ]로 표시된 네 부분이 and로 연결되어 술어 동사 covers의 목적어 역할을 한다.

어휘 direction 지도　hold 개최하다　gym 체육관
registration fee 등록비　present 주다　cover 다루다, 포함하다
one-on-one 일대일의

제 07 회 하프 모의고사 해설

문제편 p.028

ANSWER

01 ③	02 ④	03 ③	04 ④	05 ④
06 ④	07 ④	08 ②	09 ②	10 ④

01 ③

해설 ③ 문맥상 the identity를 대신하는 대명사가 필요하므로 복수인 those를 단수인 that으로 바꿔 써야 한다.

① 주어(the planet Tines)와 수동태 형태의 동사(is populated)로 이루어진 완전한 절이 이어지고 있고 <전치사 + 관계대명사> 형태의 in which는 문맥상 in the book의 의미를 대신하여 선행사와 자연스럽게 연결되므로 어법에 맞는 표현이다.

② 주어(These doglike creatures)와 동사(travel)가 있는 절 뒤에서 분사구문을 이끌고 있으므로 현재분사 giving은 어법에 맞는 표현이다.

④ 주어인 the communication path가 동사의 주체가 아닌 대상으로 해석되므로 수동태 형태인 is lost는 어법에 맞는 표현이다.

해석 내가 가장 좋아하는 공상과학 작가 중 한 명인 Vernor Vinge는 'A Fire Upon the Deep'을 집필했는데, 그 책 속에는 집단지성을 가진 동물들이 Tines 행성에 거주한다. 개와 유사한 이 생명체는 무리를 지어 이동하는데, 그 구성원들은 강력하고 광범위하게 분포된 의식을 만들어 내면서, 서로 간에 지속적인 음향 의사소통을 한다. 개체들은 죽음, 질병, 혹은 사고로 인해 무리를 떠나고, 그들을 대신하기 위해 새로운 젊은 구성원들이 모집되며, 그리하여 그 무리는 어느 한 개체의 그것(정체성)을 훨씬 뛰어넘는 자신의 정체성을 유지한다. 무리를 구성하는 각 개체는 완전히 혼자 있을 때는 지성이 부족하다. 무리는 많은 개체들과의 협력을 통해 지성을 얻는다. 그 결과 한 개체가 제 위치를 벗어나 무리에서 너무 멀리 떨어지면, 소리의 범위가 제한적이기 때문에, 의사소통 경로를 잃게 되어, 그 결과로 생기는 '단독 개체'는 지성이 전혀 없다. 단독 개체는 좀처럼 살아남지 못하고, 살아남는 것들도 아무 생각이 없는, 말 그대로 아무 생각이 없는 존재가 될 불행한 운명을 맞게 된다.

어휘 planet 행성 populate (~에) 살다
collective intelligence 집단지성 creature 생명체, 생물, 창조물
pack 무리, 꾸러미; 짐을 싸다 continuous 지속적인
give rise to ~을 만들어 내다, ~을 초래하다
distributed (광범위하게) 분포된
recruit 모집하다, 채용하다; 모집, 채용 collaboration 협력
stray 제 위치를 벗어나다 resulting 결과로서 생기는
doom 불행한 운명을 맞게 하다 mindless 아무 생각이 없는
literally 말 그대로, 글자 그대로

02 ④

해설 ④ '~보다 더 좋아하다'의 의미로 prefer 동사를 사용할 때는 <prefer + to부정사 + rather than + to부정사>, 또는 <prefer + (동명사) + to + (동명사)> 형태로 쓴다. 따라서 to staying home than to going을 to stay home rather than (to) go 또는 staying home to going으로 고쳐야 옳다.

① '~하는 것을 규칙으로 삼다'를 의미하는 <make it a rule to부정사>라는 표현이 바르게 쓰였다.

② <동사 + 목적어(사람) + 전치사 + the + 신체 부위>라는 정관사의 주요 용법대로 접촉 동사 grab의 목적어로 me가 쓰였을 때, 전치사 by 뒤에 the arm이 바르게 쓰였다.

③ '만큼'이라는 차이를 의미하는 전치사 by가 옳게 쓰였다. 전치사 owing to 뒤로 절이 아닌 명사구 the heavy rain이 바르게 쓰였다. '상승하다, 오르다'의 의미를 가진 자동사 rise가 과거분사로 바르게 쓰였다.

03 ③

해석 그 행성들 중의 하나와 혜성이 충돌할 것이라고 예언되었다.

어휘 collide with ~과 충돌하다(= crash) narrowly 아슬아슬하게
take off 이륙하다

04 ④

해석 그녀는 교인들에게 다소 반감을 가지고 있다.

어휘 antagonistic 적대하는 in favor of 우호적인
ignorant 무시하는 curious 호기심 많은 opposed 반대하는

05 ④

해석 ① A: 오, 나 배고파!
B: 우리 간단히 뭐 먹으러 가는 거 어때?
② A: 그가 노래 대회에서 무슨 상이라도 탔어?
B: 어, 그는 2등 상을 받았어.
③ A: 널 여기서 보다니 너무 좋아. 우리 어디 앉아서 얘기 좀 할까?
B: 물론, 나 너랑 대화하고 싶어.
④ A: 저는 경제학자입니다. 제가 막 국제 무역에 관한 책을 마무리했습니다.
B: 오? 저랑 같은 분야네요. 저는 연예 분야에서 일합니다.

06 ④

해설 마치 정기 검진이 우리의 신체 건강을 유지하는 데 도움이 되는 것처럼 우리가 맺는 인간관계를 때때로 점검하는 것이 그 관계의 안녕을 유지하는 데 도움이 될 수 있다는 내용의 글이다. 그러므로 빈칸에 들어갈 말로 가장 적절한 것은 ④ '점검하면서'이다.
① 만들어 내면서
② 수량화하면서
③ 바꾸어 가면서

해석 때때로 인간관계를 점검하는 것은 심각한 어려움이 발생 하는 것을 막는 데 도움을 줄 수 있다. 우리의 건강에서처럼 인간관계와 관련해서도 너무나도 자주, 무엇인가가 잘못될 때까지 우리는 모든 것이 괜찮다고 추정한다. 정기 검진을 받으러 의사를 방문하는 것이 우리 몸의 건강을 유지하는 것을 도울 수 있는 것처럼, 이따금씩 사려 깊은 '검진'은 중요한 인간관계의 안녕을 유지하는 것을 도울 수 있다. 한 인간관계의 내포된 목표와 그 목표에 도달하기 위한 전략에 대해 일반적인 관점으로 생각하는 것은 유용할 수 있다. 가능하다면

인간관계를 맺고 있는 상대편과 함께 각각의 요소를 점검하면서 우리는 관심이 필요한 영역을 확인할 수 있다. 나란히 앉아서 최근의 만남에 대해 회상하고 논의할 구체적인 질문의 목록을 만드는 것이 우리의 상호작용 방식을 개선하는 데 필요한 신선한 아이디어를 자극할 수 있다.

어휘 arise 발생하다 assume 추정하다
regular checkup 정기 검진 reflective 사려 깊은
maintain 유지하다 well-being 안녕, 복지 implicit 내포된, 암시된
strategy 전략 identify 확인하다 specific 구체적인
stimulate 자극하다 interaction 상호작용

07 ④

해설 주어진 문장은 '그러나 그의 사후에 자신의 이름을 따서 California 주 Berkeley로 명명된 서해안의 한 대학교가 정말로 생겼다.'이다. 그리고 ④ 다음에 나오는 문장에서는 그것(That)이 그가 미국에 대해 쓴 시의 한 행인 '제국의 진로는 서쪽으로 향한다'라는 것에서 유래했다는 말이 나온다. That이 가리키는 내용이 앞에 없어서 글의 흐름이 단절되다가 주어진 문장을 넣어주면 That이 주어진 문장을 가리키면서 글의 흐름이 자연스럽게 이어짐을 알 수 있다. 따라서 정답은 ④이다.

해석 철학자 George Berkeley는 자신의 비물질론을 옹호하며 자신의 생애의 모든 시간을 보내지는 않았다. 그의 삶에는 그보다 훨씬 더 많은 것이 있었다. 그는 사교적이고 호감가는 사람이었고, 그의 친구들 가운데에는 '걸리버 여행기'의 작가인 Jonathan Swift가 있었다. 노년에 Berkeley는 Bermuda 섬에 대학을 세울 야심찬 계획을 생각해냈고, 이것을 실행하기 위해 상당히 많은 돈을 그럭저럭 모금했다. 유감스럽게도 그 계획은 실패했는데, 부분적으로는 Bermuda가 본토로부터 얼마나 멀리 떨어져 있는지, 그리고 그곳으로 물자를 옮기는 것이 얼마나 어려운지 깨닫지 못했기 때문이었다. 그러나 그의 사후에 자신의 이름을 따서 California 주 Berkeley로 명명된 서해안의 한 대학교가 정말로 생겼다. 그것은 그 대학의 설립자들 중 한 사람의 관심을 끈 한 행, '제국의 진로는 서쪽으로 향한다'라는 행이 들어 있는 미국에 대해 그가 쓴 시에서 유래했다.

어휘 west coast (미국의) 서해안 sociable 사교적인
hatch 생각해내다, 부화하다 ambitious 야심찬 line (시의) 행, 시구
take one's way 나아가다 appeal 관심을 끌다 founder 설립자

08 ②

해설 (A) 여러 세대가 소요되는 유전적인 변화를 먼저 말한 다음 문화적인 특징이 전달되는 데에는 그보다는 적은 시간이 걸린다는 내용을 제시하기 위해 (A)가 있는 문장을 썼으므로 빈칸에 들어갈 연결사로는 대조를 나타내는 on the other hand가 가장 적절하다.
(B) 대중음악과 의상의 유행처럼 빨리 퍼지는 것의 예를 앞에 제시한 다음 (B)가 있는 문장부터 다른 문화적인 특징은 변화되기 어렵다는 점을 제시했으므로 빈칸에 들어갈 연결사로는 역접을 나타내는 However가 가장 적절하다. 그러므로 ②가 정답이다.

해석 상당히 강력한 자연 선택이 수반될 때에도 유전적인 변화는 항상 여러 세대가 걸린다. 반면에, 문화적인 특징은 부모로부터 자식으로 전달될 뿐만 아니라 전하는 말이나 글을 통해 어느 한 개인으로부터 다른 사람으로 전달될 수 있다. 그래서 일부 문화적인 변화는 전체 인구에 의해 상당히 빠르게 채택될 수 있다. 문화의 전달은 전염병의 전염과 다소 비슷하다. 유행성 독감과 감기는, 특히 현재 세계의 모든 나라 사람들이 서로 갖는 접촉의 양이 많은 상황에서, 매우 빨리 퍼진다. 마찬가지로 대중음악의 선호와 의상의 유행 같은 문화적인 관습은 오늘날 특히 라디오와 텔레비전이라는 매체를 통해 매우 빠르게 퍼질 수도 있다. 그러나 민족과 민족적 하위 집단의 뿌리가 깊은 다른 문화적인 특징은 변화시키기가 훨씬 더 어렵다. 이것들은 변화에 너무나 저항적이어서 선천적인 것처럼 보이는 문화 양상이다.

어휘 adopt 채택하다 transmission 전달, 전염, 양도
infection 전염병, 감염 epidemic 유행성의; 유행병
subgroup 하위 집단, 소집단 resistant 저항하는
alteration 변화, 개조 innate 선천적인, 내재적인
natural selection 자연 선택, 자연 도태 characteristic 특징, 특질
offspring 자식 pass on ~을 전달하다[넘겨주다]
word of mouth 전하는 말, 입소문

09 ②

해설 주어진 글은 지능이 낮은 평범한 사람들을 어리석다고 부르는 경향이 있다고 언급하고 있고, (B)의 They가 주어진 글의 지능이 낮은 평범한 사람들을 가리키며, 그들이 미치는 영향 때문에 그들도 우리의 관심을 받을 자격이 있다는 내용으로 이어지고 있다. 이어서 지능이 높은 사람도 영리하지 못하게 행동할 수 있음을 말하는 (C)로 이어진 다음에, 그 결과 분야에 따라 지능이 다를 수 있으므로 영리하지 못한 행동에 대한 이해가 필요하다고 결론을 짓는 (A)로 이어지는 것이 자연스럽다.

해석 이제 지능이 낮은 평범한 사람들의 행동을 생각해 보자. 우리는 그런 사람들을 어리석다고 부르는 경향이 있다. 물론 그들이 우리보다 더 높은 지위를 차지하고 있지만 않다면! (B) 때때로 중요한 사건들의 과정에 그들이 미치는 영향 때문에, 그리고 또한 정신 능력의 가장 가치 있는 특성은 그것의 결핍이라는 배경과 비교했을 때에만 온전히 인식되고 평가될 수 있기 때문에 그들은 우리의 관심을 받을 자격이 있다. (C) 게다가, 높은 수준의 일반 지능을 가진 사람조차도 때때로 피로나 격한 감정과 같은 요인의 영향 아래에서 영리하지 못하게 행동하곤 한다. 지능을 구성하는 다양한 기본적인 능력의 발달은 대체로 고르지 못한 것으로 또한 알려져 있다. (A) 따라서, 말이 유창하고 재치가 있어서 지적이라고 평가받는 사람이 수나 지각과 관련된 자료를 다루는 데는 그다지 똑똑하다고 판명되지 못할 수도 있으며 그 반대도 마찬가지이다. 그것이 바로 전형적인 '영리하지 못한' 행동에 대한 이해가 교육과 독학에서 실로 중요할지도 모르는 이유이다.

어휘 intelligence 지능 on account of ~ 때문에
eloquence 유창한 화술, 웅변 numerical 수와 관련된
typical 전형적인 exert 미치다, 발휘하다 vital 중요한
appreciate 평가하다 quality 특성 deficiency 결핍, 결함
fatigue 피로 primary 기본적인 make up ~을 구성하다

10 ④

해설 'They are found on all major land masses except Greenland and Antarctica.'라고 했으므로, ④는 글의 내용과 일치하지 않는다.

해석 전갈은 바다에서 육지로 기어 나온 최초의 포식자였으며, 그들이 하는 것에 매우 능숙하기 때문에 지난 4억 3천만 년간 거의 진화하지 않았다. 그들의 전성기인 대기에 산소가 풍부한 석탄기 동안에는, 개만큼 큰 전갈이 육지를 돌아다녔고, 바다에서는 거대한 장구애비가 그 크기의 두 배까지 자라났다. 그들의 더 어린 거미류 사촌격인 거미처럼, 전갈은 강인하고 적응력이 높아 영하의 기온과 사막 열기를 견뎌낸다. 그들은 심지어 물속에 완전히 잠긴 채 이틀간 생존할 수도 있다. 그들은 그린란드와 남극 대륙을 제외한 모든 주요 대륙에서 발견된다.

구문 • ~ and they have evolved very little in the last 430 million years because they are very good at [what they do].
→ 현재완료 형태인 have evolved는 과거부터 현재까지 지속되어 온 상태를 나타내며, 관계대명사 what이 이끄는 절은 전치사 at의 목적절로 사용되고 있다.

어휘 **predator** 포식자 **crawl** 기다 **evolve** 진화하다
prime 전성기 **atmosphere** 대기 **roam** 돌아다니다
water scorpion 장구애비 **adaptable** 적응력이 높은
put up with 견디다, 참다 **subzero** 영하의
submerge 물속에 담그다 **land mass** 대륙 **antarctica** 남극 대륙

제08회 하프 모의고사 해설

문제편 p.033

ANSWER

01	④	02	①	03	③	04	③	05	③
06	④	07	④	08	①	09	①	10	④

01 ④

해설 ④ '...한 것은 바로 ~이다'라는 의미의 'It is ~ that ...' 강조구문이 사용된 구조이므로, 밑줄 친 ④의 whose를 that으로 고쳐 써야 한다.

① 관계절인 that ~ rare의 수식을 받는 The bright red juice가 문장의 주어로 단수형이므로, 동사 is는 적절하다.

② 문장의 동사 requires는 '~해야 하는 것을 필요로 하다'라는 당위성을 나타내므로 that절에서 동사원형인 endure는 적절하다. endure 앞에 should가 생략된 것으로 볼 수 있다.

③ being은 전치사 for의 목적어 역할을 하는 동명사로, being 앞에 있는 blood는 being의 의미상 주어이다.

해석 우리가 보는 익히지 않은 고기와 아주 살짝 익힌 스테이크에서 뚝뚝 떨어지는 선홍색의 육즙은 피와 동류이기는 하지만 피는 아니다. 이것에 대해 설명하려면 독자가 잠깐의 고등학교 생물 수업을 견디는 것이 필요하다. 산소는 헤모글로빈이라고 하는 화학물질 안에서 혈류에 의해 신체에 전달되는데, 헤모글로빈은 피가 붉은색인 것의 원인에 해당하는, 철분을 기본 성분으로 하는 화합물이다. 하지만, 많은 동물들은 순환계가 전달할 수 있는 것보다 훨씬 더 빠르게 근육에 그 산소를 필요로 한다. 그래서 동물들은 미오글로빈이라고 하는, 철분을 기본 성분으로 하는 또 다른 화합물을 근육에 저장한다. 근육 조직이 아주 빠른 반응으로 요구할 때 근육은 '진짜 물질'인 헤모글로빈이 도착하는 도중에 미오글로빈을 이용한다. 우리가 먹는 고기에서 뚝뚝 떨어지는 것은 이 미오글로빈이지 피가 아니다. 아주 살짝 익힌 스테이크에는 사실 피가 거의 없다.

어휘 biology 생물(학) convey 전달하다 bloodstream 혈류
chemical 화학물질 hemoglobin 헤모글로빈, 혈색소
drip 뚝뚝 떨어지다 uncooked 익히지 않은, 날것의
rare 살짝 익힌, 설익은 relative 동류, 친척

02 ①

해설 ① would rather A than B(B보다 차라리 A를 하는 편이 낫다)와 had better A than B에서 A와 B는 원형부정사이다. 위와 같이 A와 B를 비교하는 구문에서 A와 B의 형태는 동일해야 한다. 따라서 going은 동사원형인 go의 형태가 되어야 한다.

② be willing to 기꺼이 하다 / be unwilling to ~하기를 꺼리다. 이때 be unwilling to의 to는 to부정사이므로 뒤에 동사원형을 취한 것이 옳다. interfere는 자동사로서 '~에 개입하다'가 되려면 전치사 in이 있어야 한다.

③ '~해야 소용없다'를 의미하는 동명사의 관용표현인 'It's no use -ing'가 올바르게 사용되었다.

④ '너무 ~해서 하다'를 의미하는 <so + 형용사/부사 + that ~>의 부사절 접속사 구문이 올바르게 사용되었다. ones는 앞의 keys를 받는 것인데, 바로 그 열쇠가 아니라, 여분의 다른 열쇠를 의미하므로 ones가 되어야 한다.

03 ③

해석 그는 그의 노를 물속으로 가라앉게 내버려두고 스트로크를 길게 당기기 시작했다.

어휘 commence 시작하다 swam 수영했다 drown 익사하다
crawl 기어가다

04 ③

해석 급성전염병을 앓고 있는 동물은 음식과 물을 먹지 않으며 냉담하게 된다.

어휘 apathetic 무관심한 abstract 추상적인
considerate 사려 깊은 indifferent 무관심한 steadfast 확고한

05 ③

해석 ① A : 서희야, 어디 가는 길이야?
B : 경주에 가는 길이야.
② A : 유수야, 롤러코스터 타자.
B : 그건 내 취향이 아니야.
③ A : 너무 비싸다. 바가지 쓰고 싶지 않아.
B : 이미 다 지나간 일이야.
④ A : 소현아, 운전해봤니?
B : 아니, 하지만 해보고 싶어.

06 ④

해설 다른 사람의 작품에 근거해서 공연 내용을 쓸 때는 지적 재산권에 대한 문제를 명쾌하게 해결해야 이후에 위험이 따르지 않는다는 내용의 글이다. 따라서 빈칸이 있는 문장은 각색물의 작가가 정당한 지적 재산권을 확보하지 않아서 제작이 무산되었다는 내용이 되어야 하므로 빈칸에 들어갈 말로 가장 적절한 것은 ④ '각색물'이다.

① 고전 작품
② 연설
③ 비평

해석 저작권법은 여러분이 허가 없이 다른 어떤 사람의 작품을 베끼는 것을 금지하고 있으므로 그 사람의 작품에 근거해서 공연 할 내용을 작성할 때는 매우 주의하라. 각본을 영화사나 제작자에게 가지고 올 때, 그것이 책, 희곡 혹은 어떤 사람의 인생 이야기에 근거한 것이라면 우리가 하는 충고는 그들에게 말하라는 것이다. 그렇게 하는 것은 문제를 복잡하게 하지만 지적 재산권 문제를 미리 다루는 것이 훨씬 더 좋다. 여러분의 작품에 대한 정당한 지적 재산권을 넘겨줄 수 없다면 여러분은 자신과 여러분이 함께 사업 하려고 하는 사람들의 입지를 서서히 해치는 위험을 무릅쓰게 될 것이다. 여러 제작물이 영화사 법률 담당 부서에 의해서 폐기되었는데, 그 이유는 각색물의 작가가 필요한 지적 재산권을 확보하지 않았기 때문이다. 일단 기획물이 제작될 준비가 되면 이러한 문제를 정리하는 것은 매우 힘이 들고 비용이 많이 들 수 있다.

어휘 material (공연) 내용, 자료 copyright 저작권
permission 허가, 허락 property 각본, (상연될) 극 studio 영화사

complicate 복잡하게 하다 up front 미리
deliver 인도하다, 배달하다 clean 정당한, 위법 사례가 없는
more than one 하나가 넘는, 여러 개의 kill (사업 등을) 그만두다
legal 법적인 secure 확보하다 clear up ~을 정리하다

07 ④

해설 ④ 다음 문장에서 나이와 함께 변하는 특정한 증상의 사례로 젊은 성인과 나이가 더 많은 성인에게 나타나는 이른 아침에 잠에서 깨는 증상을 비교하고 있으므로, 주어진 문장이 들어갈 가장 적절한 위치는 ④이다.

해석 사람이 성인기의 어느 한 시점에서 어떻게 행동하는가는 그 사람의 과거 경험과 (지금) 직면하고 있는 문제에 의해 크게 영향을 받는다. 성인의 행동을 평가할 때 이러한 인생 주기 요소들이 반드시 고려되어야만 한다. 예를 들어 학교로 되돌아가기를 원하는 한 중년 여성은 적응 장애를 겪고 있는 것이 아닐 수 있다. 그녀는 단지 자신의 새로운 한 측면을 계발하기를 원할 수도 있다. 그것이 전혀 그렇지 않음에도 일부 사람들은 그녀의 행동을 그녀가 자기의 현재 삶의 상황에 대처하는 능력이 없다고 해석할 수도 있다. 오히려 그녀는 자신의 삶에 대해 이성적인 평가를 하고 있는 것이며, 예를 들어 자신의 전문직에서 발전하기 위해 학위가 필요하다는 것을 깨닫고 있는 것이다. 마찬가지로 사적인 질문에 모호한 대답을 하는 한 나이 든 남자는 저항하는 것이 아닐지도 모른다. 그는 단지 낯선 사람에게 내적 자아를 밝히기를 꺼리는 자기네 세대의 속성을 반영하고 있는 것일지도 모른다. 가장 중요한 것은 특정한 증상의 의미가 나이와 함께 변할 수 있다는 것이다. 예를 들어 이른 아침에 잠에서 깨는 것과 관련된 문제는 젊은 성인에게는 우울증을 나타내는 것일 수 있지만 나이가 더 많은 성인에게는 단순히 정상적인 노화의 결과일 수 있다.

어휘 symptom 증상 adulthood 성인기
take into account ~을 고려하다 adjustment disorder 적응 장애
inability 무능, ~할 수 없음 cope with ~에 대처하다
rational 이성적인, 합리적인 degree 학위 profession 전문직, 직업
vague 모호한 resistant 저항하는 generation 세대
reluctance 꺼림, 마지못해 함 disclose 밝히다
inner self 내적 자아 awakening 잠에서 깸, 각성
depression 우울증

08 ①

해설 (A) 빈칸의 앞에는 만족이 상황에 따라 달라진다는 내용이 있고, 빈칸의 뒤에는 만족이 태도와 다르다는 말과 함께 태도의 상대적 지속성을 설명하는 내용이 있으므로, 빈칸에는 '그러므로'가 적절하다.
(B) 빈칸의 앞에는 초기에는 감정이 만족의 판단에 미치는 영향이 크지만 시간이 흐르면서 그 영향이 줄어든다는 내용이 있고, 빈칸의 뒤에는 시간이 흐름에 따라 생각이 만족의 판단에 더 큰 영향을 미친다는 내용이 있으므로, 빈칸에는 '반대로'가 적절하다.
그러므로 정답은 ①이다.

해석 소비자 만족 평가는 특정한 소비 상황과 관련 있는 경향이 있다. 즉 우리는 제공된 물건을 현재 사용하고 있는 동안에 그것에 대해 만족할 (또는 만족하지 않을) 수도 있는 것이다. 그러나 우리가 지금은 만족한다 할지라도 다음에 그것을 사용할 때는 만족하지 않을 수도 있다. 그러므로 만족은 태도와 다른데, 그것(태도)은 비교적 지속적이고 특정한 상황에 덜 의존적이다. 게다가, 조사 결과는 초기에는 감정이 만족의 판단에 더 많은 영향을 미치는 경향이 있지만, 이 영향은 시간이 흐르면서 감소한다는 것을 보여준다. 반대로, 시간이 흐름에 따라 생각이 만족의 판단에 더 많은 영향을 미친다. 제품을 사용한 후 소비자가 이전에 했던 것과 다른 속성을 판단할 수 있다는 점에서 결정 후의 평가가 결정 전의 평가와 다를 수 있다는 것을 주목하라. 예를 들어 냉동 전자레인지 피자를 먹어본 후, 여러분은 생각했던 것보다 그 맛을 덜 좋아한다고 결론을 내릴지도 모른다.

어휘 consumer 소비자 evaluation 평가
be tied to ~와 관련이 있다 specific 특정한, 구체적인
consumption 소비 offering 제공된 물건 current 현재의
relatively 비교적 enduring 지속적인, 참을성 있는 early on 초기에
attribute 속성 frozen 냉동된

09 ①

해설 인간이 다른 동물보다 도구 사용 기술을 더 많이 발전시켰다는 주어진 글 다음에, 도구 사용의 출현이 눈, 뇌, 팔다리 사이의 공동 작용의 결과임을 설명하는 (B)가 이어져야 한다. 또한, 직립 보행이 걷는 동안에도 손을 사용할 수 있게 하여 도구 사용에 도움이 되었다는 (A)가 이어진 다음에, 반대로 유인원은 앉아서 그러한 과제를 실행해야 한다고 말하는 (C)로 이어지는 것이 자연스럽다.

해석 인간 두뇌의 성장은 도구 사용의 증가와 관련이 있었을지도 모른다. 비록 인간이 도구를 사용하는 유일한 동물은 아니지만, 우리 종은 이 기술을 다른 어느 동물보다 훨씬 더 큰 정도로 발전시켰다. (B) 도구 사용의 출현은 입체적으로 보는 눈, 뇌, 그리고 팔다리 사이의 전례 없는 공동 작용의 결과였는데, 이것은 우리 인간의 조상들이 여전히 숲에 사는 종이었던 동안 처음 나타났다. (A) 직립 보행 또한 매우 도움이 되었는데, 왜냐하면 (비록 나무 사이에서 이리저리 이동하는 것은 더 어려워졌지만) 훨씬 더 광범위한 목적을 위해 팔과 손을 사용할 수 있게 되었기 때문이었다. 그 결과, 인간은 심지어 걷는 동안에도 자신의 손으로 훨씬 더 많은 과제를 수행하는 법을 배웠다. (C) 반대로 오늘날, 유인원들은 이런 일을 할 수 없으며 그러한 과제를 실행하기 위해서는 그들은 가만히 앉아 있어야 한다. 이러한 발전의 결과로, 초기 인간은 다른 더 큰 동물들에 비해서 서서히 더 강력해졌다.

어휘 species 종 upright 직립의 stride 큰 걸음 range 범위
emergence 출현 unprecedented 전례 없는
coordination 공동 작용, 공동 작업 limb 팔다리, 사지(四肢)
dwell 살다, 거주하다 great ape 유인원 execute 실행하다

10 ④

해설 젊은 남자와 화자와의 관계는 아직까지 명확하게 밝혀지지 않은 상태이므로 ④ '젊은 남성 친구와 화자(話者)와의 관계를 시 속에서 분명히 밝히고 있다.'가 글의 내용과 일치하지 않는다.

해석 William Shakespeare는 154편의 소네트를 썼으며, 그 중 많은 것들은 영문학의 위대한 업적들이다. 그 시들 중에서, 'Sonnet18'이 가장 잘 알려져 있고 가장 자주 인용된다. 그 소네트에서, 화자(話者)는 그의 연인을 여름에 비유하는데, 그 연인이 여름보다 더 좋으며 영원히 오래 살 것이라고 주장한다. 독자들은 종종 이 시(詩)는 화자의 낭만적 사랑의 대상인 어느 젊은 여인에게 보내진 것이라고 추정한다. 하지만 이 시는 확실하게 사랑에 관한 시이지만, 실제로는 최초의 Shakespeare의 소네트들 중 126개의 시를 받은 무명의 젊은 신사인 한 남성 친구를 위한 사랑의 표현이다. 비록 학자들이 오랫동안 젊은 남자의 정체와 화자와의 관계에 대한 본질에 대해 논쟁을 벌여 왔지만, 그 문제는 불확실성에 의해 쟁점이 흐려졌다. 심지어 Shakespeare가 화자인지도 명확하지 않다.

구문 • William Shakespeare wrote 154 sonnets, many of which are great achievements of English literature.
→ 관계대명사 which의 선행사는 154 sonnets이다. 관계대명사 앞에 콤마(,)가 있을 때는 계속적 용법으로 「접속사 + 대명사」로 해석한다. 따라서 many of which는 and many of them(=154 sonnets)이다.

제09회 하프 모의고사 해설

문제편 p.037

ANSWER

01 ③	02 ②	03 ①	04 ②	05 ④
06 ②	07 ④	08 ②	09 ④	10 ④

01 ③

해설 (A) '~하는 경우에, ~한 곳[상황]에서'라는 의미를 나타내는 접속사인 where가 적절하다.

(B) <have(사역동사) + 목적어 + 목적보어> 구조에서 two people이 행위(do)의 주체가 되므로 동사원형인 do가 적절하다.

(C) following the checklist의 수식을 받는 The person이 문장의 주어이고 might do가 동사이므로, 주어를 부가적으로 설명해 주는 현재분사인 feeling이 적절하다.

해석 체크리스트는 행동의 정확성을 높이고 오류를 줄이는 것으로 입증된 강력한 도구이다. 체크리스트는 많은, 복잡한 요구 사항이 있는 상황에서 특히 중요한데, 방해 요소가 있는 경우에는 훨씬 더 그러하다. 한 가지 과업에 많은 사람들이 관련된 상황에서는, 책임의 소재가 명확하게 설명되어야 하는 것이 필수적이다. 한 명은 지시 사항을 읽고, 다른 사람은 그것을 실행하는 식으로, 두 사람이 함께 팀으로 체크리스트를 실행하게 하는 것이 항상 더 낫다. 대신에 만약 혼자서 체크리스트를 실행하고, 그러고 나서 나중에 두 번째 사람이 항목들을 점검하면, 그 결과는 그만큼 탄탄하지 않다. 체크리스트를 따라 실행하는 사람은, 어떤 오류든 발견될 것이라고 확신하고서, 너무 빨리 단계들을 진행할지도 모른다. 그러나 똑같은 편견이 점검하는 사람에게도 영향을 미친다. 첫 번째 사람의 능력을 확신하기에, 점검하는 사람은 흔히 빠르게, 결코 철저하지 못하게 일을 한다.

어휘 checklist 체크리스트, 확인 사항 대조표 accuracy 정확성
multiple 많은 interruption, 방해(요소), 중단
spell out ~을 상세히 설명하다 execute 실행하다
confident 확신하는 bias 편견, 편향 affect 영향을 미치다
less than 결코 ~아닌 thorough 철저한

02 ②

해설 ② don't do/know A no more B than CD는 'C가 D가 아니듯 A도 B가 아니다'를 의미하는 양자부정의 표현이다. 이때 than 이후는 부정의 의미지만 부정부사를 사용하지 않는다. 따라서 you don't about her mother you know/do about her mother로 바꿔 써야 한다.

① talk A out of B는 'A를 설득해서 B를 그만두게 하다'를 의미하는 표현으로 바르게 쓰였다.

③ outnumber는 완전타동사로 '~보다 수가 더 많다'의 의미이다. 이 문장에서는 수동태가 되어 '~보다 열세이다'의 의미로 사용되었다. 뒤의 two to one은 부사구로써 by two to one으로도 사용될 수 있다.

④ a, an에는 '동등한, 같은'의 의미가 있어, Two girls of an age는 Two girls of the same age의 의미이다. not always는 부분부정으로 '반드시 ~한 것은 아니다'의 의미이다.

03 ①

해석 자동차 엔진의 기능은 심장의 기능과 동등하다.

어휘 comparable ~에 필적하는, 동등한 (= equivalent)
similar 유사한 contradictory 모순적인 opposite 반대의

04 ②

해석 청중들은 연주 후에 열정적으로 박수를 쳤다.

어휘 applaud 박수치다 crawl 기어가다 clap 박수치다
crave 열망하다 clamor 아우성치다

05 ④

해석 ① A: 우리 몇 시에 점심 먹어요?
B: 정오 전에는 준비가 될 거에요.
② A: 당신에게 여러 번 전화했었어요. 왜 안 받았어요?
B: 아, 제 핸드폰이 꺼졌던 것 같아요.
③ A: 올 겨울에 휴가 가실건가요?
B: 그럴지도 몰라요. 아직 결정하지 않았어요.
④ A: 여보세요. 전화를 못 받아서 미안해요.
B: 메시지를 남기시겠습니까?

06 ②

해설 Lev Kuleshov가 촬영한 실험에서 나오는 숏들이 각각 다른 장소에서 촬영된 것이지만 그것들이 합쳐졌을 때 배우들이 몇 발자국으로 이동할 수 있는 장소에서 촬영한 것 같은 통일된 효과를 만들어 낼 수 있다는 내용의 글이다. 그러므로 빈칸에 들어갈 말로 가장 적절한 것은 ② '통일체'이다.
① 부족, 결핍
③ 과잉
④ 분할

해석 소련의 감독인 Lev Kuleshov에 의해 촬영된 한 짤막한 실험은 영화의 편집 효과를 보여 준다. 그것은 다섯 개의 숏으로 구성된 장면으로, 각각의 숏은 다른 장소에서 개별적으로 찍힌 것이었다. 특정한 순서로 조합되었을 때 그것들은 실제로 존재하지 않는 공간의 통일체를 만들어 냈다. 그 영화는 한 소년이 소녀에게 다가가고, 그들이 만나고, 그 소년이 멀리 있는 한 건물을 가리키고, 그 두 명은 그 건물을 향해 출발하고 마침내 두 명은 함께 여러 층의 계단을 올라가는 모습을 보여 주었다. 처음 세 개의 숏은 모스크바의 서로 다른 구역에서 촬영되었다. 네 번째 숏은 미국의 한 오래된 영화에서 가져온 백악관의 사진이었다. 다섯 번째 숏은 레닌그라드의 한 교회 계단에서 촬영되었다. 그 숏들이 결합되었을 때 실제로는 수천 마일 떨어진 장소들이 합쳐져서 배우들이 몇 걸음으로 이동할 수 있는 작은 지역에 집중되어 있는 것처럼 보이도록 만들어졌다.

어휘 film 촬영하다 demonstrate 보여 주다
editing effect 편집 효과 consist of ~으로 구성되다
shot 숏(한 대의 카메라가 계속해서 잡는 장면) location 장소, 위치
assemble 조합하다 sequence 순서, 배열 existence 존재

point to ~을 가리키다 in the distance 멀리, 먼 곳에
in actuality 실제로 cover 이동하다 pace 걸음, 속도

07 ④

해설 이 글은 나이 차이에 따라 달라지는 문제 해결 전략에 관한 내용이다. ④ 앞에는 더 젊은 나이의 성인의 문제 해결 전략이 나오고 ④ 뒤에는 주어진 상황에 따라 더 젊은 나이의 성인과는 다른 전략을 사용하는 예시가 나온다. 그러므로 더 젊은 성인과는 달리 문제 해결 전략을 다양화하는 더 나이든 성인에 대한 첫 언급인 주어진 문장이 들어갈 위치는 ④가 가장 적절하다.

해석 우리가 일상의 문제를 해결하는 방법에 영향을 주는 한 가지 중요한 요소는 문제가 발생하는 상황이다. 우리가 두 형제자매 사이에 발생하는 가족 갈등을 해결할 때, 직장에서 프로젝트를 주도하는 역할에 관한 갈등을 해결할 때 우리가 사용하는 것과 동일한 전략을 사용하는가? 대답은 아니오이다. 그러나 흥미롭게도 나이 차이는 더 젊은 나이의 성인은 문제 해결 상황 전반에 걸쳐 유사한 전략, 즉 문제 해결을 위해 독자적 행동을 사용하는 경향이 더 많다는 것을 보여준다. 반면에 나이가 더 많은 성인은 문제 해결 상황을 고려해 자신들의 전략을 다양화하는 경향이 더 많다. 그들은 (예를 들어 가족 갈등과 같은) 대인 관계에서의 갈등 문제에서는 (다시 말해 감정 관리와 같은) 감정 조절 전략을 더 많이 사용하는 반면 (예를 들어 결함 있는 상품을 다루는 것과 같은) 보다 수단적 상황에서는 (제품의 반품과 같은) 독자적 행동 전략을 사용한다. 연구자들은 우리가 나이가 들고 더 많은 일상의 경험을 축적함에 따라 문제의 상황에 더 민감해지고 그것에 맞게 전략을 사용한다고 주장한다.

어휘 vary 다양하게 하다 self-action 독자적 행동
regulate 조절하다 instrumental 수단이 되는, 기계적인
defective 결함이 있는 merchandise 상품 accumulate 축적하다

08 ②

해설 (A) 빈칸의 앞에는 말과 개들 중 몇몇은 우리에게 자연적인 충동을 아주 쉽게 전달한다는 내용이 나오고, 뒤에는 이성이 없는 동물이 어떤 것을 자연적인 충동이 아닌 생각의 결과를 단어나 기호로 나타낼 정도로 완벽에 도달한 사례가 없다는 내용이 나오므로, 빈칸에는 '그럼에도 불구하고'가 가장 적절하다.
(B) 빈칸의 앞에는 모든 인간이 말을 사용하지만 어떤 동물도 말을 사용하지는 않는다는 내용이 나오고, 뒤에는 이것이 인간과 동물의 진정한 본질적 차이로 받아들여질 수 있다는 내용이 나오므로, 빈칸에는 '그러므로'가 가장 적절하다. 따라서 정답은 ②이다.

해석 동물에게 사고가 존재하지 않는다는 것을 우리에게 설득할 수 있는 모든 주장 중, 내 생각에 최고의 것은 다음과 같다. 단일 종 내에서 어떤 동물들은 인간들 사이에서와 다를 바 없이 다른 것들보다 더 완벽한데, 말과 개의 경우에서 볼 수 있는 것처럼 그것들 중 몇몇은 배우는 것을 다른 동물들보다 훨씬 더 빠르게 익힌다는 것을 사실로 인정한다. 그것들이 모두 소리나 몸의 다른 동작으로 분노, 두려움, 굶주림 등과 같은 자연적인 충동을 우리에게 쉽게 전달한다는 것을 또한 사실로 인정한다. 그럼에도 불구하고 이성이 없는 그 어떤 동물도 진정한 언어를 사용할 수 있을 정도의 그런 완벽한 상태에 이르렀음이, 다시 말해, 자연적인 충동 때문이 아니라 오로지 사고 때문이라고 밖에는 여길 수 없는 어떤 것을 단어나 기호로 나타냈음이 관찰된 적은 없었다. 왜냐하면 말은 몸 안에 숨겨진 유일하게 분명한 사고의 표시이고, 모든 인간이 그것을 사용하지만, 어떤 동물도 그렇지 않기 때문이다. 그러므로 이것은 인간과 동물 사이의 진정한 '본질적 차이'로 받아들여질 수 있다.

어휘 argument 주장 persuade 설득하다 beast 동물, 짐승
chief 최고의, 주된 no differently than ~와 다를 바 없이
impulse 충동 anger 분노
and the like 기타 등등, 기타 같은 종류의 것
attribute ~ to ... ~을 … 때문으로 돌리다 conceal 숨기다, 감추다
make use of ~을 사용하다 take ~ to be ... ~을 …라고 여기다
differentia 본질적 차이

09 ④

해설 음식을 훈련시키는 과정이 음식에 대한 식욕을 더 증진시킬 수 있다는 주어진 글 다음에, 그 예로 싫어하는 음식에 선호하는 음식이나 감미료를 섞어 싫어하는 음식의 선호도를 증가시킨다는 내용의 (C)가 이어져야 한다. 이어서 설탕과 함께 먹은 후 브로콜리나 콜리플라워를 선호하게 되었다는 유사한 예와 안타깝게도 설탕을 활용하는 부모는 거의 없다는 내용인 (B)가 이어진 다음, 대신에 부모들은 자녀가 싫어하는 음식을 디저트 보상을 통해 먹도록 유인하려 하지만 오히려 역효과를 낼 수 있다는 내용인 (A)가 이어지는 것이 자연스럽다.

해석 (음식을) 훈련시키는 과정이 때때로 음식을 싫어하게 만드는 것처럼, 그러한 과정은 또한 음식이 식욕을 더 증진시키도록 할 수도 있다. (C) 예를 들어, 싫어하는 음식에 대한 우리의 선호도를 증가시키는 한 가지 강력한 방법은 그것을 우리가 매우 선호하는 어떤 음식이나 감미료와 섞는 것이다. 이것은 일부 사람들이 블랙커피를 좋아하게 되는 방법일 수 있다. 그들은 처음에 블랙커피를 크림과 설탕과 함께 마시고 그러고 나서 커피의 맛 자체가 즐겁게 됨에 따라 차츰 그 추가 재료들을 제거한다. (B) 유사하게, 한 연구에 따르면 대학생들은 브로콜리나 콜리플라워를 설탕과 함께 몇 번 먹은 후에 그것들을 더 선호하게 되었다. 안타깝게도, 아이들의 식습관을 개선하기 위해 그러한 방법을 사용하는 부모들은 거의 없는데, 아마도 그들은 설탕이 건강에 좋지 않다고 인지하고, 나중에 설탕을 뺄 수 있다는 것을 깨닫지 못하기 때문일 것이다. (A) 대신에, 부모들은 흔히 자녀들에게 디저트를 보상으로 제공함으로써 싫어하는 음식을 먹도록 유인하려고 시도하는데, 그것은 싫어하는 음식과 그 이후의 디저트 사이의 대조가 전자를 훨씬 더 싫어하게 만들 수 있다는 점에서 쉽게 역효과를 내는 전략이다.

어휘 appetitive 식욕을 증진시키는 entice 유인하다, 유도하다
backfire 역효과를 일으키다 subsequent 그 이후의
cauliflower 콜리플라워, 꽃양배추 improve 개선하다
withdraw 빼내다, 회수하다 eliminate 제거하다 ingredient 재료

10 ④

해설 In her time she was a celebrity로 보아 생전에 이미 인정받았음을 알 수 있으므로 ④ '살아 있는 동안에는 작가로서 그다지 인정을 받지 못했다.'가 글의 내용과 일치하지 않는다.

해석 Aphra Behn은 영문학에 있어 최초의 여성 직업 작가였다. 그녀는 Canterbury 근처에서 1640년에 태어났다. 1664년에, 그녀는 네덜란드계의 상인인 Johan Behn과 결혼했으나, 그 결혼은 그다지 오래 지속되지 않았다. 1966년에 빚으로 인한 수감이 그녀가 수입을 위해 글을 쓰도록 이끌었다. Behn은 일련의 성공적인 희곡들을 썼다. 그녀의 최초 소설인 '강요된 결혼'은 1671년에 출판되었다. Behn의 소설 Oroonoko(1688)는 노예가 된 아프리카 왕자의 이야기였는데, 현재 그것은 영국 소설의 발달에 있어서 하나의 초석으로 간주된다. 희곡과 산문뿐만 아니라 Behn은 시도 썼고, 프랑스어와 라틴어에서 온 작품들도 번역했다. 살아 있는 동안에 그녀는 유명 인사였고, 직업 작가로서의 독립성과 양성 평등에 대한 그녀의 관심으로 인해 비범했

다. Behn은 1689년4월 16일에 죽었고 웨스트민스터 사원에 묻혔다.

구문 • Behn's novel Oroonoko (1688) was the story of an enslaved African prince, now considered a foundation stone in the development of the English novel.
→ now (being) considered ~에서 being이 생략된 분사 구문이다. 다시 쓰면 and it is now considered ~로 바꾸어 쓸 수 있다.

어휘 parentage 태생, 가문, 혈통 imprisonment 수감, 감금
lead ~ to ... ~가 …하도록 이끌다 prose 산문
in one's time ~가 살아 있는 동안 celebrity 유명 인사
unusual for ~가 비범한 independence 독립
concern 관심, 염려 equality 평등 abbey 사원

제 10 회 하프 모의고사 해설

문제편 p.041

ANSWER

01 ④	02 ④	03 ②	04 ④	05 ④
06 ②	07 ②	08 ③	09 ②	10 ④

01 ········· ④

해설 By ~routine은 By(~함으로써)가 이끄는 전치사구이고, Pur bottles가 문장의 주어이다. 따라서 Pur bottles 다음에 동사가 필요하므로 밑줄 친 ④의 helping을 help로 고쳐야 한다.

① '~에 주의하다'라는 의미의 be careful 뒤에 절이 이어지고 있으므로 명사절을 이끄는 접속사 that은 적절하다.

② 명사구인 an easy mistake를 수식하는 역할을 해야 하므로 to부정사 to make는 적절하다.

③ 형용사인 frustrating을 수식하는 역할을 해야 하므로 '매우'라는 뜻의 부사 highly는 적절하다.

해석 아이들은 따뜻한 우유나 우유 대체품을 (젖)병으로 자주 마신다. 부모들과 아이를 돌보는 사람들은 액체가 갓난아기의 입을 데게 할 정도로 그렇게 뜨겁지 않게 주의해야 한다. 불행히도, 이것은 한밤중에 병을 전자레인지에 데울 때 저지르기 쉬운 실수이다. 병을 적당한 온도로 식히는 것은 느린 과정이고, 배고픈 아이가 당신의 품 안에서 울어대고 있을 때에는 매우 좌절감을 줄 수 있다. 온도와 색깔을 연결한 최근의 획기적인 상품들이 이 문제를 해결하였다. Royal Industries의 Pur 분과[사업본부]에서는 아기 제품을 20년 넘게 만들어 오고 있다. 거기서 만든 최신 젖병은 젖병 안에 든 액체가 화씨 100.4도에 도달하면 색깔이 변한다. 피곤한 부모들이 전자레인지를 끄고 그 과정에서 (온도를 확인하기 위해) 손목에 액체를 조금 떨어뜨리는 일반적인 과정인 다음 단계로 옮겨 가도록 알려 줌으로써, Pur병은 액체의 온도가 딱 맞는다고 부모들이 확신하도록 도와준다.

어휘 frequently 자주 substitute 대체품 caregiver 돌보는 사람
liquid 액체 infant 갓난아기, 유아
microwave 전자레인지에 데우다; 전자레인지 cool 식히다
frustrating 좌절감을 주는, 답답하게 하는 link 연결하다, 관련짓다
division (조직의) 분과, 부 baby bottle 젖병 turn off ~을 끄다
move on to ~로 옮겨 가다[이동하다]

02 ········· ④

해설 ④ 비교하는 두 대상이 Your son's hair와 your hair가 되어야 하므로, as you에서 대명사의 주격인 you 대신 your hair를 대신하는 소유 대명사인 yours라고 써야 한다.

① as 형용사 원급 as가 사용된 원급 비교의 문장이다. Jane is not as young as she looks young에서 이 중복된 young을 생략하고 구성된 올바른 문장이다.

② 비교급 비교가 사용된 문장으로, 가주어 it이 의미하는 to make a phone call과 than 뒤에 오는 to write a letter를 비교하고 있다. 이 두 비교 대상의 형태가 일치하므로 올바른 문장이다.

③ 비교급 비교가 사용된 문장으로, 'You have more money than I have much money.'에서 주절과 중복된 형태인 have much money가 생략된 올바른 문장이다.

03 ········· ②

해석 나는 그가 능력 있는 요리사라고 생각하지 않는다.

어휘 competent 유능한, 능력 있는 lazy 게으른
proficient 능숙한 inefficient 비효율적인 turn to ~에 의존하다

04 ········· ④

해석 집을 페인트칠하는 것을 끝마치고 난 후, 그들은 청소하는 힘든 작업을 직면했다.

어휘 arduous 고된, 힘든(= difficult) rewarding 보상하는
resolute 단호한 boring 지루한 laborious 힘든

05 ········· ④

해설 'How long~?'은 거리를 물어보는 의문문이 아니라 기간의 정도를 알고 싶을 때 사용하는 의문문이다. 따라서 A가 "How long have you been away from home?"(얼마나 오래 집에서부터 멀리 떨어져 있었어?)에 B가 "It's about ten miles."(대략 10마일이야)라고 거리를 대답했으므로 적절하지 않은 대화이다. 따라서 정답은 ④이다.

해석 ① A: 제가 좀 도와드릴까요?
B: 그냥 보고 있는 거예요, 감사합니다.
② A: 영화는 몇 시에 시작해?
B: 4시 정각에.
③ A: 나는 푸드 코트에서 내 지갑을 잃어버렸어.
B: 분실물 센터에 가보자.
④ A: 얼마나 오래 집에서부터 멀리 떨어져 있었어?
B: 대략 10마일이야.

06 ········· ②

해설 지성이 감정에게 원하는 것을 얻기 위한 중간 단계의 목표를 차례로 제시하면, 감정은 그것을 원하게 된다는 내용이므로, 빈칸에 들어갈 말로 가장 적절한 것은 ② '지성에 의해 형성된'이다.
① 비교하여 바뀐
③ 보상에 의해 강화된
④ 전달과정에서 감소된

해석 지성은 감정에 명령을 내릴 수는 없지만, 그것은 현재 존재하는 감정적인 에너지의 방향을 돌릴 수 있다. 예를 들어, 만일 감정이 X를 원하면, 지성은 Y를 하는 것이 X를 가져다줄 것이라고 지적함으로써 감정을 설득하여 Y를 하는 것을 원하게 할지도 모른다. 감정이 Y를 하는 것이 X를 감정에게 가져다 줄 것이라고 확신하자마자, 그들이 X에 대하여 느꼈던 열망은 Y로 이동할 것이다. 그런 다음 지성은 감정에게 Z를 함으로써 Y를 얻을 수 있다고 지적하고, 다시 한 번, 열망이 이동할 것이다. 이런 방식으로, 열망은 지성에 의해 형성된 욕구의 연쇄 고리를 따라 흘러간다. 그렇게 하는 것이 그 자체로 기분이 좋지

않다고 할지라도, 그리고 실제로 그렇게 하는 것이 기분이 나쁘다 할지라도, 우리는 그렇게 함으로써 이런 연쇄 고리의 도구적 욕구를 충족하고자 하는 동기를 부여 받게 된다.

어휘 command 명령하다, 지시하다 channel (~의 방향을) 돌리다
point out ~을 가리키다, ~을 지적하다 anxiety 열망
with respect to ~에 대하여, 관하여 transfer 이동하다
fulfill 충족하다

07 ②

해설 ② 앞에 있는 문장은 일반적으로 식량이 부족한 시기의 사막 메뚜기에 관한 설명이고, ② 뒤의 the abundant food supply는 주어진 문장에서 언급된 major vegetation growth를 통해 풍부해진 먹이를 가리킨다. 그리고 주어진 문장의 everything changes는 ② 다음에 오는 At first와 바로 상응한다. 그러므로 주어진 문장이 들어가기에 가장 적절한 곳은 ②이다.

해석 사막 메뚜기는 식량원의 입수 가능성과 지역 메뚜기 개체군의 밀도에 따라 현저히 다른 두 가지 방식으로 산다. 그들이 원래 사는 사막의 서식지에서 보통 그렇듯 식량이 부족할 때는 메뚜기들이 위장을 위해 고안된 색채를 갖고 태어나며 혼자 살아간다. 드물긴 하지만 상당량의 비가 내리는 기간이 와서 초목이 크게 성장하게 되면, 모든 것이 변한다. 처음에는 그 메뚜기들이 그저 풍부한 식량 공급량을 맘껏 먹어치우면서 계속 혼자 산다. 그러나 그 여분의 초목이 죽어 없어지기 시작하면, 메뚜기들은 자신들이 (수가 많아져서) 서로 혼잡하게 있다는 것을 알게 된다. 갑자기, 밝은 색을 띠고 함께 있기를 갈망하는 새끼 메뚜기들이 태어난다. 서로를 피하고 위장과 무활동을 통해 포식자들로부터 몸을 숨기는 대신 이 메뚜기들은 떼를 짓고, 함께 먹으며, 순전히 숫자를 통해 자기네 포식자들을 압도한다.

어휘 vegetation 초목, 식물 remarkably 현저히
availability 입수 가능성 density 밀도 scarce 부족한
solitary 혼자의 loner 혼자 있는 동물[사람]
feast off 맘껏 먹어치우다 abundant 풍부한 predator 포식자
inactivity 무활동, 움직이지 않음 swarm 떼; 떼를 짓다
overwhelm 압도하다 sheer (크기·정도·양을 강조하여) 순전한

08 ③

해설 (A) 배움의 장소로서 미래의 학교는 배우고자 하는 것을 무엇이건 배울 수 있도록 하는 곳이 될 것이라는 내용이 앞에 나오고 (A)를 포함하는 문장에서는 그것을 언제든지 할 수 있도록 해줄 것이라는 점층적 내용이 이어지므로 빈칸에는 추가의 의미를 나타내는 '더욱이'가 가장 적절하다.
(B) 앞선 문장에서는 학교가 24시간 열려 있게 될 것이라는 내용이 오고 (B)를 포함하는 문장에서는 새벽 2시에 대수를 공부할 수 있다는 사례가 나오므로 빈칸에는 '예를 들어'가 가장 적절하다. 그러므로 정답은 ③이다.

해석 미래의 학교는 누구라도 배우고 싶어 하는 어떤 것에든 접근할 수 있도록 허용할 일련의 교수학습의 장소로 이루어질 것인데, 그것(배우고자 하는 것)은 학교의 공통 교육과정에 현재 포함된 모든 과목뿐만 아니라 그렇지 않은 과목들도 상당히 더 많이 포함하거나, 포함할 수 있을 것이다. 더욱이 그 (교수학습의) 장소는 학생이 배워보고 싶어 할 때는 '언제든지' 원하는 정보에 접근할 수 있도록 허용할 것이다. 그 학교들은 인근 지역 도처에 흩어져 있고 하루 24시간 개방되어 있을 것이다. 예를 들어 대수를 배우고자 하는 사람이 목요일 새벽 2시에 잠을 이룰 수 없다면, 그는 가서 마음껏 대수를 공부할 수 있을 것이다. 어떤 것이든 배우고 싶어 하는 사람이면 누구든 원하는 때 언제든지 그것을 배우고자 할 수 있을 뿐만 아니라 어떤 시험에서도 떨어지거나 교사나 다른 학생들로부터 조롱당하지 않고 필요한 만큼 여러 번 학습을 반복할 수 있을 것이다.

어휘 consist of ~로 이루어지다
station (특정 서비스가 제공되거나 이루어지는) 장소·건물
permit 허용하다 presently 현재 curriculum 교육과정
a good deal 상당히, 많이; 상당량 have access to ~에 접근하다
scatter 흩어지게 하다 to one's heart's content 마음껏, 흡족하게
redo 반복하다, 다시 하다
subject to ~을 당하는[겪기 쉬운] ridicule 조롱, 조소

09 ②

해설 침팬지를 비롯한 유인원이 거울 앞에서 자기 인식을 한다는 주어진 글 다음에, (B)의 They가 주어진 글의 침팬지와 유인원을 지칭하고 있고 내용 또한 그들이 전에 볼 수 없었던 곳을 조사한다는 것이므로 (B)가 이어져야 한다. 그 뒤로 동물의 이마에 빨간 점을 찍은 후 거울 앞에서의 그들의 행동을 지켜보는 내용인 (C)가 이어진 후 침팬지와 유인원은 자신의 이마에 있는 점을, 원숭이는 거울의 점을 만지는 내용인 (A)가 이어지는 것이 자연스럽다. 그러므로 주어진 글 다음에 이어질 글의 순서로 가장 적절한 것은 ②이다.

해석 자기 인식은 침팬지와 다른 유인원에서 관찰된다. 침팬지들이 거울 앞에 놓일 때, 그들이 자기 자신들을 보고 있다는 것을 알아내는 데는 몇 분밖에 걸리지 않는다. (B) 그러고 나서 그들은 입 속, 머리 꼭대기, 그리고 전에는 볼 수 없었던 다른 모든 곳을 조사하면서 얼마간의 시간을 보낸다. 원숭이는 자신이 자신의 이미지를 보고 있다는 것을 결코 알아내지 못한다. 즉, 그들은 인간이 이미지를 인식할 때 하는 것처럼 전혀 행동하지 않는다. (C) 동물의 이마에 빨간 점을 찍고 나서 그 동물을 거울 앞에 둘 수 있을 것이다. 그런 다음 우리는 그 동물이 거울의 점을 만지는지, 아니면 자신의 머리 위에 있는 점을 만지는지 알아보기 위해 지켜본다. (A) 자신의 이마에 있는 점을 만지는 것은 그 동물이 거울에서 자신의 이미지를 보고 있음을 이해하고 있다는 것을 보여 준다. 침팬지는 자기 자신의 이마에 있는 점을 만질 것이다. 모든 유인원 종들은 자기 자신의 이마를 만지는 것이 발견된 반면에 모든 원숭이 종은 거울의 점을 만진다.

어휘 self-awareness 자기 인식 ape 유인원
figure out ~을 알아내다, ~을 이해하다 forehead 이마
recognize 인식하다

10 ④

해설 'During World War I the Ottoman Empire fought on the losing side.'에서 오스만 제국이 1차 세계대전 패전국이었음을 알 수 있으므로 ④ '1차 세계대전 승전국 중 하나로 전쟁 후 터키 공화국으로 다시 태어났다.'가 글의 내용과 일치하지 않는다.

해석 1300년대 오스만 튀르크족은 또 다른 이슬람 제국을 건설하였다. 술탄(sultan)이라 불리는 오스만 군주들은 1453년에 Constantinople을 점령하고 그곳을 오스만의 수도로 삼았다. 1600년대에 이르러 오스만 제국은 서남아시아 대부분을 포함하였고, 동유럽 일부와 북아프리카 대부분 지역까지 확장되었다. 하지만, 정치 분쟁, 부패, 그리고 다른 나라들과의 경쟁으로 제국은 서서히 쇠약해졌다. 시간이 흐르면서, 제국 국경 안에 있던 소수 민족들 또한 독립을 계속 요구하기 시작했다. 1차 세계대전 중 오스만 제국은 패전한 쪽에서 싸웠다. 전쟁 후, Mustafa Kemal이라는 이름의 장군이 정부를 인계받았다. 그는 터키 공화국을 세웠고 Ankara에 수도를 세웠다. Turkey를 넘어, 이라크, 시리아, 레바논과 팔레스타인을 포함한 이전 오스만 영토들은 영국과

프랑스의 지배를 받게 되었다. 2차 세계대전 후에 이들 지역들은 독립을 얻었다.

구문 • The Ottoman rulers, called sultans, took Constantinople in 1453 and made it the Ottoman capital.
→ called 앞에는 who were가 생략되었으며, 앞에 나온 The Ottoman rulers를 부연 설명하고 있다. it은 Constantinople을 가리키며, the Ottoman capital은 made의 목적격보어에 해당한다.
• After the war, a general [named Mustafa Kemal] took over the government.
→ the war는 World War I을 가리키며, 과거분사 named가 이끄는 어구가 앞에 나온 명사 a general을 뒤에서 수식하고 있다. named 앞에 who was가 생략되었다.

어휘 **establish** 설립하다, 세우다 **empire** 제국 **stretch** 뻗다 **struggle** 분투, 투쟁 **corruption** 부패 **rivalry** 경쟁, 대항 **border** 국경 **independence** 독립 **general** 장군, 장성 **republic** 공화국 **former** 이전의 **territory** 영토 **region** 지역

제 11 회 하프 모의고사 해설

문제편 p.045

ANSWER

01 ②	02 ②	03 ④	04 ②	05 ④
06 ④	07 ③	08 ②	09 ②	10 ④

01 ②

해설 (A) early-stage entrepreneurs를 수식하는 관계절이므로, 관계대명사 who가 적절한 표현이다.

(B) 관계절인 that ~ participate가 수식하는 Each venture가 주어이고, '40,000달러를 지급받다'라는 의미가 되어야 맥락상 적절하므로, is given이 적절한 표현이다.

(C) 분사구문인 making ~ opportunities에서 less ~ opportunities가 목적보어인데, less fearful과 마찬가지로 and more 다음에도 보어의 역할을 할 수 있는 형용사가 와야 하므로 open이 적절한 표현이다.

해석 Start-UP Chile라고 하는 새로운, 대담한 실험이 칠레에서 기획된다. 칠레 정부는 현지 지역 사회를 기업가 정신으로 물들일 목적으로 새로운 벤처 사업을 시작하고 있는 시작 단계의 기업가들을 전 세계에서 말 그대로 수입하고 있다. Start-UP Chile는 신규 회사에게 사업을 시작하기 위해 여섯 달 동안 칠레로 올 기회를 제공한다. 참여하도록 선발된 각 벤처 기업은 Start-UP Chile 공동 작업 구역에서의 공간뿐 아니라 그들의 현지 경비를 지불할 40,000달러를 지급받는다. 참여자들은 자신들이 하고 있는 것을 공유하고 자신들의 사업을 도울 현지 인재들을 고용하도록 권장된다. 그 목적은 칠레 사람들에게 전 세계에서 온 역할 모델들을 접해 보게 함으로써 그들을 고무시켜 그들 자신의 회사를 시작할 생각을 해 보게 하는 것이다. Start-UP Chile는 말 그대로 칠레인들의 마음을 바꾸어, 그들이 실패를 덜 두려워하고 기회에 더 노출되도록 만들고 싶어 한다.

어휘 bold 대담한 chilean 칠레의 literally 말 그대로, 그야말로
venture 벤처(사업) infect 물들이다, 감염시키다.
entrepreneurial 기업가의 expense 경비, 비용
collaborative 공동의, 합작의 hire 고용하다 expose 접하게 하다
fearful 두려워하는

02 ②

해설 ② '기껏해야'는 at the most 또는 at most라고 써야 한다. 따라서 at the least but little을 ~ at the most but little이라고 써야 한다.

① <The 비교급 + 주어 + 동사, the 비교급 + 주어 + 동사>의 표현이 올바르게 사용되고 있다. The older + you(주어) + grow(동사), the more difficult + it(주어) + becomes(동사) + to learn a foreign language(진주어)이다.

③ 'A가 아니라 B'라는 의미의 'not A but B'의 형태가 옳게 사용되었고, 이때 A와 B가 문법적으로 올바른 병렬 관계, 즉 모두 똑같이 to부정사구로 구성되어 있다. '누군가 좋아하는 것'을 의미하는 명사절이 what one likes라는 올바른 구문으로 쓰였다.

④ 명사절 접속사 what이 올바르게 사용되어 명사절 what you possess를 구성하고 이 명사절이 주어로 바르게 쓰였다. '너의 것'을 의미하는 소유대명사 yours도 적합하다.

어휘 at the least 최소한, 적어도 compared with ~와 비교하여
ignorant 무지한, 무식한 possess 소유하다 personality 인격, 인성

03 ④

해석 김씨는 계획안 A, 이씨는 계획안 B를 작성하였는데, 이 둘은 서로 보완적이다.

어휘 complementary 보충적인

04 ②

해석 대부분의 낙타들은 건조한 서식지에서 발견된다.

어휘 arid 건조한, 메마른 dirty 더러운 sandy 모래의
harsh 거친

05 ④

해석 ① A: 혼자 가고 싶지 않아.
B: 내가 함께 가 줄까?
② A: 나 조금 피곤해.
B: 잠시 휴식이 필요한 것 같다.
③ A: 더 이상 참을 수 없어.
B: 진정해.
④ A: 내가 행운을 빌어 줄게.
B: 손가락을 언제 다쳤니?

06 ④

해설 배가 고플 때 의지력이 약해지고 그런 상황에서는 건강에 좋은 음식을 선택하기 어렵다는 내용의 글이므로 빈칸에 들어갈 말로 가장 적절한 것은 ④ '음식과 관련된 좋은 선택을 하고'이다.
① 근육을 빠르게 만들고
② 혈당 수준을 낮추고
③ 열량을 효율적으로 소모하고

해석 근육처럼 의지력도 용량이 제한되어 있고 광범위하게 사용되면 그것은 기운이 다 빠질 수 있다. 또한 근육처럼, 여러분의 뇌가 의지력을 사용하기 위해 활용하는 일차적인 연료는 혈당이다. 그래서 여러분의 혈당이 낮으면 (즉, 여러분이 배고플 때인데, 다이어트 중일 때는 거의 항상 그렇다.) 여러분의 의지력은 그 어느 때보다 더 약하고, 그것을 해결하는 유일한 방법은 먹는 것이다. 음식과 관련된 결정을 내릴 때 여러분은 이것이 유발할 수 있는 어려움을 알 수 있다. 운동을 방정식에 대입하는 것은 다이어트를 하는 사람들이 더 많은 열량을 의도적으로 소모하기 위하여 (즉, 더 많은 혈당을 사용하기 위하여) 활용하는 것인데, 이는 상황을 더 심각하게 만들 뿐이다. Baumeister와 Tierney는 이것을 영양의 진퇴양난이라고 부르는데, 여러분이 더 적게 먹고 더 많이 운동할수록, 여러분은 결국 음식과 관련된 좋은 선택을 하고 체중 감소를 유지할 가능성이 더 낮아지게 될 것이다.

어휘 willpower 의지력 capacity 용량, 능력

exercise 사용하다, 발휘하다; 운동 extensively 광범위하게
worn out (특히 힘든 노동·운동으로) 기운이 다 빠진, 매우 지친[지쳐 보이는]
primary 일차적인 equation 방정식 problematic 문제가 되는
nutritional 영양의

07 ③

해설 주어진 문장에서는 또 다른 항해 보조 기구를 언급하고 있다. 그리고 ③ 다음에 이어지는 문장에서 이 보조 기구에 대해 설명하고 있으므로 주어진 문장이 들어가기에 가장 적절한 곳은 ③이다.

해석 아무도 선원의 나침반이 언제 어디에서 발명되었는지는 말할 수 없지만 바이킹족은 그것 없이도 그럭저럭 지낼 수 있었던 것 같았는데, 그 이유는 스칸디나비아 반도에 나침반이 알려지기 전에 그들이 북대서양을 이미 횡단한 것 같았기 때문이다. 훨씬 더 전에도 미노스인과 페니키아인과 같은 다른 해상 문명은 나침반 없이 육지가 보이지 않는 곳에서 대양을 항해했다. 초기 뱃사람들은 아마 별, 일출과 일몰, 그리고 탁월풍의 패턴을 이용한 항해법을 알았을 것이다. 그러나 바이킹족은 또 다른 항해 보조 도구를 갖고 있었는지도 모른다. 스칸디나비아의 전설은 '태양의 돌'이라는 것에 관해 언급하고 있다. 몇몇 과학자들은 이것들이 편광성이 있는 광물이었다고 믿는다.

어휘 navigation 항해 aid 보조 도구 mariner 선원
compass 나침반 maritime 해상의 seaman 뱃사람
refer to ~에 관해 언급하다 polarizing property 편광성
obscure 가리다, 덮어 감추다

08 ②

해설 (A) 연구자가 연구를 위해 현지로 가져가야 할 장비를 정할 때 근거가 되는 조건들이 앞에서 제시된 뒤에 그 중 한 가지 예로 구체적인 장비가 열거되고 있으므로 빈칸에는 '예를 들어'가 가장 적절하다.
(B) 조건이 특수한 상황에서는 거기에 맞는 특수한 장비가 필요하다고 말한 다음에 이에 관해 잘 알고 있을 인근에서 비슷한 연구를 해온 사람에게 조언을 구해야 한다는 내용이 나오고 있으므로 빈칸에는 '그러므로'가 가장 적절하다. 따라서 정답은 ②이다.

해석 연구자가 현지로 가져가는 측정 장비의 종류와 양은 대개 현지 조사의 목적, 기후, 지리의 특성과 그가 다른 사람으로부터 얻을 수 있는 지도와 자료의 특성에 달려 있다. 예를 들어 만일 제안된 연구가 농업에 초점을 맞추고 있으면 필수 장비에는 강우계, 지온계, 토양 색상첩이 포함될 것이다. 만일 기후가 열대이면 잘 부식되지 않는 기구와, 필요 이상의 수분을 제거할 실리카 겔과 열대 지방용 특별 (장비) 세트가 어울리는 물건일 것이다. 만일 가파르고 거친 지형을 오르는 것이 특별한 문제를 일으킨다면 가벼운 장비가 필요하다. 그러므로 장비의 필요 사항을 계획할 때 중요한 단계는 인근에서 유사한 연구를 해 본 사람들의 조언을 구하는 것이다. 그런 확인이 있었더라면 과거의 연구자들이 자신들의 너무나 훌륭한 강우계를 자료 제공자의 개인적인 장식품으로 등장하게 하는 슬픔은 피했을지도 모른다.

어휘 measurement equipment 측정 장비 geography 지리
obtain 얻다 agriculture 농업 rain gauge 강우계, 우량계
soil thermometer 지온계
color chart 색상첩(색상들을 도표로 나타낸 것)
implement 기구, 도구 silica gel 실리카 겔(제습제의 한 종류)
excess 필요 이상의, 과도한
the order of the day (특정한 때·장소에) 어울리는 것, 유행[풍조]
steep 가파른 seek 구하다, 찾다
spare (슬픔·상해·죽음 등을) 피하게[면하게] 해 주다 grief 슬픔
turn up as ~로 등장하다[나타나다] informant 자료[정보] 제공자

09 ②

해설 이 글은 업무 준비가 되어 있는 졸업생들에 대한 선호도가 높아지고 있다는 내용을 담고 있다. 직무 준비도에 대한 논쟁이 있고, 일과 교육이 질적으로 다르다고 보는 사람들이 있다는 내용의 주어진 문장 다음에, 교육은 일반적인 훈련을 제공할 뿐 구체적 직업 훈련은 학업 이후에 시작될 수 있다는 내용의 (B)가 이어지고, 그렇지만 업무 준비가 되어 있는 졸업생에 대한 수요가 증가하고 있으며 고용주들이 업무 현장 경험을 긍정적으로 생각한다는 (C)가 이어진 후, 업무 현장 경험의 또 다른 이점을 제시하고 업무 경험은 직무 준비도를 향상시킨다는 결론을 담고 있는 (A)가 마지막으로 오는 흐름이 자연스럽다. 따라서 글의 순서로 ② (B) – (C) – (A)가 가장 적절하다.

해석 '직무 준비도'를 점점 더 강조하는 것은 많은 논쟁의 대상이다. 어떤 사람들은 일과 교육이 질적으로 다른 사회 현장이라고 믿는다. (B) 교육은 단기적으로 그리고 장기적으로 모두 유용한 기술과 지식을 제공하지만, 업무를 위한 광범위하거나 일반적인 훈련만 제공할 수 있다. 특정 직업을 위한 구체적인 훈련은 학업 이후에만 시작될 수 있다. (C) 하지만 업무 현장에서의 조직의 관행을 아주 잘 알고 있는 일할 준비가 되어 있는 졸업생들에 대한 수요가 증가하고 있다. 고용주들은 공부하는 동안 업무 현장을 접한 것이 학생들에게 업무 현장이 어떻게 운영되는지와 다양한 직장 상황에서 그들에게 무엇이 기대되는지에 대한 귀중한 통찰을 얻을 수 있는 기회를 제공한다고 믿으며 업무 경험을 중요하게 여긴다. (A) 고용주들은 업무 경험이 졸업생들의 소프트 스킬을 향상시키고, 자신감을 높이며, 그들의 학업을 취업과 연관시키는 데 도움을 주어, 그들을 더 성숙하게 하고, 일에 대해 보다 현실적인 기대를 하게 한다고 말한다. 미래의 취업을 위해 (사람들과) 연락하고 네트워크를 만들 수 있는 기회는 또 다른 이점이다. 다시 말해, 업무 경험은 직무 준비도를 향상시킨다.

어휘 emphasis 강조 qualitatively 질적으로
employer 고용주, 고용인
soft skill 소프트 스킬(남들과 잘 소통하는 자질)
confidence 자신감 rounded 성숙한, 원숙한 realistic 현실적인
advantage 이점, 장점 generic 일반적인
undertake 시작하다, 착수하다
familiar with ~을 아주 잘 아는, ~에 익숙한 practice 관행, 관례
workplace 업무 현장, 직장 exposure 접(하게)함, 직접 체험하게 함
acquire 얻다 insight 통찰, 통찰력

10 ④

해석 1896년 Washington D.C.에서 태어난 미국 작가인 Marjorie Kinnan Rawlings는 시골을 다룬 주제와 (시골을)배경으로 하는 소설을 썼다. 그녀가 어렸을 때, 그녀의 이야기 중 하나가 The Washington Post에 실렸다. 대학교를 졸업한 후 Rawlings는 저널리스트로 일하면서 동시에 소설가로 자리매김 하려고 애썼다. 1928년에 그녀는 Florida주 Cross Creek에 있는 오렌지 과수원을 구입했다. 이것은 The Yearling과 자전적인 책인 Cross Creek을 포함해서 그녀의 일부 작품의 영감의 원천이 되었다. 1939년에 한 소년과 어미 잃은 아기 사슴에 관한 이야기였던 The Yearling은 퓰리처상 소설 부문 수상작이 되었다. 나중에, 1946년에 The Yearling은 같은 제목으로 영화화되었다. Rawlings는 1953년에 세상을 떠났고, 그녀가 Cross Creek에 소유한 땅은 Florida 주립 공원이 되어 그녀의 업적을 기리고 있다.

제 12 회 하프 모의고사 해설

문제편 p.049

ANSWER

01 ②	02 ④	03 ④	04 ③	05 ①
06 ②	07 ④	08 ②	09 ④	10 ④

01 ②

해설 The person이 문장의 주어이고 would stand가 동사이다. 따라서 주어인 The person을 수식하는 역할을 해야 하므로 ② acts를 acting으로 고쳐 써야 한다.

① 실현성이 희박한 일을 가정하는 조건절이므로, were to는 적절하게 사용되었다.

③ makes의 주어이면서 문장의 주어 역할을 해야 하므로, '~하는 것'이라는 의미의 선행사를 포함한 관계대명사 What은 적절하게 사용되었다.

④ 부정의 의미를 지닌 문장 뒤에서 연속적으로 부정의 의미를 나타내고 있으므로 Nor는 적절하게 사용되었다.

해석 우리는 신호의 힘에 대한 이상한 믿음을 가지고 있다. 차가 없는 행성에서 어떤 방문객이 지구를 방문하게 된다면, 그는 도로 위에 있는 이상한 페인트 칠에 정말 어리둥절해할지도 모른다. 아이들의 '빨간불, 초록불' 놀이를 기억하는가? 신호등 역할을 하는 사람은 다른 (놀이) 참가자들에게 등을 진 채로 서서 '초록불'이라고 말하곤 했다. (놀이) 참가자들은 앞으로 움직이곤 했다. 그리고 나서 그가 '빨간불'이라고 말하곤 휙 돌아섰다. 그가 여러분을 보기 전에 멈추지 않으면, 여러분은 '퇴장'당했다. 이 놀이를 가능하게 하는 것은 아이들이 항상 제 시간에 멈추지 않는다는 것이다. 실제 생활에서 어른들도 또한 그렇게 하지 않는데, 실제 생활에서는 '멈춰야 하나, 가야 하나?'와 같은 노란불 같은 것들이 있기 때문에 훨씬 더 복잡하다. 도로 위의 차선이나 공중에 있는 신호등은 도시가 고소당하지 않게 해 줄 수는 있지만, 운전자가 잘못된 행동을 하는 것을, 어쩌면 심지어는 누군가를 죽이는 것을 막기 위해서 아무것도 하는 것이 없다.

어휘 puzzled 어리둥절해하는 announce 말하다, 알리다
spin around 휙 돌아서다, 돌다 complicated 복잡한 sue 고소하다
misbehave 잘못된 행동을 하다

02 ④

해설 ④ The number of는 '~의 수'라는 의미의 표현이다. '많은' Whit best의 표현은 A number of라고 써야 한다.

① by far가 비교급인 larger를 올바르게 수식하고 있다.

② 비교급의 표현으로서 부정문에서 any more than으로 쓰면 '~와 마찬가지로 … 아니다'를 의미한다.

③ 4분의 3을 말하는 Three-quarters의 뒤에 전치사 of를 취하면 뒤에 나오는 명사가 동사의 수를 좌우하는 주어가 된다. 따라서 전치사 of 뒤에 나오는 what 명사절이 주어이므로 동사도 단수인 comes가 바르게 쓰였다.

어휘 evolve 진화하다, 발달하다
not A any more than B A도 B도 아니다(양자부정)
via ~을 통하여 the number of ~의 수 in order that ~하기 위하여
keep abreast ~에 뒤지지 않고 따라가다

03 ④

해석 내 친구는 나에게 몇 장의 초대권을 보내줬다.

어휘 complimentary 칭찬의, 무료의 splendid 멋진
enigmatic 수수께끼 같은 compatible 호환되는, 어울리는

04 ③

해석 만일 내가 신체적인 공격을 받는다면, 그것은 나로 하여금 상응하는 폭력을 동원해 보복하는 것을 허락할 것이다.

어휘 assault 기습 공격하다 endorse 승인하다 divulge 누설하다
assail 공격하다 resent 분개하다

05 ①

해석 ① A: 어제 본 영화는 어땠니?
B: 잠깐, 제발 내게 내용을 말하지 말아줘.
② A: James, 올해 네 목표는 뭐니?
B: 그게, 난 바이올린을 배우고 싶어.
③ A: Peter, 네 그룹 프로젝트는 어떻게 되어가고 있어?
B: 별로야. 그게 생각보다 더 어려워.
④ A: 네 모자 보기 좋은데. 어디서 샀니?
B: 지난 토요일에 벼룩시장에서 샀어.

06 ②

해설 글의 내용은 전문가용 장비는 그것을 설계하는 사람이 그 제품을 실제로 사용하는 사람이므로 일반 장비보다 더 사용하기 쉽고 간단한 경향을 보인다는 것이므로 빈칸에 들어갈 말로 가장 적절한 것은 ② '그 제품 자체를 사용할'이다.

① 구매자와 긴밀하게 작업할

③ 그들 자신의 작품을 만들도록 독려 될

④ 다양한 스타일의 제품을 생산할

해석 나는 소비자에게 판매되는 전자 장비와 전문가에게 판매되는 장비를 비교하는 것이 흥미롭다는 것을 알았다. 훨씬 더 비싸지만 전문 장비는 더 단순하고 사용하기 쉬운 경향이 있다. 가정용 비디오 레코더는 수많은 플래시 라이트, 많은 버튼과 설정, 그리고 시간을 설정하고 미래의 녹화를 프로그래밍하기 위한 복잡한 메뉴를 가지고 있다. 전문가용 녹음기는 필수품만 갖추고 있으므로 더 잘 작동하면서 사용하기가 더 쉽다. 이 차이는 부분적으로, 디자이너들이 그 제품 자체를 사용할 것이기 때문에 발생하고, 그래서 그들은 무엇이 중요하고, 그렇지 않은지 알게 된다. 장인들이 직접 만든 도구들은 모두 이런 특성을 가지고 있다. 하이킹 혹은 산악등반장비의 디자이너들은 어느 날 그들의 삶이 그들 자신의 디자인의 특징과 행태에 의존하고 있다는 것을 자기도 모르게 알게 될 것이다.

어휘 electronic 전자의 equipment 장비, 용품
professional 전문가, 전문직 종사자 flashing light 섬광등
program 설정하다 essentials 필수 사항 property 특징, 특성

07 ④

해설 ④ 앞에서는 Francis Galton의 시대 이래로 지능의 척도로 단순한 반응 시간을 사용했다는 내용이 나오고, ④ 다음에는 지능의 척도로 속도 외의 것이 있다고 말하고 있으므로, 글의 흐름에서 논리적 단절이 생긴다. 단순한 반응 시간 척도와 지능의 척도 사이의 상관관계의 정도가 약했다고 기술된 주어진 문장이 ④에 들어가면 앞뒤의 연결이 자연스러워짐을 알 수 있다. 그러므로 ④가 정답이다.

해석 지능에서 개인별 차이가 순전히 정보 처리 속도 하나만으로 추적되어 밝혀질 수 있다고 믿는 사람들은 단순한 반응 시간과 관련 과업을 이용하는 경향이 있어 왔다. 단순한 '반응 시간' 패러다임에서는, 자극이 제시된 다음에 개인이 단순히 가능한 한 빨리 한 가지 반응을 하도록 요구된다. 예를 들어 우리가 여러분에게 개구리 사진이 나타날 때마다 여러분의 키보드에 있는 스페이스 바를 누르라고 말할 수 있을 것이다. 그런 다음에, 우리는 여러분에게 펭귄, 물고기, 개구리, 기린, 그리고 개구리를 보여줄 수 있을 것이다. 여러분의 반응 시간은 개구리가 매번 보인 후에 여러분이 스페이스 바를 얼마나 빨리 누르는가에 의해 측정될 것이다. 이 패러다임은 심리측정학의 아버지인 Francis Galton의 시대 이래로 지능의 척도로 널리 사용되어 왔다. 그러한 초기의 지지에도 불구하고, 단순한 반응 시간 척도와 지능의 다양한 표준 척도 사이의 입수된 상관관계의 정도는 약했다. 지능에는 순전히 속도 한 가지보다 훨씬 더 많은 것이 있는 것 같다.

어휘 correlation 상관관계, 연관성 measure 척도, 조치
intelligence 지능 be traced back to ~로 추적되어 밝혀지다
sheer 순전한, 매우 얇은, 가파른 paradigm 패러다임, 이론의 틀
giraffe 기린 pure 순전한, 깨끗한

08 ②

해설 (A) 계속되는 불평등의 주된 요인이 앞에서 언급된 tax policy, greater overseas competition 등이 아니라고 한 후, 빈칸이 있는 문장에서 주된 요인에 해당하는 것이 무엇인지 말하고 있으므로, 빈칸에는 '그 대신'이 가장 적절하다.
(B) 대부분의 선진국에서 불평등이 심화되고 있는 경향에 대해 기술한 후, 스웨덴, 핀란드, 독일과 같은 선진국의 소득 불평등을 예로 들고 있으므로, 빈칸에는 '예를 들면'이 가장 적절하다.
그러므로 정답은 ②이다.

해석 지난 몇 십 년간 우리는 세금 정책의 변화, 더 커진 해외 경쟁, 지속적인 정부의 낭비, 그리고 월스트리트의 속임수를 보아왔다. 그러나 자료와 연구 결과를 볼 때, 우리는 이런 것들 중 어느 것도 증가하는 불평등의 주된 요인이 아니라고 결론을 내린다. 그 대신 주된 요인은 우리 경제 체제를 뒷받침해주는 기술에 있어서의 기하급수적인, 디지털화된, 복합적인 변화이다. 대부분의 선진국에서 유사한 경향이 분명하다는 사실이 이런 결론을 확고히 해준다. 예를 들면 스웨덴, 핀란드, 독일에서는 실제로 지난 20년에서 30년 동안 미국에서보다 소득 불평등이 더 급속히 심해졌다. 이런 국가들은 소득 분배에 있어 덜 불평등한 상태에서 시작했기 때문에 미국보다는 덜 불평등한 상태가 지속되었지만, 이런 내재적인 경향은 때로는 현저하게 서로 다른 기관, 정부 정책, 그리고 문화에 이르기까지 세계적으로 유사하다.

어휘 policy 정책 driver 요인, 추진 요인 inequality 불평등
combinatorial 복합의, 조합의, 결합의 solidify 확고히 하다
income 소득 distribution 분배 underlying 내재하는, 잠재적인
markedly 현저하게, 두드러지게 institution 기관

09 ④

해석 분명히, 도식적인 지식은 여러분의 이해를 이끌어 주고 기억할 수 없는 것들을 재구성할 수 있게 하여 여러분에게 도움을 준다. (C) 하지만 도식적인 지식은 또한 인식과 기억에 오류를 조장하여 여러분에게 해를 끼칠 수 있다. 게다가, 도식에 의해서 발생하는 오류의 '유형'은 상당히 예측 가능하다. 도식은 여러분의 경험의 광범위한 양식을 간추려 주며 그래서 본질적으로, 주어진 상황에서 어떤 것이 전형적이거나 평범한지 여러분에게 말해 준다는 것을 명심하라. (B) 따라서, 도식적인 지식에 대한 어떠한 의존이라 하더라도, 그것은 어떤 것이 '일반적'인 것인지에 대한 이러한 정보에 의해 형성될 것이다. 그러므로 어떤 상황이나 사건을 보면서 여러분이 알아차리지 못하는 것이 있으면, 여러분의 도식이 그 환경에서 일반적으로 무엇이 그 자리에 있는가에 관한 지식으로 이러한 '공백'을 채우도록 여러분을 이끌어 줄 것이다. (A) 마찬가지로, 여러분이 기억할 수 없는 것이 있으면, 여러분의 도식이 그 상황에서 무엇이 전형적인가에 관한 지식으로 그 공백을 채워 줄 것이다. 결과적으로, 도식에 의존하는 것은 불가피하게 세상을 실제보다 더 '평범한' 것으로 보이게 할 것이고, 과거를 실제 그랬던 것보다 더 '규칙적인' 것으로 보이게 할 것이다.

10 ④

해설 심지어 피라루쿠의 거친 비늘조차 귀중하게 여겨지며, 사포처럼 줄로 사용된다(Even the pirarucu's tough scales are considered valuable and are used as files, like sandpaper.)고 했으므로, 글의 내용과 일치하는 것은 ④이다.

해석 피라루쿠는 길이가 10피트에 이르고 무게는 400파운드가 넘는 세계에서 가장 큰 민물고기 중 하나이다. 그것은 진정한 강의 괴물이다! 그것의 크기 때문에 arapaima, 즉 '드래곤 피시'라고 불린다. 모든 물고기는 물속에서 숨 쉴 수 있다. 그렇지 않은가? 이것은 아니다. 물속에서 산소를 얻기 위해 아가미를 사용하는 대부분의 물고기와 달리, 피라루쿠는 공기를 들이마시기 위해 매 10분 정도마다 수면으로 올라와야 한다. 이는 이용 가능한 산소가 거의 없는 아마존강의 탁한 호수에서 그것이 생존하는 것을 돕는다. 피라루쿠는 토착 어민이 가장 좋아하는 음식 중 하나이다. 그 물고기의 모든 부위를 먹는다. 심지어 피라루쿠의 거친 비늘조차 귀중하게 여겨지며, 사포처럼 줄로 사용된다. 그러나 피라루쿠는 멸종 위기에 처해 있다. 이 멋진 거대한 물고기가 장래에 오랫동안 반드시 존재하게 하기 위해 오직 특정 토착민만이 매년 제한된 수의 피라루쿠를 잡는 것이 허락된다.

제 13 회 하프 모의고사 해설

문제편 p.053

ANSWER

01 ②	02 ②	03 ②	04 ④	05 ④
06 ①	07 ②	08 ②	09 ②	10 ④

01 ②

해설 (A) 주어인 The rest가 The rest of the nutrients를 가리키는 복수의 의미이므로 동사로 복수형인 are를 써야 한다.

(B) 「배수 (ten times) as ~ as ...」 구문으로 '…보다 (몇) 배 ~'의 의미를 나타내므로, as가 적절한 표현이다.

(C) 문장의 동사가 필요하므로 requires가 적절하다. requires를 쓰면 The cultivation of those feed crops는 주어, land ~ problems는 목적어가 되는 적절한 문장을 형성한다. requiring을 쓰면 requiring land ~ problems가 The cultivations ~ crops를 수식하게 되는데, 문장이 명사구로만 형성되어 적절하지 못하다.

그러므로 차례로 are, as, requires가 결합한 ②가 정답이다.

해석 식물 기반[채식 위주의] 식사는 지구가 더 쉽게 호흡하도록 해준다. 인간의 직접적 소비를 위한 작물 재배는 농장 동물을 살찌우기 위해 곡물이나 콩을 사용하는 것보다 훨씬 더 효율적이다. 소나 다른 동물이 섭취하는 영양분의 작은 부분만이 그 동물의 근육에 남아 있다. 나머지는 그 동물들의 움직임, 신진대사, 몸의 따뜻함, 그리고 다른 생명 기능에 동력을 공급하기 위해 다 사용된다. 몇십 년 전에 'Scientific American'은 1파운드의 베이컨을 만드는 데 콩으로부터 같은 양의 인공 베이컨을 만들기 위해 사용되는 것보다 (사료용 곡물의 형태로) 열 배나 많은 농경지가 필요하다고 보고했었다. 그런 사료용 작물의 재배는 토지와 물을, 그리고 환경 문제를 증가시키는 살충제와 다른 화학 물질을 필요로 한다.

어휘 cultivation 재배, 경작 crop 작물, 농작물
consumption 소비 efficient 효율적인, 능률적인 grain 곡물
fatten up ~을 살찌우다 nutrient 영양분 take in ~을 섭취하다
muscle 근육 crop land 농경지 feed grain 사료용 곡물

02 ②

해설 ② <A as B>는 'A라기보다는 B'를 의미하므로 사람의 재산을 의미하는 what he has가 A의 자리에, 사람의 인격을 의미하는 what he is가 B의 자리에 위치하는 것이 옳다. 따라서 not so much in what he has as in what he is라고 써야 한다.

① 동사인 leave가 간접목적어로 him, 직접목적어로 nothing to live on을 취하는 4형식의 문장이다. nothing이라는 명사를 to live on이 수식하고 있는데 '~을 먹고 살다'라고 할 때 live on의 형태를 취하므로 nothing to live on의 구문이 옳다.

③ '~함에 따라'를 의미하는 접속사 as로 시작되는 부사절이 올바르게 사용되고 있다.

④ '~이 부족한'을 의미하는 short of ~ 라는 표현이 사용되고 있고, '그래서, 그 결과'를 의미하는 부사절 접속사인 so that 역시 올바르게 사용되고 있다. '가능한 한'을 의미하는 원급 비교 형태의 표현인 <as 형용사/부사 원급 as possible>도 정확하게 사용되고 있다.

어휘 come to ~하게 되다 be short of ~이 부족하다

03 ②

해석 위 예시에 나타난 바와 같이, 그것은 포괄적인 용어로서 약 4가지 정도의 다른 의미를 갖는다.

어휘 comprehensive 포괄적인 understandable 이해될 만한
broad 광범위한 apprehensive 걱정하는

04 ④

해석 그들은 그 진술에 동의했다.

어휘 assent 동의하다(= consent) resent 화내다
object 반대하다 pretend ~인 체하다

05 ④

해석 ① A: 회사에서 긴 하루를 보낸 후, 나는 정말 피곤해.
B: 나도 마찬가지야!

② A: 우리가 지난 금요일에 갔던 술집 이름 기억나?
B: 이런, 생각이 날 듯 말 듯해.

③ A: 이 영화를 보게 되서 너무 신나.
B: 나도 그래. 그 영화는 모든 비평가들로부터 최고의 평점을 받았어.

④ A: 몸이 좀 안 좋아.
B: 사실 지금은 비가 안 와.

06 ①

해설 글의 내용이 로스쿨은 대학에서 건물이나 도서관, 학사 일정에 있어서 다른 분야와는 분리되어 독자적으로 존재해 왔다는 것을 지적하고 있으므로 빈칸에 가장 적절한 말은 ① '독자적인 영역이다'이다.

② 항상 분명해야 한다

③ 사람들이 올바르게 행동하기를 요구한다

④ 정의에 부합한다

해석 전통적으로 로스쿨은 대학교에서 다른 단과대학으로부터 거리를 유지하는 경향이 있어 왔으며 주로 그들만의 건물을 갖고 있다. 법학 도서관은 다른 대학 도서관으로부터 분리되어 있고 법률과 관련된 문헌들 외에 다른 것은 거의 가지고 있지 않는데, (이는) 법과 다른 지식 체제와의 정보상의 거리를 조성하는 환경인 것이다. 학생들의 분리도 거의 절대적이었다. 법학의 학부 프로그램은 좀처럼 없다. 법학 수업은 거의 전적으로 로스쿨 학생으로 채워져 있으며, 이 학생들도 또한 로스쿨 밖에서는 아무것(수업)도 듣지 않는다. 적어도 내가 속한 대학(기관)에서는 법학 강좌들이 별도의 일정표에 올라와 있고 로스쿨은 심지어 그 대학교의 나머지 다른 대학과는 다른 학사 일정표를 따른다. 3년 동안 이러한 분리된 세계에 빠져 있던 변호사가 법은 독자적인 영역이라는 신념을 가지고 나아가는 것은 그리 놀랄 일이 아니다.

어휘 separate 분리된 literature 문헌
promote 조성하다, 촉진하다 undergraduate 학부

be peopled with (사람들로) 가득 채워지다 exclusively 전적으로
in turn 또한, 번갈아 institution 기관 timetable 일정표, 시간표
academic calendar 학사 일정표 go forth 나아가다, 시작하다
domain 영역 unto oneself 독립하여, 독자적인

07 ②

해설 애완동물을 얻는 다양한 출처를 설명하고 있는 글이다. 주어진 문장은 애완동물의 유형과 그것을 얻는 장소의 사례로서, 바닷물고기가 들어 있는 수조나 청개구리와 같은 흔치 않은 것은 전문 애완동물 소매점에서만 구입할 수 있다는 내용을 담고 있다. 'For more common companion animal species'로 시작되는 ② 이후에는 더 흔한 반려동물에 있어서는 선택할 수 있는 장소가 많다는 것과 구체적인 장소들이 언급되어 있다. 그러므로 주어진 문장이 들어가기에 가장 적절한 곳은 ②이다.

해석 사람들은 다양한 장소로부터 그리고 많은 다양한 상황 하에서 애완동물을 얻는다. 여러분이 집으로 가져오는 데 관심을 갖고 있는 동물의 유형은 여러분이 애완동물을 얻게 되는 장소에 크게 영향을 줄 수 있다. 예를 들어, 바닷물고기 수조나 특정 유형의 청개구리를 얻는 데 관심이 있다면, 여러분은 전문 애완동물 소매점에 한정될 것이다. 더 흔한 반려동물 종에 있어서는 선택의 여지가 엄청날 것이다. 가장 흔히 이용되는 애완동물의 출처들 중 일부에는 동네에서 '길 잃은 동물'을 들여오는 것뿐만 아니라 친구나 친척, 동물 육종가, 동물 보호소, 신문, 온라인 출처, 그리고 애완동물 판매점과 대형 매장 등이 포함된다. 하지만 알맞은 동물을 찾기 위한 모든 공급원이 동등하게 되어 있지 않아서, 이러한 선택권들 거의 모두에 긍정적인 면과 부정적인 면이 있을 수 있다. 애완동물을 찾는 데 가장 흔히 사용되는 출처에 대한 일반적인 장단점을 잘 알아두는 것이 이러한 결정을 내리는 데 있어서 여러분과 여러분 가족에게 유용할 수 있다.

어휘 saltwater fish 바닷물고기 tree frog 청개구리
specialty 전문 retail store 소매점 circumstance 상황
companion animal 반려동물 overwhelming 엄청난, 압도적인
animal breeder 동물 육종가, 동물 사육자
animal shelter 동물 보호소 superstore 대형 매장
stray 길을 잃은 동물, 주인이 없는 동물
be informed of ~을 잘 알고 있다, ~에 정통하다
pros and cons 장단점, 찬반양론

08 ②

해설 (A) 여성 농부의 소득이 남성 농부의 소득보다 더 적은 요인이 교육이나 능력이 아니라 여성을 제한하는 사회 문화적 요인 때문이라는 내용이 연결되므로, 빈칸에는 '오히려'가 가장 적절하다.
(B) 땅의 소유가 불가능해서 농업 증진 프로그램과 계획에서 여성이 배제된다는 내용을 아프리카의 농업 개발 프로그램의 사례를 통해 설명하고 있으므로, 빈칸에는 '예를 들어'가 가장 적절하다.
그러므로 ②가 정답이다.

해석 보통 여성 농부는 남성 농부보다 일은 더 오래 하고 소득은 더 적다. 이것은 그들이 교육을 더 적게 받았거나 덜 능숙하기 때문이 아니다. 오히려 그것은 (여성을) 제한하는 사회 문화적 요인 때문이다. 우선, 대부분의 여성 농부는 자급적 농업이나 현금 수익을 거의 만들어내지 못하는 지역 시장을 위한 식량 생산에 종사한다. 둘째, 그들은 남성보다 은행의 신용거래 이용 기회가 더 적다. 그들이 잡종 종자와 비료 같은 '녹색 혁명' 기술을 습득할 수 있게 해 줄 수 있을 국고 보조 이율 또한 비교적 여성은 이용하기가 어렵다. 셋째, 몇몇 사회에서 여성은 땅을 소유할 수 없고 그래서 지주들을 목표로 한 농업 증진 프로그램과 계획에서 배제된다. 예를 들어 아프리카의 많은 농업 개발 프로그램은 공동 토지를 개인 보유지로 전환하는 것을 토대로 한다. 여성이 공동 토지는 이용할 수 있지만, 개인 보유지(를 소유하는 것으)로부터는 배제되기 때문에 이 전환은 여성에게 불리하게 영향을 끼친다.

어휘 as a rule 보통, 대체로 competent 능숙한, 유능한
restrict 제한하다, 방해하다 access 이용 기회[권리] credit 신용거래
subsidize 보조금을 주다 rate 이율, 비율 acquire 습득하다, 얻다
hybrid seed 잡종 종자 fertilizer 비료 comparatively 비교적
inaccessible 이용하기 어려운 exclude 배제하다, 제외하다
agricultural 농업의 landowner 지주 conversion 전환, 개조
holding 보유 자산, 소장 자산 adversely 불리하게, 반대로

09 ②

해설 주어진 글은 보통 일벌들이 알을 낳지 않는 현상을 제시한다. (B)에서 However로 흐름을 바꾸어, 절박한 상황을 제시하고 (C)에서 In that case로 연결해 그 상황에서 일벌들이 알을 낳기 시작하게 된다는 내용을 제시한다. (A)에서 they로 (C)의 some of the workers를 받아, 일벌들이 수벌만을 낳게 되는 상황을 설명하는 흐름으로 글이 이어지는 것이 가장 적절하다.

해석 일벌들은 '보통은' 알을 낳지 않는다. 그것은 여왕벌의 페로몬이 일벌들의 생식계를 억제하기 때문이다. (B) 그러나, 만일 여왕벌이 죽고 그 여왕벌을 대체하도록 훈련될 수 있는 유충이 없으면, 그것은 바뀔 수 있다. 양봉업자가 새로운 여왕벌을 가지고 개입하지 않는다면, 그 벌집은 운이 다한 것이다. (C) 그 경우, 여왕벌이 없게 된 소멸되어가는 군체는 그것이 운명을 다하기 전에 예상치 못한 전략을 사용하여 유전자를 퍼뜨리려 하는데, 그것은 일벌 중 일부가 알을 낳기 시작하는 것이다. (A) 그러나, 그것들은 짝짓기하지 않았기 때문에, 그것들의 수정되지 않은 알은 오직 수벌만 생기게 한다. 아마 그것들 중 몇몇은 운이 좋아서 적극적인 여왕벌을 찾아, 죽어가는 꿀벌 떼의 유전자를 전하게 될 것이다.

10 ④

해설 55개 줄의 반원형의, 단으로 배열된 좌석이 언덕 경사면을 깎아서 만들어졌다(Fifty-five rows of semicircular tiered seats were carved into a hillside, ...)라고 했으므로, 글의 내용과 일치하는 것은 ④이다.

해석 Epidaurus 극장은 일반 대중이 즐기도록 의도된 고대 그리스 시민 건축물의 한 사례였다. 극장 예술은 고대 그리스 문화와 종교의 중요한 부분이었는데, 그 이유는 종교 의식이 음악 및 무용과 결합되어 있었고 공공장소에서 행해졌기 때문이다. 비극과 희극을 포함하여 그리스 연극은 Epidaurus 극장과 같은 야외 장소에서 공연되었다. 극장의 중심부에는 중앙 공연장인 원형의 orchestra가 있었다. 55개 줄의 반원형의, 단으로 배열된 좌석이 언덕 경사면을 깎아서 만들어졌는데, 이것은 14,000명이나 되는 관객들이 orchestra를 잘 볼 수 있게 해 주었다. Epidaurus 극장의 디자인은 매우 효율적이어서 오늘날에도 여전히 사용되고 있으며 음향 효과는 너무나 완벽하여 그곳에서 공연이 이루어질 때 전기 음향 장치가 필요하지 않다.

ANSWER

01 ④	02 ④	03 ③	04 ②	05 ④
06 ②	07 ④	08 ③	09 ③	10 ④

01 ④

해설 (A) would come 앞에 나온 내용이 주어의 역할을 해야 하므로 주어부를 이끌 수 있는 형태인 동명사 Examining을 써야 한다.
(B) 'Picasso's Guernica, a huge (11-ft.×25.6-ft.) painting in black, white, and grey'를 선행사로 하는 관계대명사 that을 써야 한다. what은 선행사를 포함하는 관계대명사이므로 여기에 쓸 수 없다.
(C) 주어인 Images가 복수이므로 dominate를 써야 한다.

해석 한 전통적 정의에 따르면, '미학'은 아름다움, 특히 예술에서의 아름다움을 다루는 철학의 분야이다. 예를 들어, '모나리자'나 꼭대기가 눈으로 덮인 산이 주는 즐거운 특징들을 살펴보는 것이 미학의 범위에 포함될 것이다. 그렇지만, 예술 작품들과 자연물들이 아름답다는 것에 의한 것 외에 다른 방식으로 우리의 관심을 끌 수 있으므로 그러한 정의는 너무 좁아 보인다. 아름다움에 대한 감탄을 불러일으키는 대신에, 예술가들은 어리둥절함, 충격, 심지어 혐오감을 불러일으킬 수도 있다. 스페인 내란 동안에 있었던 독일과 이탈리아의 전투기들에 의한 스페인 시민 대량 학살에 대한 반응으로 피카소가 그린 검은색, 흰색, 회색으로 이루어진 거대한(11피트×25.6피트) 그림인 피카소의 '게르니카'에 대해 생각해 보자. 해체된 시신들과 소리치는 사람들의 이미지가 캔버스를 지배한다. 이 작품은 널리 칭송되고 있으나 아름답기 때문이 아니다. 그러므로 미학에 대한 더 나은 정의는, 미학이란 사물이 경험되면서 사람들을 즐겁게 하는 방식을 다루는 철학의 분야라는 것이 될 것이다.

어휘 definition 정의, 의미 aesthetics 미학
snow-capped 꼭대기가 눈에 덮인 evoke 불러일으키다
admiration 감탄, 존경 puzzlement 어리둥절함, 얼떨떨함
disgust 혐오감, 역겨움 disjoint 해체하다 corpse 시체, 송장
dominate 지배하다

02 ④

해설 ④ to control과 동명사 making이 등위접속사 and로 연결되었다. 등위접속사로 연결할 때는 병렬 구조를 이루어야 하므로 문법적으로 형태가 같아야 한다.
① 'When the dinner was ready ~'의 부사절을 분사구문으로 전환한 형태이다. 접속사인 When을 생략하고 주어인 the dinner가 주절의 주어와 일치하지 않으므로 남겨둔 후, 동사인 was, 즉 be동사에 -ing를 붙여 바르게 전환하였다.
② who 이하는 간접의문문이다. 주어는 that, 동사는 is이므로 간접의문문 어순인 의문사(who) + 주어(that) +동사(is)의 구문으로 바르게 사용되었다.
③ 부정부사인 rarely는 '거의 ~하지 않는'의 의미로 다른 부정부사와 함께 쓰지 않는다. 또한 prove는 불완전자동사로 뒤에 형용사 보어를 취할 수 있다. 보어인 fatal이 형용사로 바르게 사용되었다.

어휘 dining hall 식당 fatal 치명적인 process 과정
improvement 발전, 진전 objective 목표, 목적

03 ③

해석 그 정부는 선거 결과가 나오자마자 패배를 인정했다.

어휘 concede 인정하다, 양보하다 compromise 타협하다
conceal 은닉하다 modify 수정하다

04 ②

해석 두 대륙이 비슷하다고 추측하는 것은 잘못된 생각이다.

어휘 assume 가정하다, 받아들이다 pretend ~인 체하다
suppose 가정하다 assert 단언하다 assemble 모으다

05 ④

해설 ④ A: 지루하면 함께 농구하자.
B: 그들이 오기를 원하는지를 그들에게 물어 보고 있었다.
의미상 통하지 않는다. 문맥상 적절한 표현은 'You took the words out of my mouth.'(나도 똑같은 말을 하려고 했다)이다.

06 ②

해설 동물의 각 기관이 각자 기능을 하면서 전체로서의 동물의 생존과 건강에 이바지하는 것처럼 사회의 각 구성 요소도 각자의 기능을 수행하면서 전체 사회의 생존과 안정에 이바지한다는 것이 Herbert Spencer의 관점이다. 따라서 빈칸에 들어갈 말로 가장 적절한 것은 ② '하나의 유기체인 사회의 일부분'이다.
① 정체성을 표현하는 수단
③ 안전을 보장하는 사회적 장치
④ 생존을 위한 다양한 형태의 인간의 노력

해석 영국의 사회학자인 Herbert Spencer는 어떻게 사회가 작동하는가에 관한 (이전의 사회학자들과는) 다른 관점을 가지고 있었다. 그는 사회가 살아있는 유기체에 비유될 수 있다고 믿었다. 심장, 폐, 뇌 등등처럼 동물의 각 부위는 수행할 각자의 기능을 가지고 있지만, 모든 부위가 서로 의존하고 있어서 한 부위에서의 변화가 다른 모든 부위에 영향을 끼친다. 게다가, 각 부위는 전체로서의 동물의 생존과 건강에 이바지한다. 만약 한 기관이 병에 걸리면, 나머지 다른 기관들은 그 동물의 생존을 지키려고 더 열심히 작동함으로써 적응한다. 마찬가지로, Spencer의 관점에서, 사회의 각 부분은 각자의 기능을 수행하면서 전체의 생존과 안정에 이바지한다. 가족, 종교, 정부, 그리고 산업은 모두 하나의 유기체인 사회의 일부분으로 간주된다.

어휘 compare 비유하다 organism 유기체 lung 폐
perform 수행하다 interdependent 서로 의존하는
affect 영향을 끼치다 contribute to ~에 이바지하다 organ 기관
adapt 적응하다 ensure 지키다, 반드시 ~하게 하다 stability 안정
industry 산업

07 ④

해설 주어진 문장에서 '그 행동(that behavior)'이 가져오는 부정적인 결과를 역접의 연결사 But이 이끌고 있으므로, 그 앞에는 긍정적인 내용이 등장했다고 추측할 수 있다. 그러므로 주어진 문장이 들어가기에 가장 적절한 곳은 ④이다.

해석 자기파멸적 행동은 삶이 우리에게 알려주고자 하는 가르침을 우리가 배우지 못할 때 일어난다. 그것은 충동이 자각을 이기고, 즉각적 희열이 지속적 만족감을 이기며, (고통의) 경감이 해결을 이긴다는 것을 나타낸다. 자기파멸적 행동은 보통 우리 자신의 기분을 더 나아지게 하려는 노력으로 시작된다. 그것은 하나의 대응 기제이다. 위기, 위협 또는 잠재적으로 혼란스러운 상황에 직면했을 때, 우리는 우리 자신을 보호하려 한다. 우리는 긴장을 덜어주거나 우리가 다치지 않게 해줄 무언가를 단단히 붙잡는다. 그 행동 자체가 당시에는 타당하고 적절해 보이며, 실제로도 그것은 단기적인 (고통의) 경감을 유발하는 데 성공할지 모른다. 하지만 그 행동은 항상 되돌아와 우리를 괴롭힌다. 그러면 실은 우리가 위협적이거나 혼란스러운 상황 중에서 단순히 균형감을 잃었을 뿐인데도 우리는 어리석거나 바보스럽거나 약하다고 자신에게 악담을 하게 된다.

어휘 haunt 괴롭히다, 문제를 일으키다 impulse 충동
relief (고통, 걱정 등의) 경감, 완화, 제거 resolution 해결
attempt 노력, 시도 coping mechanism 대응 기제
upsetting 혼란스러운 grasp for ~을 단단히 붙잡다
appropriate 적절한 bring about ~을 유발하다, 초래하다
curse 악담하다, 욕하다 in truth 실은, 사실은
perspective 균형감, 시각, 견지
in the midst of ~하는 중에, ~의 한가운데에 threatening 위협적인

08 ③

해설 (A) 앞에서 공공정책을 만드는 데 관심이 있는 사람들이 대중의 필요와 요구를 이해하고 대중을 보호하기 위해 소비자 행동을 연구한다고 했으며, (A) 뒤에서는 포장 식품 산업에서 화학물질이나 방부제의 사용을 늘렸으며 소비자들이 가공식품 속에 포함된 성분에 대해 더욱 관심을 갖게 된 것을 예로 들고 있으므로 (A)에는 For example이 적절하다. (B) 앞에는 소비자들이 건강상의 위험과 영양에 대한 관심으로 가공식품 속에 포함된 성분에 대해 더욱 관심을 가지게 되었다고 말하고, (B) 뒤에서는 이러한 관심의 결과로 미국식품의약국 규정이 식품 판매업체에게 영양성분표를 요구하게 되었다는 내용이 나오므로 (B)에는 As a result가 가장 적절하다.
그러므로 정답은 ③이다.

해석 소비자를 위한 공공정책은 소비자를 보호하기 위해, 사업 관행에 적용되는 법과 규정을 제정하는 것이다. 공공정책을 만드는 데 관심이 있는 사람들은 대중의 필요와 요구를 이해하고, 동시에 부당하거나 비윤리적이거나 위험한 사업 관행으로부터 대중을 보호하기 위해, 소비자 행동을 연구한다. 예를 들어, 포장 식품 산업에서 제조업체들이 좀 더 오래가고 더 편리한 형태의 포장 식품을 개발해옴에 따라 화학물질과 방부제의 사용이 꾸준히 증가해 왔다. 이에 대한 반응으로 소비자들은, 가공식품의 잠재적인 건강상의 위험과 합성 첨가물이 영양에 미치는 영향 때문에 가공식품 속에 포함된 성분에 대해 점점 더 큰 관심을 가져왔다. 그 결과로, 미국 식품의약국 규정은 현재 식품 판매업체에게 '영양성분표'의 형태로 식품 포장지에 영양 정보를 제공할 것을 요구한다.

어휘 establishment 제정, 확립 regulation 규정
govern (법 등이) ~에 적용되다, 지배하다 practice 관행, 관례
unethical 비윤리적인 preservative 방부제
manufacturer 제조업체, 생산 회사 ingredient 성분, 재료
potential 잠재적인 consequence 영향, 결과
u.s. food and drug administration (fda) 미국식품의약국
nutrition facts label 영양성분표

09 ③

해설 주어진 문장에서 입지가 부동산의 시장 가치를 결정한다고 했고, (C)에서 어떻게 한 장소가 다른 장소에 비해 나아지게 되는가 물으며 자연적인 이점을 그 답으로 제시했고, (A)에서는 앞서 언급한 자연적 이점을 'These natural advantages'라고 하며 그것이 부동산 가격을 상승시킨다 했고, (B)에서 앞서 언급한 방식을 'In this way'라고 하며 주변 지역까지 부동산 가격이 상승된다고 했다. 따라서 (C) - (A) - (B)의 흐름으로 글이 이어지는 것이 가장 적절하다.

해석 부동산 업계에서, 입지는 부동산의 시장가치를 결정하는데 있어 매우 중요하다. 빈민가 지역에 있는 좋은 집은 아무리 좋은 집이라도 비싼 가격으로 팔리지 않을 것이다. (C) 하지만 어째서 일부 장소들이 다른 장소들보다 더 나아지게 되는가? 대개 그 것은 자연적인 이점과 함께 시작된다. 한 지역이 편리하게 주요사업체 근처에 위치해 있거나, 바다나 강 근처에 있거나, 약간의 언덕이 있어, 좋은 전망을 제공할 수 있다. (A) 이러한 자연적인 이점들은 사람들이 그것들을 많은 노력을 기울여 찾아내어 다른 부동산보다 조금 더 많은 돈을 지불하기에 충분하다. 일부 부동산들이 높은 가격을 유인하면, 그들은 근처의 다른 부동산의 가격을 상승시킨다. (B) 이러한 방식으로, 한 지역의 평균 가격은 서서히 변해서 인근 지역에서보다 더 비싸지게 될 것이다. 사람들은 당연히 가격이 더 높은 지역이 살기에 분명 더 좋을 것이라고 생각한다. 그렇게 해서 그 과정은 강화된다.

10 ④

해설 땅에서는 두 개의 뒷발을 이용하여 옆으로 깡충깡충 뛰어 이동한다고 했으므로 ④가 글의 내용과 일치하지 않는다.

해석 Verreaux's sifaka는 Madagascar 남서쪽 숲에 산다. 이 종은 대략 12마리까지의 개체 수로 구성되는 작은 무리를 지어 산다. 무리는 거의 동등한 수의 다 자란 수컷과 암컷을 포함한다. 무리는 작은 영역을 방어한다. 그들은 영역의 경계를 표시하기 위해 자신의 냄새를 이용한다. sifaka는 건기가 한창인 12월에 짝짓기를 한다. 단 한 마리의 새끼가 5개월 후에 태어나며 7개월 후에 젖을 뗀다. sifaka는 뛰어올라서 나무들 사이를 헤집고 이동한다. 그들이 점프할 수 있는 거리는 그 동물의 짧은 팔뚝 아래의 작은 날개 모양의 피부에 의해 약간 증대된다. 땅 위에서, sifaka는 두 개의 뒷발로 옆쪽으로 깡충깡충 뛰어 이동한다. 팔뚝은 균형을 위해 옆쪽으로 내민다. Verreaux's sifaka는 뿌리를 제외하고 온갖 종류의 식물성 물질을 먹는다. 우기에는 쉽게 소화되는 부드러운 과일과 꽃을 먹기를 선호하지만 건기에는 나무, 나무껍질과 잎에 의존한다.

제 15 회 하프 모의고사 해설

문제편 p.061

ANSWER

01 ②	02 ④	03 ③	04 ①	05 ③
06 ④	07 ②	08 ②	09 ①	10 ④

01 ②

해설 (A) '…하는 것은 단지 과학에서뿐만이 아니다'라는 의미를 나타내려면 「It is ~ that ...」 강조 구문이 사용되어야 하므로 that이 적절하다.
(B) '~부터 …까지'라는 의미의 「from ~ to ...」가 사용된 구조이므로 전치사 to 뒤에서 동명사인 identifying을 써야 적절하다.
(C) '아주 ~해서 …하다'라는 뜻의 「so ~ that ...」이 사용된 구조에서 형용사인 persuasive를 수식하는 역할을 해야 하므로 부사인 powerfully가 적절하다.

해석 우리가 논리를 사용하고 오용하는 것은, 물론, 단지 과학에서뿐만이 아니다. 논리는 우리가 우리의 사고를 정리하고 세상을 이해하는 방식이다. 선과 그림자의 특정한 배열을 입체적 상자로 인지하는 것에서부터 얼굴이 우호적 또는 적대적이라고 인식하는 것에 이르기까지, 성장하면서 우리의 눈은 우리가 보는 것들을 해석하는 법을 배운다. 따라서 논리는 우리가 세상을 살아가는 방법을 찾는 데 도움을 준다. 논리적 논쟁은 또한, 만약 우리가 논리를 사용하는 것이 양호하다면, 우리의 이해가 실제로 옳은지를 점검해보는 귀중한 방법이다. 그리고 물론, 그것은 우리의 생각을 다른 사람들에게 정당화시키는 매우 효과적인 방법이 될 수 있다. 정말로, 논리는 매우 강력하게 설득력이 있는 것처럼 보일 수 있어서 우리 모두는 그것을 우리의 일상 대화에서 항상 사용한다.

어휘 misuse 오용하다, 남용하다 make sense of ~을 이해하다
recognize 인지하다, 알아보다 arrangement 배열
three-dimensional 입체적인, 삼차원의 identify 인식하다, 확인하다
friendly 우호적인 hostile 적대적인 invaluable 귀중한
insight 이해, 통찰력 justify 정당화하다 persuasive 설득력 있는

02 ④

해설 ④ <it - that ...> 강조 구문이다. 우리말에서 '~이 아니고, ~이다'를 영어로 옮기면 <not A but B> 구문이 되어야 한다. 따라서 not 뒤로 the strongest of the species, '또한 아닌'을 의미하는 nor 뒤로 the most intelligent가 언급된 후, or가 아닌 but이 위치해야 한다.
① 기억동사 remember는 to부정사와 동명사를 모두 목적어로 취할 수 있다. 하지만 이미 한 것을 기억한다고 표현할 때는 동명사, 앞으로 할 것을 기억하고 있다고 표현할 때는 to부정사를 취한다. 과거의 일을 기억하는 것이므로 remember 뒤로 동명사 형태인 meeting이 옳다. <take + 간접목적어 + 직접목적어>로 표현하면 '~에게 …만큼의 시간이 걸리게 하다'라는 의미가 된다. 또한 가주어 it과 진주어 to부정사가 옳게 사용되었다.
③ my umbrella의 안쪽이 바깥쪽으로 뒤집힌 것이므로 inside out은 알맞다. home은 '집으로'를 의미하는 부사로 완전자동사 walk 뒤에 바르게 쓰였다.

03 ③

해석 많은 수의 유명한 상원의원들이 숙련된 조정자이다.

어휘 conciliator 조정자(= arbitrator) parliamentarian 하원의원
mediator 중재자

04 ①

해석 Smith 씨는 4명의 임원으로 구성된 팀과 함께 CEO 역할을 맡게 될 것이다.

어휘 assume ~를 떠맡다(= take on) undertake 떠맡다
presume 가정하다 efface 지우다 take down 받아 적다

05 ③

해설 ③의 A가 '리조또는 어떠냐?'고 물었기 때문에, B는 '맛있다/없다' 등의 대답이 선행이 되어야 한다. 동시에 yes 또는 no는 의문사가 포함된 문장에 대한 답으로 옳지 않다.

해석 ① A: 내일로 예약하고 싶어요.
B: 네. 몇 시를 원하세요?
② A: 주문하시겠어요?
B: 네, 수프로 할게요.
③ A: 당신의 리조또 어때요?
B: 네, 우리는 버섯과 치즈가 들어간 리조또를 먹어요.
④ A: 디저트 드시겠어요?
B: 저는 괜찮아요, 감사해요.

06 ④

해설 빈칸을 포함한 문장 다음에 제시되는 두 가지 예에서, 자신이 바라는 직업 변경을 실제로 이룬 사람들을 만나볼 것을 조언하고 있으므로, 빈칸에 들어갈 말로 가장 적절한 것은 ④ '자신이 향하기를 바라는 곳과 일치하는'이다.
① 창의적 정신을 고취하는
② 한 단계를 넘는 단계를 포함하는
③ 달성하기에 불가능한 것처럼 보이는

해석 우리 세계관의 한계를 벗어날 수 있는 최고의 방법 중의 하나는 우리의 동료 집단을 바꾸어, 경력과 일상의 삶이 우리 자신의 것과는 아주 다른 사람들과 이야기해 보는 것이다. 여러분이 정말로 새로운 직업을 추구하고 싶다면, 비록 현재의 동료들이 좋은 사람들이더라도 그들과 시간을 덜 보내는 것이 현명할지도 모른다. 더 구체적으로 말하자면, 여러분은 자신이 향하기를 바라는 곳과 일치하는 직업 변경을 한 사람들과 대화를 가짐으로써 막대한 것을 배울 수 있다. 여러분이 정말로 Steiner 학교에서 가르치는 일에 마음이 끌린다면, 한때 변호사나 의사였던 Steiner 학교 교사를 찾아 그들을 점심 자리로 데려갈 수 있는가? 여러분이 지루해 하는 교수이고 정원 디자이너가 되기를 바라고 있다면, 여러분은 이와 같은 변화를, 아니면 어떤 다른 큰 변화를 이룬 동료 학자를 찾기 위해 할 수 있는 모든 일을 해야 한다.

어휘 escape 벗어나다, 모면하다 confine 한계
shift 바꾸다, 이동하다 pursue 추구하다 career 직업

current 현재의 colleague 동료 company 함께 있는 사람들
specifically 구체적으로 enormous 막대한 academic 교수

07 ②

해설 주어진 문장은 생활 연령과 생물학적 연령의 차이를 설명하기 전에 위치하는 것이 자연스럽다. 또한, 주어진 문장에서 'this apparent variation (이러한 외견상의 차이)'이 가리키는 바는 사람들 간에 나타나는 노화 속도의 차이를 가리킨다. 그러므로 주어진 문장이 들어가기에 가장 적절한 곳은 ②이다.

해석 '노화'는 우리가 항상 쓰는 단어라서, 우리는 막연히 그것이 무슨 뜻인지에 대해 어느 정도의 생각을 하고는 있지만, 우리가 조금 더 정확해지려고 하는 바로 그때 문제가 시작된다. 예를 들어, 어느 인구 집단 내에서 어떤 사람들은 빨리 나이를 먹는 것처럼 보이고, 또 어떤 사람들은 더 느리게 나이를 먹는 것처럼 보인다. 노화의 속도에 있어서 이러한 외견상의 차이를 설명하기 위해, 과학자들은 '생활' 연령과 '생물학적' 연령을 구별하는 것을 좋아한다. 생활 연령은 단순한 시간의 흐름, 즉 생일 케이크 위에 있는 양초의 개수로 측정된다. 생물학적 연령은 출생부터 고령으로 인한 죽음에 이르기까지의 길을 얼마나 멀리 여행해 왔는지를 표현하려 한다. 생활 연령상으로는 60세이지만 일반적인 50세가 가진 외모와 체력을 가진 여성은 평균보다 더 느린 생물학적 노화 속도를 갖고 있을지 모른다. 하지만 생물학적 연령은 측정하기가 그렇게 쉬운 개념은 아니며, 의학과 생물학에서 노화란 정말로 무엇인가에 대한 정의는 수년 동안 전문가들을 괴롭혀왔다.

어휘 apparent 외견상의, 얼핏 보아 ~같은 variation 차이, 변화
rate 속도 distinction 구별 fair 어느 정도의, 상당한
in general terms 막연히, 일반적인 말로 precise 정확한
chronological age 생활 연령(한 사람이 실제 산 햇수)
measure 측정하다 stamina 체력 typical 일반적인, 보통의

08 ②

해설 (A) 앞에서 고등학교에 관한 영화가 깊이 관심을 두지 않는 관객에게 단순한 오락거리에 지나지 않는다고 말했고 (A) 뒤에서 전체적으로 살펴볼 때, 고등학교 영화 장르가 오락을 뛰어넘어 미국 문화에 대해 가르침을 준다고 했으므로 (A)에는 역접의 연결사 however가 적절하다.
(B) 앞에서 고등학교 영화가 문화적으로 의미가 있다고 말했으며, (B) 뒤에서 고등학교 영화가 미국인들이 교육, 청소년기, 계층의 불평등에 대해 어떻게 이해하는가를 우리에게 가르쳐 줄 수 있다고 했으므로 앞에서 한 말에 대해 표현을 다르게 하여 말할 때 사용하는 연결사 That is가 (B)에 들어가야 한다. 그러므로 정답은 ②이다.

해석 깊이 관심을 두지 않는 관객에게 고등학교에 관한 영화는 단순한 오락거리에 지나지 않을 수 있다. 그러나 영화를 전체적으로 살펴볼 때, 고등학교 영화 장르는 오락을 넘어서 미국 문화에 대한 더 깊은 교훈을 가르치는 패턴을 보여준다. 영화가 반드시 고등학교의 경험을 정확하게 반영하는 것은 아니다. 할리우드는 통상적으로 극적이거나 코믹한 효과를 극대화하기 위해 현실을 왜곡하고 꾸며낸다. 영화는 또한 두 시간 내에 이차원의 캔버스[스크린]에 복잡한 사회적 관계들을 표현해야 한다. 그럼에도 불구하고, 비록 영화가 실제 고등학교와 실제 청소년의 정확한 사회적 기록은 아니라 할지라도, 이러한 고등학교 영화는 여전히 문화적으로 의미가 있다. 다시 말해서, 이런 영화들은 미국인들이 교육, 청소년기, 그리고 계층의 불평등을 어떻게 이해하는지에 관해서 우리에게 가르침을 줄 수 있는 어떤 것을 가지고 있는 것이다.

어휘 collectively 전체적으로, 집합적으로 reflect 반영하다
twist 왜곡하다, 비틀다 maximize 극대화하다
frame 표현하다, 틀에 넣다 complicated 복잡한
two-dimensional 이차원의 precise 정확한 adolescent 청소년
make sense of ~을 이해하다 adolescence 청소년기

09 ①

해설 주어진 글은 여느 발달한 산업 분야와 마찬가지로 건설 분야에도 선도적인 생각을 하는 사람들과 그들의 새로운 아이디어를 받아들이고 전파하는 기술 전문가 집단이 있다는 내용이다. 기술 전문가 집단의 구성원과 집단의 소규모적 특징을 설명하는 (B)가 주어진 글 다음에 이어지고, 매체의 막대한 주목을 받지만 실제 건설 현장에서는 그들의 혁신이 반영되지 않는다는 내용과 그 이유를 설명하는 (A)가 온 후, 그 이유에 대해 부가적으로 설명하고 있는 (C)가 연결되는 것이 가장 자연스럽다.

해석 충분히 발달한 산업의 모든 분야와 마찬가지로, 건설 분야는 동향[유행]을 혁신하고 탐지하는 비교적 소수의 선도적인 생각을 하는 사람들과 혁신과 새로운 아이디어를 받아들이고 전파하는 그보다 더 큰 무리의 기술 전문가들로 특징지어진다. (B) 이 전파하는 집단은 건축가, 상담역[컨설턴트], 설계자, 엔지니어로 구성되어 있다. 건설 분야에서 이 전파하는 집단은 매우 작고, 비교적 보수적이며, 여러 집단으로 나뉘어 있다. (A) 그러나 그 집단, 특히 건축가들은, 혁신과 진보적인 사고를 함에 있어 매체의 막대한 주목을 받는다. 하지만 대부분의 건설 공사에 있어서, 그렇게 높은 수준의 기술적인 정교함은 불필요하며, 비용이 많이 들기 때문에 지지받지 못한다. (C) 대부분 건물은 기능적인 목적을 위해 지어지는 것이지, 기술의 한계를 진전시키거나 탐구하기 위해 지어지지 않는다. 흥미롭거나 기교가 뛰어난 전면을 가진 실용적인 건물은 대부분 용도에 아주 충분하다.

10 ④

해설 그녀는 프랑스어를 독학했다(She taught herself French ~)고 했으므로 ④가 글의 내용과 일치하지 않는다.

해석 미국의 대통령 일가들 중 한 가문의 여성 가장으로서, Abigail Adams는 두 명의 대통령, 즉 자기 남편 John Adams와 자기 아들 John Quincy Adams에게 강하게 영향을 미쳤다. 그녀는 또한 미국에서 편지를 가장 훌륭하게, 그리고 가장 많이 쓴 사람 중의 한 명으로 인정받고 있다. Abigail은 1744년 11월 11일 매사추세츠 주 Weymouth에서 태어났다. 회중파 교회의 목사 William Smith와 그의 아내인 Elizabeth의 세 딸들 중 한 명인 Abigail은 몸이 허약한 아이여서 학교에 다닐 수 없었다. (몸집이) 자그마하고, 조용하고, 내성적이며, 꿰뚫어 보는 듯한 검은 눈을 가진 그녀는 또한 의지가 강하고 이해가 빠르며 호기심이 많았다. 정규 학교 교육을 받지 못했음에도 불구하고, Abigail은 문학, 역사, 철학을 공부하기 위해 책이 잘 갖춰진 아버지의 서재를 이용한 독서광이었다. 그녀는 독학으로 프랑스어를 배웠고, 그녀가 아주 좋아했던 그리고 '가르침과 놀이를 함께 하는 행복한 방법'을 선호했던 외할머니의 개인 지도를 받았다.

제 16 회 하프 모의고사 해설

문제편 p.065

ANSWER

01 ②	02 ③	03 ①	04 ①	05 ①
06 ②	07 ④	08 ④	09 ②	10 ④

01 ②

해설 주어가 the few, highly coveted jobs with professional organizations로 복수이므로, ②의 is를 are로 고쳐야 한다.

① 내용으로 보아 the process of job advancement와 연결되어 '~의 형태가 되다'의 의미가 되도록 수동태 형태인 be shaped로 적절하게 사용되었다.

③ 형용사 tough를 수식하므로 부사 형태인 increasingly로 적절하게 사용되었다.

④ 주어, 동사를 갖춘 앞부분에 연결되고 내용상 the salaries가 exceed의 목적어이므로 분사구문의 능동형인 exceeding으로 적절하게 사용되었다.

해석 스포츠 분야에서 일자리가 향상되는 과정은 피라미드 형태라고 (사람들은) 흔히 말한다. 넓은 바닥에는 청소년 또는 고등학교 운동 경기 팀과 관련 있는 일자리가 많은 한편, 좁은 꼭대기에는 전문 조직과 관련있는 몇 안 되는 매우 선호되는 일자리들이 있다. 그래서 전체적으로 보아 많은 스포츠 관련 직업이 있지만, 상위 단계로 올라가면서 경쟁은 점점 더 치열해진다. 다양한 직위에서의 봉급은 이러한 피라미드 모델을 나타낸다. 예를 들어, 고등학교의 미식축구와 농구 코치들은 대개 방과 후 업무에 대해 약간의 추가 보수를 받는 교사들이다. 하지만 큰 대학에 있는 똑같은 종목의 코치들은 대학 총장의 연봉을 능가하여 일 년에 일백만 달러보다 많이 버는 전국적인 유명 인사가 될 수 있다. 전미 미식축구 연맹과 전미 농구 협회는 한 단계 더 높은데, 거기서 헤드 코치(감독)는 최고 연봉을 받는 대학 감독보다 몇 배 더 벌 수 있다.

어휘 advancement 향상, 승진, 발전, 진보 field 분야
pyramid 피라미드 base 바닥, 기초 athletic 운동 경기의
competition 경쟁
work one's way up 상위 단계로 올라가다, (회사에서) 승진하다
reflect 나타내다, 반영하다 typically 대개, 전형적으로
celebrity 유명 인사, 명사 exceed 초과하다 association 협회
head coach 헤드 코치, 감독
counterpart 상대(편), 대응 관계에 있는 사람[것]

02 ③

해설 ③ 등위상관접속사 <not A but B>의 구문으로, 이때 A와 B는 문법적으로 같은 것이 놓여야 한다. 즉 병렬관계를 이루어야 하므로 but 이하의 looks but (consist) in looking이 되어야 한다.

① 복합관계대명사인 Whatever로 시작하는 <Whatever + 주어 + 동사>는 명사절을 구성할 수 있으므로 동사인 is의 주어로 사용된 것이 올바르다. 또한 명사절 주어는 단수 취급하므로 동사도 단수 형태인 is가 맞다.

② '그리고 또한 ~ 아니다'를 의미하는 nor의 뒤에는 「동사 + 주어」의 어순인 도치가 발생하므로 동사인 came과 주어인 any of my inventions를 도치한 did any of my inventions come이 올바른 어순이다.

④ '보수를 받지 않는다'는 의미이므로 수동태인 aren't paid가 올바르게 쓰였고, 두 개의 because 종속절이 <not A but B>로 바르게 연결되어 있다.

03 ①

해석 그는 그 문제에 대해서 간결한 진술을 했다.

어휘 concise 간결한 terse 간략한 redundant 장황한
inclusive 포괄적인 gorgeous 아주 멋진

04 ①

해석 그 여자는 그녀의 가장 친한 친구가 그녀에 대한 나쁜 소문을 퍼트렸다는 것을 알게 되어 놀랐다.

어휘 astound 놀라게 하다(= amaze, astonish)
irrigate 물을 공급하다 tremble 떨다

05 ①

해설 'the exam results'(시험 결과)에 대해 물어보았는데 B가 "They really cut corners when they built an extension."(그들은 증축 공사를 할 때 정말로 절차를 무시했어.)라는 질문에 적합하지 않은 대답을 하고 있으므로 ①이 가장 어색한 대화이다.

해석 ① A: 시험 결과 들었니?
B: 그들은 증축 공사를 할 때 정말로 절차를 무시했어.
② A: 내일이 디데이야. 정말 긴장돼.
B: 행운을 빌어, 샘! 네 수행능력이 뛰어날 거라고 확신해.
③ A: 이 지갑을 사는 게 어때? 멋져 보여.
B: 이 지갑을 살 형편이 안 돼! 가격이 엄청나.
④ A: 얼마나 자주 영화 보러가?
B: 아주 가끔만 가.

06 ②

해설 가족이나 친척은 처음 보는 경우에도 가족이나 친척이라는 이유로 신뢰하게 된다는 글의 흐름이므로 ② '신뢰감을 가지는 것'이 빈칸에 들어갈 말로 가장 적절하다.

① 오류를 지적하는 것
③ 오랜 관습을 고수하는 것
④ 기여를 요구하는 것

해석 많은 사람들이 배우자와 같은 인위적으로 맺어진 관계에서 신뢰를 형성하는 것은 매우 어렵다고 느끼지만 자신의 부모나 형제자매를 신뢰하는 것은 아주 자연스럽고 안전하다고 느끼는 것은 불행한 일이다. 때로 이러한 신뢰가 어떤 생물학적 혈연관계에서 비롯된 것인지, 아니면 기본적으로 함께 성장하는 기간 동안에 형성된 것인지를 생각해 볼 필요가 있다. 그러나 또한 (사촌이나 먼 친척의 경우처럼) 함께 자란 적도 없고 전에 만난 적조차도 없는 사람들이, "오, 하지만 그는 가족이니까"라고 말하는 경우처럼 서로를 쉽게 신뢰하고 의지하는 상황도 존재하는데, 그들은 마치 그것이 전혀 모르는 낯선 사람에 대해서도 신뢰감을 가지는 것을 정당화해 줄 어떤 연대 의식을 나타내게 되어

있는 것처럼 그렇게 한다.

어휘 spouse 배우자 sibling 형제자매, 동기
biological 생물학적인, 생물학의 relative 친척
togetherness 연대감, 친근감
entrust one's faith in ~에 대하여 신뢰감을 가지다
identify 찾다, 발견하다 gene 유전자

07 ④

해설 주어진 문장은 과도한 산화가 몸에 미치는 해로운 영향에 관한 내용이 시작되기 전에 위치하는 것이 자연스럽다. 그러므로 주어진 문장이 들어가기에 가장 적절한 곳은 ④이다.

해석 산화는 원자와 분자와 접촉하게 되면서 전자를 잃는 과정이며, 그것은 우주의 가장 기본적인 화학적 반응 중 하나이다. 사과를 잘랐는데 그것이 공기와 접촉하면서 갈색으로 변하거나 자동차의 범퍼가 녹슬면, 여러분의 산화 작용을 목격하고 있는 것이다. 산화는 우리 몸속에서도 발생한다. 그것의 일부는 자연적이고 좋은 것인데, 산화는 몸속에서 에너지의 이동을 촉진한다. 산화는 또한 해로울 수 있는 몸 안의 이물질을 물에 녹게 하여 (그러므로 소변을 통해 몸에서 빠져나갈 수 있게 하여) 제거해 준다. 하지만 과도한 산화가 여러분의 새 자동차를 고물 자동차로 바꾸고 사과 조각을 퇴비로 바꿔버리는 것처럼 제어되지 않은 과도한 산화는 인간에게 있어 건강과 장수의 적이다. 산화는 활성 산소라고 불리는 무언가를 만드는데, 그것은 우리가 아는 바로는 노화를 부추기고 암을 조장하는 원인이 된다.

어휘 longevity 장수, 오래 지속됨 junker 고물 자동차
molecule 분자 electron 전자 rust 녹슬다, 부식하다
witness 목격하다 at work 작용 중인 facilitate 촉진하다, 조장하다
foreign substance 이물질 water-soluble 물에 녹는, 수용성의
urine 소변

08 ④

해설 (A) 앞에는 정원을 가꾸는 데 완벽한 토양이 있어야 하는 것은 아니라고 했으며, (A) 뒤에서 비옥하고 유기물이 많으며 경작하기 쉬운 토양이 최선이라고 했으므로 (A)에는 역접의 연결사 However가 가장 적절하다.
(B) 앞에서 정원을 가꾸기에 좋지 않은 토양을 언급했으며 (B) 뒤에도 식물을 기르는 데 효과적이지 못한 토양에 대해 말하고 있으므로 추가적인 언급을 할 때 사용하는 연결사 Furthermore가 가장 적절하다.
그러므로 정답은 ④이다.

해석 일부의 믿음과는 반대로, 생산적인 정원을 만들고 가꾸기 위해서 완벽한 토양이 필요한 것은 아니다. 그러나 식물의 뿌리에 영양분을 제공하는 유기물로 가득한 비옥하며, 파고 경작하기 쉬운 토양을 갖는 것이 가장 좋다. 푸석푸석하고 배수가 잘 되는 토양이 좋은 정원을 가꾸는 데 이상적이다. 땅을 흠뻑 적시는 많은 비가 내린 후에 물이 쉽게 빠지지 않는 마당의 한 부분이 있다면, 과도한 물이 정원의 식물들을 익사시킬 가능성이 아주 많으므로, 그곳에 정원을 만들지 않는 것이 최선이다. 뿐만 아니라, 진흙이나 모래 일색인 토양도 식물을 기르는 데 그만큼[배수가 되지 않는 토양만큼] 효과적이지 않다. 이러한 유형의 토양을 영양분이 더 풍부하고 비옥하게 만들기 위해서는, 그것들[토양]의 질을 증진시킬 수 있는 퇴비와 같은 유기물을 더하라.

어휘 contrary to ~와는 반대로 fertile 비옥한, 기름진
organic material 유기물 cultivate 경작하다
well-drained 배수가 잘 되는 soaking 흠뻑 적시는
drown 익사시키다 consistency 일색, 한결같음

09 ②

해설 제시된 단락에서 오늘날 살고 있는 삶을 밝혀주는 자원이라고 했고 B에서는 이전 시대와 사상가들은 오늘날 우리가 직면하는 문제와 유사한 것들을 이미 직면했었으므로 우리는 역사에서 배운다고 했으니 오늘날 살고 있는 삶을 밝혀준다는 의미와 연결된다.

해석 "왜 역사를 가르치나요?" 내가 주장하건데, 거기에 있기 때문은 아니다. 오히려 역사는 오늘날 우리가 살아가는 삶을 조명할 수 있는 자료이기 때문에 가르쳐야 한다. 우리는 역사로부터 배울 수 있다. 왜냐하면 초기의 시대와 사상가들은 오늘날 우리에게 직면한 문제들, 생각들, 상황들에 직면해 있었기 때문이다. 우리는 과거 시대가 우리와 유사한 개념과 관점에 전념할 때와 그들이 그들의 차이점으로 주목할 만한 관점을 가질 때 둘 다에서 배울 수 있다. 오직 바보만이 새로운 상황에 직면했을 때 그의 과거 경험을 무시할 것이다. 우리의 집단적인 역사를 무시하는 것도 마찬가지로 어리석은 일일 것이다. 역사가 교양교과뿐만 아니라 초중등교육과 중등교육 이후에도 중심적인 위치를 차지해야 하는 이유다.

어휘 primary 주요한 collective 집단적인
occupy 종사하다, 점유하다 secondary education 중등교육

10 ④

해설 'Hugh wrote thirteen other books about the kindly doctor, as well as a number of other books for children. The Doctor Dolittle stories are still some of the best loved of all time.'에서 hugh는 다른 작품도 썼다는 것을 알 수 있다.

해석 휴 존 로핑은 영국에서 아일랜드인 아버지와 영국인 어머니 사이에서 태어났다. 휴는 상상력이 풍부한 아이였고 그의 형제 자매들에게 이야기를 들려주기 위해 이야기를 만드는 것을 좋아했다. 그는 또한 동물들을 사랑했고 어렸을 때 많은 애완동물을 키웠다. 동물에 대한 휴의 관심은 닥터 둘리틀의 탄생으로 이어졌다. 닥터 둘리틀은 쾌활하고 매력적인 의사로 시작했는데 그는 모험을 하면서 더욱 진지해졌다. 이것은 아마도 휴의 삶과 비슷했을 것이다. 그의 성년기에는 몇 가지 슬픔이 있었다. 그의 첫 번째 부인은 뉴베리 상을 수상하는데 큰 성공을 거둔 지 4년 후인 1927년에 사망했다. 그는 재혼했지만, 그의 두 번째 아내는 1년도 채 되지 않아 죽었다. 그의 첫 닥터 두리틀의 책이 출판된 후 27년 동안, 휴는 그 친절한 의사에 대한 다른 13권의 책들과 어린이들을 위한 많은 다른 책들을 썼다. 닥터 두리틀 이야기는 여전히 역사상 가장 사랑받는 이야기들 중 일부이다.

제 17 회 하프 모의고사 해설

문제편 p.069

ANSWER

01 ④	02 ②	03 ④	04 ②	05 ③
06 ④	07 ④	08 ①	09 ①	10 ③

01 ④

해설 (A) than others가 likely 다음에 끼어든 것이므로 to suffer가 적절하다. be likely to는 '~할 가능성이 있다, ~할 것 같다'의 의미이다.

(B) 「aware of + 명사」, 「aware that + 주어 + 동사 ~」로 쓰이는데, about 50 percent of marriages가 주어이고 end가 동사이므로 aware 뒤에 접속사 that이 오는 것이 적절하다.

(C) '놀랍게도'라는 뜻으로 뒤따르는 절의 내용을 수식하므로 부사인 surprisingly가 적절하다.

해석 우리의 일부는 비관론자이고, 우리의 일부는 현실주의자이지만, 우리의 대부분은 낙관론자이다. 위험에 관하여 우리의 대부분은 우리가 보통을 넘는다고 믿는데, 우리가 대부분의 사람들보다 덜 취약하다고 생각한다는 것을 의미한다. 여러분은 자동차 사고, 심장마비, 이혼을 포함한 삶의 불행으로 고통받을 가능성이 다른 사람들보다 더 적다고 생각할 가능성이 있다. 대부분의 사람들은 결혼의 약 50퍼센트가 이혼으로 끝난다는 것을 알고 있지만, 신랑 신부는 대체로 자신들이 이혼하게 될 가능성은 그보다 훨씬 더 낮다고 생각한다. (실제로 더 잘 알고 있을 이혼 (전문) 변호사들조차 자신들이 이혼하게 될 가능성을 몹시 낮게 추정한다.) 어쩌면 더 놀랍게도, 한 연구에 따르면 흡연자들은 흡연 인구가 마주치는 통계상의 위험을 낮게 추정하지 않지만 그럼에도 불구하고 자신의 개인적 위험은 보통의 비흡연자의 그것보다 덜하다고 믿는다.

어휘 realist 현실주의자, 사실주의자 with respect to ~에 관하여
vulnerable 취약한 bride 신부 groom 신랑
typically 대체로, 전형적으로, 일반적으로
underestimate 낮게 추정하다, 과소평가하다 statistical 통계상의
nonetheless 그럼에도 불구하고

02 ②

해설 ② '너무 ~해서 ~하다'를 의미하는 such ~ that의 부사절 접속사 구문이 바르게 쓰였다. such ~ that 접속사의 경우 such 다음에 관사가 바로 오는 어순에 주의해야 한다. <such + a/an + 형용사 + 명사>의 어순 역시 바르게 쓰였다.

① 문맥상 양보구문으로, 접속사 as를 이용한 양보구문은 <형용사 + as/though + 주어 + 동사>의 어순으로 쓴다. 양보구문에는 as를 써야 하므로 as if를 as though로 고쳐야 한다.

③ keep은 3형식과 5형식 모두 가능해서 뒤에 분사나 동명사가 나올 때 주의해야 한다. keep이 '~가 …하는 것을 방해하다/막다'라는 뜻을 전달할 때는 3형식으로 쓰이는데 이때 목적어 뒤에 <from + 동명사>를 써서 <keep + 목적어 + from + 동명사>의 형태로 표현해야 한다. 그러므로 advancing from을 advancing으로 고쳐야 한다.

④ 전치사 on의 목적어로 if 명사절이 쓰였다. if 명사절은 타동사의 목적어로만 쓰이며, 주어와 전치사의 목적어로는 쓰지 못한다. or not과 if를 바로 이어서 if or not으로 쓸 수 없다. if 명사절에서 or not은 if 명사절의 끝에 와야 한다. 반면 같은 의미를 가진 whether 명사절은 주어로도 쓰며, 동사 및 전치사의 목적어로도 쓰일 수 있고, or not은 whether와 바로 이어져도 되고, whether 명사절의 끝에 와도 된다. 따라서 if를 whether로 고쳐야 한다.

03 ④

해석 학교는 그에게 상을 주었다.

어휘 confer 수여하다 compromise 타협하다 corrupt 부패하다
collaborate 협력하다

04 ②

해석 Luke Sky Walker와 Leia 공주가 Darth Vader의 군대로부터 벗어나면서 대담하고 죽음도 두려워하지 않는, 자유로의 도약을 할 때 청중들은 환호했다.

어휘 audacious 대담한, 철면피의 prudent 신중한 bold 용감한
hilarious 즐거운 transparent 투명한

05 ③

해설 be fed up은 '물리다, 싫증나다'의 의미이다.

해석 ① A: 시험에 대한 마지막 질문은 힘들지 않았니?
B: 그래, 그건 좀 까다로웠어.

② A: 안녕, 엘라 존스 좀 바꿔주세요. 제가 그녀의 남편입니다.
B: 바로 연결해 줄게.

③ A: 미나는 왜 그녀의 일에 그렇게 진절머리가 나니?
B: 그녀는 과식한 것처럼 느껴.

④ A: 찬희? 런던에는 무슨 일로 왔어?
B: 사업차 막 도착했어.

06 ④

해설 창의력을 자극하려면 수렴적 사고보다는 확산적 사고를 유도하는 질문을 해야 한다는 내용의 글이므로 ④ '어떤 문제에 대한 다양한 해결책들에 대해 생각해 보도록'이 빈칸에 들어갈 말로 적절하다.

① 가능한 한 많은 좋은 책들을 읽도록
② 다른 사람의 입장이 되어 보도록
③ 동일한 아이디어에 대한 생각을 정교하게 하도록

해석 확산적 사고를 배제하고 수렴적 사고를 사용하는 쪽으로 너무 많이 기울어지고 싶은 유혹에 저항하라. 우리는 심지어 비교적 답이 열려있고 매우 주관적일 수 있는 생각이나 제안에 대해서도 아이들에게 무엇이 옳고 그른 것인지를 말해주는 오류를 범하기 쉽다. 우리는 또한 확산적 사고를 증진하는 질문을 던지고 있는지 확인해보면서, 우리가 질문을 말로 표현하는 방식을 살펴보아야 한다. 예를 들어, '콜라주를 만들기 위해 그림들을 붙이기 위해서 접착제를 사용하자.'라고 말하는 대신에 '우리가 이것을 특별하게 만들기 위해서 이것을 여기에다 어떻게 붙일 수 있을까 의문이네.'라고 말할 수 있을 것이다. 단

지 우리가 하는 말을 달리 표현함으로써, 우리는 그저 하나의 올바른 해결책을 제시하는 것이 아니라, 오히려 아이들에게 어떤 문제에 대한 다양한 해결책들에 대해 생각해 보도록 권장할 수 있다.

어휘 resist 저항하다 temptation 유혹
to the exclusion of ~을 배제[제외]하고
open-ended 답이 열려있는, 자유해답식의 subjective 주관적인
promote 증진하다, 장려하다
collage 콜라주(색종이나 사진 등의 조각들을 붙여 그림을 만드는 미술 기법 또는 그렇게 만든 그림)

07 ④

해설 밤하늘의 빛과 홀로그램의 원리를 통해 부분과 전체 간의 관계를 설명하고 있는 글이다. ④ 다음 문장의 주어인 'This holographic image'가 가리키는 것은 주어진 문장의 'the three-dimensional image created by interacting laser beams'이다. 그러므로 주어진 문장이 들어가기에 가장 적절한 곳은 ④이다.

해석 생체 내에서 부분과 전체 간의 관계를 인식하기 위해, 우리가 자연을 미시적인 수준에서 연구할 필요는 없다. 밤하늘을 올려다보면, 서 있는 곳에서 보이는 하늘 전부를 보게 된다. 하지만 눈의 동공은 완전히 열려도 가로로 1센티미터가 안 된다. 어찌 된 일인지, 하늘 전체로부터 오는 빛이 눈이라는 작은 공간에 담겨있는 것이 분명하다. 그리고 동공이 단지 절반 크기이거나, 고작 4분의 1 크기일지라도, 여전히 그러할 것이다. 밤하늘 전체로부터 오는 빛은 공간이 아무리 작을지라도 모든 공간에 존재한다. 이것은 교차하는 레이저 광선에 의해 만들어지는 3차원의 상에 분명히 나타나는 현상과 정확히 동일하다. 이러한 홀로그램의 상은 무한히 절반으로 쪼개어질 수 있으며, 각 조각은 아무리 작을지라도 전체의 상을 여전히 담고 있을 것이다.

어휘 evident 분명한, 눈에 띄는 appreciate (제대로) 인식하다
microscopic 미시적인, 미세한 부분에까지 이르는 pupil 동공
present 존재하는, 있는 entirety 전체, 전부 indefinitely 무한히
physicist 물리학자

08 ①

해설 (A) 앞에서는 두 문화가 접촉할 때 모든 문화 요소를 교환한다면 오늘날 세계의 모든 문화는 동일할 것이라고 했고, (A) 뒤에는 그런 것이 아니라 단지 적은 수의 문화적 요소가 한 문화에서 다른 문화로 확산된다고 했으므로 (A)에는 앞에 언급한 것과 다르며 대체되는 것을 제시할 때 사용하는 연결사 Instead가 들어가야 한다.
(B) 앞 문장에서 혁신적인 것이 사회의 필요와 일치할 때에도 그것이 받아들여지는 것을 보장할 수 없다고 말했으며, (B) 뒤에서는 그것의 예로 미국인들이 미터법을 거부해 온 것을 말하고 있으므로 (B)에는 사례를 제시할 때 사용하는 For example이 적절하다.
그러므로 정답은 ①이다.

해석 두 문화가 접촉할 때, 그 두 문화가 모든 문화 항목을 교환하는 것은 아니다. 만약 그렇다면, 오늘날 세계에는 전혀 문화적 차이가 없을 것이다. 대신에 단지 적은 수의 문화적 요소들만 늘 한 문화에서 다른 문화로 확산된다. 어떤 문화 항목이 받아들여지는가는 그 항목의 용도 및 이미 존재하는 문화적 특성과의 양립 가능성에 대체로 달려있다. 예를 들어, '흰머리를 피하려고' 고안된 남성용 머리 염색약은 나이가 들어감에 따라 사람의 지위가 올라가는 아프리카의 시골 지역으로 확산될 것 같지는 않다. 어떤 혁신적인 것이 어떤 사회의 필요와 일치할 때조차도, 여전히 그것이 받아들여질 것이라는 보장은 없다. 예를 들어, 미국의 관습적 단위(예컨대, 인치, 피트, 야드, 마일 등)를 사용하는 미국의 대부분의 사람들은, 그러한 변화가 미국인들로 하여금 세계의 다른 나라들과 더 효율적으로 접촉할 수 있게 할 터임에도 불구하고, 미터법 채택에 저항해 왔다.

어휘 come into contact 접촉하다 diffuse 확산시키다, 확산하다
trait 특성 dye 염색약; 염색하다 elevate 올리다, 높이다
with advancing years 나이가 들어감에 따라 innovation 혁신
consistent 일치하는, 일관된 guarantee 보장, 확약, 보증서
resist 저항하다 interface with ~와 접촉[접속]하다
efficiently 효율적으로

09 ①

해설 주어진 글은 우울증 환자에게 놀이는 낯선 개념처럼 보인다는 내용이다. 그래서(So) 실험자는 주변 사람들에게 놀이에 대한 실험을 하기로 결심했다는 내용인 (B)가 오고, 실험 후 많은 피험자들이 놀이가 어른들에게 무엇인지를 생각해 내는 데 어려워진다는 결과를 발견했다는 (A)가 이어진 후, 이러한 조사 결과(This finding)가 놀이에 대한 일반적인 생각과 관련이 있고 놀이에 대한 정의를 새롭게 할 필요가 있다는 내용인 (C)가 이어지는 것이 가장 자연스러운 글의 순서이다.

해석 우리가 우울할 때, 놀이는 낯선 개념처럼 보일 수 있다. 때때로 내 우울증 환자들에게 내가 '놀이'라는 단어를 말할 때 마음속에 무엇을 그리는지 물어보면, 그들은 멍한 눈으로 나를 빤히 바라본다. (B) 그래서 나는 몇몇 가족과 친구들뿐만 아니라 나와 같이 일하는 많은 사람들과 함께 놀이에 대한 실험을 하기로 결심했다. 실험은 간단했다. 나는 그들 모두에게 놀이가 그들에게 무엇을 의미하는지를 물어보았다. (A) 나와 이야기를 나눈 많은 피험자들이 어른들에게 놀이가 무엇인지를 생각해 내는 데 어려움을 겪는다는 것을 발견했는데, 왜냐하면 그것은 아이들의 놀이와 다르고, 그것이 그들이 알고 있는 유일한 놀이였기 때문이다. (C) 이러한 조사 결과는 놀이에 대한 일반적인 생각과 관련이 있다. 생산성을 중시하는 문화에서, 어른들의 놀이는 부정적이고 비생산적이며 방종한 활동으로 혹은 심지어는 성인용 등급의 것으로 정의되는 것처럼 보인다. 나는 우리가 놀이에 대한 정의를 새롭게 할 필요가 있다고 생각한다.

10 ③

해설 'Cohn was nineteen by this time, with a doctorate in botany and a position at the University of Breslau.'에서 19세 때 이미 식물학 박사학위를 소지하고 있었다는 것을 알 수 있으므로 ③이 글의 내용과 일치하지 않는다.

해석 (현재 폴란드의 Wroclaw인) Silesia의 Breslau에 있는 독일계 유대인 집단 거주지에서 태어난 Ferdinand Cohn은 신동으로서, 두 살 이전에 글을 읽을 수 있었고 14세에 대학교에 다녔다. 그러나 그의 학사학위는 그의 유대인 혈통 때문에 수여되지 않았으며 베를린에서 교직을 얻을 수 없었는데, 아마도 (이것도) 또한 그의 유대인 뿌리 때문이었을 것이다. 성공한 상인인 그의 아버지가 값비싼 고품질의 현미경을 준 후 미시 세계에 대한 Cohn의 관심이 생겨났다. Cohn은 이 무렵 열아홉 살이었고, 식물학 박사학위를 가지고 Breslau 대학교에서 근무하고 있었다. 그의 새로운 현미경은 그의 소중한 연구 도구 중 하나가 되었다. 그는 1859년 식물학 부교수로 임명되었으며, 1870년대에 이르러서는 그의 시대에 가장 앞선 세균 학자로서 많은 학생들과 젊은 과학자들을 자신의 강의에 끌어들였다. 그는 지금 세균학이라는 학문의 창시자로 간주되고 있다.

제 18 회 하프 모의고사 해설

문제편 p.073

ANSWER

01 ③	02 ④	03 ④	04 ①	05 ④
06 ③	07 ③	08 ③	09 ③	10 ②

01 ③

해설 (A) 문맥상 having의 목적어는 cats이고 의미상 주어는 owners이므로 동일한 지시 대상을 가리키지 않는다. 그러므로 themselves가 아닌 them을 쓰는 것이 적절하다.

(B) and에 의해 refine existing breeds와 연결되어 began to에 이어지는 구조이므로 develop을 쓰는 것이 적절하다.

(C) 주어인 a Maine Coon에 대한 술어 동사가 필요하므로 won을 쓰는 것이 적절하다.

해석 19세기에 도시 중산층의 부상으로, 많은 고양이가 더 이상 전업으로 쥐를 잡는 동물로서의 역할을 할 필요가 없어졌다. 점차, 고양이들은 그저 그들의 아름다움, 우아함과 그들이 줄 수 있는 애정을 위해 주변에 그들을 두려는 주인들에 의해 길러졌다. '고양이 애호'라는 현상이 이어졌다. '애호가들'의 애완동물들은 고양이 쇼에서 리본을 (상으로) 타기 위해 경쟁했고, 품종 개량가들은 기존의 품종을 개량하고 새로운 품종을 개발하기 시작했다. 170마리의 고양이가 전시에 나왔던 최초의 기록된 고양이 쇼는 런던의 Crystal Palace에서 1871년에 개최되었다. 고작 18년 후 그때보다 세 배가 넘는 수의 고양이들이 전시되었고, 2만 명의 고양이 애호가들이 참석했다. 미국의 고양이 애호가들도 자기들 나름의 그런 쇼를 1895년에 뉴욕의 Madison Square Garden에서 열어 곧 그 선례를 따랐다. 양키 혈통 품종인 Maine Coon이 최초로 쇼의 1등상을 받은 것은 아마 놀랍지도 않을 것이다. 오늘 날 고양이 애호는 건재하고, 전 세계 수백 개의 클럽이 고양이 쇼를 한다.

어휘 mouser 쥐를 잡는 동물 grace 우아함 affection 애정
phenomenon 현상 fancy 애호, 기호 breeder 품종 개량가
refine 세련되게 하다 existing 현재의, 기존의 breed 품종
on exhibit 출품되어, 전시되어
follow suit 선례를 따르다, 남을 흉내 내다 ancestry 혈통
alive and well 건재하여, 남아서

02 ④

해설 ④ '~하면서'라는 시간의 의미를 전달하는 부사절 접속사는 as이다. as though는 '마치 ~처럼'을 의미하므로 접속사 선택이 적절치 않고, 동사의 시제도 과거인 got이 아니라 현재형인 get이 적합하다. 따라서 as they get old라고 써야 한다.

① '~했어야 했다'라고 과거의 일에 대한 아쉬움을 표현할 때 「should have pp.」의 구문을 사용한다.

② 강조구문이 올바르게 사용되어 강조하고자 하는 'not talent but passion'이 it과 that 사이에 올바르게 위치하고 있다.

③ '시간을 엄수하는 것'을 의미하는 동명사 주어인 being punctual이 올바르게 사용되었다.

어휘 punctual 시간을 지키는 strict 엄한, 엄격한

03 ④

해석 경찰은 도난품을 압수했다.

어휘 confiscate 압수하다 locate 위치를 확인하다
release 풀어주다 seize 꽉 쥐다

04 ①

해석 그 운전자는 차를 갑자기 세워서 사고를 피하려고 했다.

어휘 avert 피하다 prevent 예방하다 control 통제하다
yearn 열망하다 spur 박차를 가하다

05 ④

해석 ① A: 오늘 밤 우리 캠핑에 함께하시지요?
B: 죄송합니다만, 저는 당분간 외출 금지입니다.
② A: 네가 또 다른 영화를 만들고 있다고 들었어! 내가 참여할 수 있을까?
B: 물론이지. 토요일에 Kimberly's에서 배우와 직원 미팅이 있어.
③ A: 네가 만약 그 팀의 리더가 되길 요청받는다면 넌 뭐라 말할 거니?
B: 내가 판단할 일이 아니야.
④ A: 토요일 아주 이른 시각에 넌 무엇을 포장하고 있니?
B: 네가 이걸 해낼(이해할) 수 없다는 것은 유감스러운 일이다.

06 ③

해설 매끄러운 상호 작용을 익히지 않은 아이들은 게임에 마구 뛰어들어서 흐름을 방해하지만, 사교적으로 더 능숙한 아이들은 잠시 기다리고 지켜본 다음 자연스러운 기회에 매끄럽게 들어가며, 이것이 어른에게도 적용된다는 내용의 글이다. 따라서 빈칸에는 ③ '우리가 함께 일하는 사람의 사교적 리듬과 타이밍을 깨닫는 것'이 가장 적절하다.

① 조직 안에서의 정치적 그리고 사회적 흐름을 판단하는 것
② 자기 계발과 성장을 위한 기회를 많이 갖는 것
④ 자기들 공동체의 미래 욕구를 예상하고 인지하는 것

해석 우리가 처음으로 공감을 배우는 것은 우리가 어머니나 아버지의 팔에 안길 때인 유아기에 시작된다. 이런 기본적인 정서적 유대는 협력하여 게임이나 집단에 환영받고 들어가는 방법을 배우는 토대를 마련한다. 우리가 이런 정서적 교육과정을 완전히 익히는 정도는 우리의 사교능력의 수준을 결정한다. 매끄러운 상호 작용을 위한 중요한 신호들을 포착하지 못하는 놀이터의 아이들을 예로 들어보자. 게임에 참여하고자 할 때, 그들은 흔히 마구 뛰어들며, 그리하여 그 흐름을 방해한다. 반면에, 사교적으로 더 능숙한 아이들은 잠시 기다리고 지켜본다. 그들은 처음에는 게임에 맞추어 가다가 자연스러운 기회에 매끄럽게 들어간다. 그것은 어른에게도 마찬가지다. 우리가 함께 일하는 사람의 사교적 리듬과 타이밍을 깨닫는 것이 극히 중요하다.

어휘 empathy 공감, 감정이입 primary 기본적인, 주요한
bond 유대 groundwork 토대, 기초
master 완전히 익히다, 숙달하다 curriculum 교육 과정
competence 능력, 능숙함 crucial 중대한, 결정적인 cue 신호
disrupt 흐름을 방해하다, 혼란케 하다 skilled 능숙한, 숙련된

awhile 잠시, 잠깐　tune in to ~에 맞추다
opening 기회, 호기, 깨진 틈　essential 극히 중요한, 필수적인

07 ③

해설 주어진 문장은, 식물의 이산화탄소 흡수량에 물이 영향을 미친다고 말하고 있다. 그러므로 물이라는 요인이 중요하다는 결론을 내기 전에 이 문장이 들어가는 것이 적절하다. 그러므로 주어진 문장이 들어가기에 가장 적절한 곳은 ③이다.

해석 비록 기후 변화에 인간이 미치는 영향의 정도가 여전히 논의되고 있지만, 자동차, 가정, 그리고 공장은 대기를 덥게 만들고 이러한 인간의 영향은 기후 변화의 속도를 증가시켰다. 오늘날 과학적 지식에 근거할 때, 지구 온도가 더 증가하는 것을 막기 위해 온실가스를 줄여야 할 필요가 있다. 식물이 대기로부터 흡수하는 이산화탄소(CO_2)의 양을 최초로 측정하고 있는 최근 두 연구는 지구 온난화가 이전에 생각했던 것만큼 기존의 생태계에 극적인 영향을 끼치지 않는다고 말한다. 식물은 온도가 증가할 때 여전히 많은 CO_2를 흡수할 수 있는 것이 분명하지만, 식물이 그만큼의 물을 얻지 못할 때 더 적은 CO_2가 흡수된다. 그러므로 물의 이용 가능성이 온도의 변화를 최소화하는 것보다 더 중요하다고 여겨진다. 대체로 지구 온도의 상승을 제한하기 위해 애쓰는 CO_2 목표량과 대책에 초점을 맞추는 지금까지의 모델은 그래서 틀렸을 수 있다. 어쩌면 세계의 수자원을 보호하는 쪽으로 더 치중할 필요가 있다.

어휘 extent 정도, 규모　dramatic 극적인, 인상적인
availability 이용 가능성, 입수 가능성　minimize 최소화하다, 축소하다
to date 지금까지　strive 애쓰다, 노력하다, 힘쓰다
safeguard 보호하다, 지키다

08 ③

해설 (A) 앞에서는 미학이 주로 미술에 초점을 맞춘다고 하였고, (A) 뒤에서는 미적 감상이 예술에 국한되지 않는다고 말하고 있으므로 (A)에는 역접 연결사 However가 가장 적절하다.
(B) 앞에서는 미에 대한 감상이 자연을 넘어서 일상적인 환경에까지 도달한다고 하였고, (B) 뒤에는 환경 미학이 필요하게 되었다고 말하고 있으므로 (B)에는 인과 관계를 나타내는 연결사 Thus가 들어가야 한다.
그러므로 정답은 ③이다.

해석 미학은 사물이 우리의 감각에 영향을 줄 때, 특히 즐거운 방식으로 영향을 줄 때, 그 사물에 대한 우리의 감상과 관련된 철학의 분야이다. 따라서 그것[미학]은 흔히 미술에 주로 초점을 맞추는데, 그 미술 작품들은 전통적으로 우리의 감각을 즐겁게 하기 위해 만들어진다. 그러나 우리의 미적 감상의 많은 부분은 예술에 국한되지 않고 세계 전체를 향한다. 우리는 예술뿐만 아니라 넓은 지평선, 불타오르는 일몰과 우뚝 솟은 산과 같은 자연도 감상한다. 게다가 우리의 감상은 오염되지 않은 그대로의 자연을 넘어서 더 일상적인 우리의 주변, 즉 비 오는 날 저녁 인근 공원의 호젓함, 분주한 아침 시장의 혼란함, 도로에서 보는 광경에까지 미친다. 그러므로 환경 미학의 필요성이 있게 되는데, 그러한 경우에 우리의 미적 감상은 우리 주변, 즉 우리 환경을 포함하기 때문이다.

어휘 aesthetics 미학　appreciation 감상, 감사, 평가
as such 따라서, 그러므로　frequently 흔히, 자주
be confined to ~에 국한되다　surroundings 주변 환경
solitude 호젓함, 고독(함)　chaos 혼란, 혼돈

09 ③

해설 주어진 글에는 필자가 다리를 다쳤고 카세트 레코더를 샀다는 내용이 제시되어 있다. (C)에서 아버지로부터 그 레코더를 사용하여 굴뚝새의 소리를 녹음하여 틀어 놓아 보라는 제안을 받고 그렇게 하였다는 내용이 제시된 다음 (C)의 마지막 부분에 나온 the wren을 (A)에서 him으로 받아 그 새가 자신의 영역을 지키기 위해 카세트 레코더를 공격하는 모습을 묘사하고 (B)에서 that sort of behaviour로 (A)의 내용을 받아 카세트 레코더가 없을 때에도 그와 비슷한 행동을 한다는 설명을 제시하는 흐름으로 글이 진행되는 것이 가장 적절하다.

해석 나는 지난 겨울 스키를 타면서 언덕을 처음으로 내려오다가 다리가 부러졌는데, 불운하고도 서투른 아이들에게 보상하기 위해 마련된 학교 보험 증서로부터 돈을 약간 받았다. 나는 그 수입으로 카세트 레코더를 샀다. (C) 아버지께서는 나에게 집 뒤의 잔디밭에 앉아 굴뚝새의 노래를 녹음한 다음 다시 틀어 놓고 무슨 일이 일어나는지 보라고 제안했다. 그래서 나는 봄볕이 밝게 비치는 곳으로 나가 굴뚝새가 노래로 자신의 영역에 대한 권리를 맹렬하게 주장하는 것을 몇 분간 녹음했다. (A) 그런 다음 나는 그 새에게 자신의 목소리를 듣도록 했다. 참새 크기의 3분의 1인 그 조그만 새가 스피커로부터 조금 떨어진 곳에서 이리저리 공격하며 나와 카세트 레코더를 향하여 급강하 폭격을 시작했다. (B) 우리는 그런 종류의 행동을 많이 보았는데 심지어 테이프 레코더가 없을 때도 그랬다. 만일 더 큰 새가 우리 새집 근처 나무 어디에 감히 앉아 쉬려고 하면, 십중팔구 급강하는 굴뚝새에게 맞아서 앉은 자리에서 떨어졌을 것이다.

10 ②

해설 1940년에 나치가 덴마크를 침공했을 때, Victor Borge는 스웨덴에서 공연을 하고 있었다(When the Nazis invaded Denmark in 1940, he was performing in Sweden)고 했으므로, ②는 글의 내용과 일치하지 않는다.

해석 1909년에 덴마크의 코펜하겐에서 태어난 Victor Borge는 코미디언이자 피아니스트였다. 처음에는 음악회에서 연주하는 음악가였던 Victor Borge는 곧 코미디와 고전 음악을 결합한 공연 스타일을 개발했다. 1940년에 나치가 덴마크를 침공했을 때, 그는 스웨덴에서 공연을 하고 있었고, 얼마 후에 용케도 미국으로 탈출했다. 미국에 도착했을 때, 그는 영어를 한마디도 하지 못했다. 그는 영화를 보면서 영어를 배워서 곧 미국 관객들을 위해서 자신의 농담을 어떻게든 (영어로) 옮길 수 있었다. 1948년에 Victor Borge는 미국 시민이 되었고, 몇 년 후에 자신이 진행하는 쇼인 Comedy in Music을 제안받았다. 그 쇼는 브로드웨이 역사상 가장 장기간 공연된 원맨쇼로 남아 있다. 그는 90세에도 여전히 일 년에 60회의 공연을 했다. 그는 2000년 12월 23일에 미국 코네티컷 주의 Greenwich에 있는 자신의 집에서 생을 마감했다.

제 19 회 하프 모의고사 해설

문제편 p.077

ANSWER

01 ④	02 ②	03 ③	04 ④	05 ②
06 ③	07 ④	08 ②	09 ②	10 ④

01 ④

해설 ④ 문맥상 '그것(성공)이 일어날 것에 대한 준비를 하라'라는 의미가 되어야 하므로 it을 의미상의 주어로 하는 to부정사가 와야 한다. 따라서 happens를 to happen으로 고쳐야 한다.

① 문장에 이미 술어 동사 becomes가 있기 때문에 situation과 becomes 사이에 있는 표현은 분사구가 되어야 한다. 상황이 인식의 주체가 아니라 대상이므로 과거분사 perceived가 적절하다.

② those는 the pastures를 대신하는 대명사이므로 적절하다.

③ 동사 appears의 주어 역할을 하고, at의 목적어 역할을 하려면 선행사가 포함된 관계절을 이끄는 what이 필요하다.

해석 모든 상황은 제대로 인식될 때 기회가 된다. 그러나 여러분이 성공하고자 한다면, 그것에 따라 행동을 해야 한다. 멀리 있는 목초지는 바로 가까이에 있는 것들보다 언제나 더 초록색으로 보이지만 진정한 기회는 바로 여러분이 있는 곳에 있다. 그러한 기회가 나타날 때 여러분은 그것을 이용해야 한다. 성공은 여러분의 주변에 있지 않고, 운이나 기회에 있지 않고, 혹은 다른 사람들의 도움에 있는 것이 아니다. 성공은 여러분 자신 안에만 있다. 어떤 사람의 '행운'인 것처럼 보이는 것을 다시 한 번 쳐다보라. 여러분은 운이 아니라 준비, 계획 세우기 그리고 성공을 낳는 사고를 발견할 것이다. 여러분이 기회에 대한 준비가 되어 있을 때 성공할 기회가 반드시 온다. 실패의 시기가 성공의 씨앗을 뿌릴 최적의 시기이다. 올해가 여러분의 성공의 해가 될 거라고 다짐하고, 그것이 일어날 것에 대한 준비를 하라.

어휘 properly 제대로, 적절히 perceive 인식하다, 인지하다
act on ~에 따라 행동하다 take advantage of ~을 이용하다
sow 씨를 뿌리다

02 ②

해설 ② whomever, whoever 등의 복합관계대명사 명사절과 부사절을 이끌 수 있다. 이 문장에서는 명사절을 이끌어 전치사 to의 목적어로 사용되었다. to가 전치사이므로 뒤에는 whomever라는 목적격이 와야 할 것 같으나, 사실상 'whomever ~ questionnaire'라는 명사절 전체가 to의 목적어이다. 또한 whomever 뒤에 바로 동사가 나온 것으로 보아 whomever는 명사절 목적격 whomever를 주격 whoever로 고쳐야 한다.

① 보증이 만기된 것이 먼저이므로 과거완료로 바르게 표현하였다. expire는 자동사이므로 절대로 수동태가 될 수 없으며 능동형으로 사용된 것이 맞다. 또한 '무료의, 공짜의'를 의미하는 'free of charge'라는 표현 역시 확인해 두자.

③ If가 나오고, 주절에 would가 오면 우선적으로 가정법임을 알 수 있다. 또한 주절에 온 now를 통해 가정법 혼합시제가 사용된 것임을 유추할 수 있다. 부사절은 last month를 통해 과거의 일임을 알 수 있으며, 따라서 가정법 과거완료의 시제가 바르다. 또한 주절은 now를 통해 현재의 일임을 알 수 있으며 가정법 과거시제가 바르게 쓰였다. 가정법 혼합시제가 잘 사용되었다.

④ what is worse는 '설상가상으로, 엎친 데 덮친 격으로'를 의미하는 표현이다. 아버지가 돌아가시고 거기에 어머니가 병에 걸리셨다는 내용이 what was worse로 바르게 표현되었다.

어휘 warranty 보증(서) expire 만료되다 free of charge 무료의
complete 완성하다 questionnaire 설문지, 질문지
ask for 요청하다 pass away 죽다 what is worse 설상가상으로

03 ③

해석 대학 총장과 도시 산업체와의 우호적인 관계는 몇몇 단과대학에 대한 기부를 초래했다.

어휘 congenial 상냥한, 우호적인(= amiable) gracious 우아한
haphazard 우연한 confidential 비밀의

04 ④

해석 나는 그러한 비생산적인 논쟁에 질려버렸다

어휘 barren 불임의, 비생산적(↔ fertile) silly 어리석은
stubborn 완고한 aggressive 공격적인
unproductive 비생산적인

05 ②

해설 '회의와 전혀 관련 없는 주제를 가져왔다'는 A의 발언에 대해서 '그가 저에게 잘해줬어요' 라는 표현으로 답변을 하는 것은 대화의 흐름상 자연스럽지 않다.

해석 ① A: 이 소포를 내 사무실로 가져다 놓아 주시겠어요?
B: 제게 맡기세요.

② A: Jinmo는 그 컨퍼런스와 관련 없는 사안을 꺼냈어요.
B: 그는 저에게 잘해줬어요.

③ A: 문을 열어도 괜찮을까요?
B: 물론 괜찮죠.

④ A: 그녀의 일이 잘 되어가고 있나요?
B: 제가 알기로는 그렇지 않요. 지금 유동성에 있어서 문제를 가지고 있어요.

06 ③

해설 서로 다른 점을 지닌 사람들이 조직을 이룸으로써 더 큰 힘이 생길 수 있으므로 차이를 존중하라는 내용이므로 빈칸에는 ③ '차이'가 가장 적절하다.

① 체계
② 창의성
④ 순응

해석 점점 더 상호의존적으로 되어가는 세계에서는 차이에 가치를 두는 것이 중요하다. 세계적 차원이 아니라 단지 어느 작은 마을에 있는 어느 직장에서 일하고 있다 하더라도 함께 일하는 사람들 사이에 나이가 많거나 어리거나, 키가 크거나 작거나, 흑인이거나 백인이거나, 부유하거나 가난하거나 등과 같은 다양성이 점점 증가한다는 것을 알게 될 것이다. 어떤 것에 다른 것보다 더 많은 가치를 두어서는 안 되는데 그들 모두 전체를 이루는 데 필요하기 때문이

다. 그것은 시너지 효과라고 하는데 전체는 개별 부분의 총합보다 크다는 의미이다. 그것에 가치를 두어라. 그것은 모든 당사자에게 초기의 어느 정도 적응을 필요로 하겠지만 결국에는 이익이 된다. 동질성은 과거의 것이다. 이질성은 그것의 가치를 증명했는데, 더 많은 두뇌, 더 많은 가치, 더 많은 관점, 더 나은 해결책, 더 큰 결과물, 더 많은 창의성, 그리고 늘어난 이해이다. 그것들은 단지 통 안에 있는 모든 청어가 똑같은 것은 아니라는 사실을 받아들이는 것의 이점의 일부분일 뿐이다.

어휘 crucial 중요한 increasingly 점점 더
interdependent 상호의존적인 diversity 다양성
synergy 시너지 효과, 동반 상승효과 sum 총합 initial 초기의
adjust 적응하다 pay off 이익이 되다, 결실을 얻다
in the long run 결국, 장기적으로 output 결과물, 산물
embrace 받아들이다, 포용하다 barrel (가운데 부분이 불룩한) 통

07 ④

해설 주어진 문장에서 However에 의해서 문맥 전환을 한 후 옛날 지도가 다양한 목적으로, 다양한 형태로 만들어졌음을 확신할 수 있다고 기술되고 있으므로, 주어진 문장의 앞에는 옛날 지도에 대해 확신하지 못하는 내용이 기술되는 것이 좋다. ④의 다음 문장에는 also가 사용되면서 현대인이 확신할 수 있는 내용이 추가로 기술되고 있다. 그러므로 ④가 정답이다.

해석 정확히 어떻게, 언제, 왜, 어디에서 최초의 지도들이 만들어지게 되었는가는 알기 어렵다. 선사 시대와 역사 시대의 초기에 그려진 것 중 대부분은 남아 있지 않으므로, 우리가 오늘날 발견하는 것이 예전에 거기에 있었던 것을 완전히 나타내지 않을 수도 있다. 현대의 관찰자에게 다른 문제들이 있다. 선사시대에 만들어진 지도는 그림의 의미를 설명하거나 그림의 내용을 기술하는 표제를 동반할 리 없다. 하지만 우리는 마치 오늘날처럼 옛날에 지도가 다양한 목적을 위해 만들어졌고 다양한 형태를 취했다는 것을 확신할 수도 있다. 일반 사람들의 믿음과는 반대로, 여러 시대를 통하여 지도가 사용된 모든 목적들 중에서 중요성이 가장 적은 단일한 목적이 길 찾기였다는 것도 명백할 수 있다. 해도는 유럽의 중세가 되어서야 비로소 나타났으며, 18세기가 되어서야 비로소 육로 여행자들이 보통 지형도를 가지고 다니게 되었다.

어휘 be representative of ~을 나타내다[대표하다]
contrary to ~와는 반대로
through the ages 여러 시대를 통하여, 대대로
sea chart 해도 come into existence 나타나다
carry about ~을 가지고 다니다

08 ②

해설 (A) 경제성이 있는 댐 건설 지점을 거의 모두 개발한 산업화된 국가와 그렇지 못한 아프리카의 국가들을 대비시키고 있으므로 In contrast(그에 반해서)를 써야 한다.
(B) 네팔은 많은 양의 포장수력을 지니고 있으나 그 중 아주 적은 부분만을 개발한 상태여서, 미국의 해결책이 네팔에게는 적합하지 않을 것이므로 Thus(그러므로)를 써야 한다.

해석 여러 나라는 서로 다른 경제 발전의 단계에 처해 있으며, 따라서 그 나라들의 댐에 대한 필요성도 각각 다르다는 것을 인식하는 것이 중요하다. 또한, 미국과 같은 산업화된 국가는 자국의 가장 좋고 가장 경제성이 뛰어난 댐 건설 지점을 거의 모두 개발했다. 그에 반해서, (남아프리카 공화국을 제외하고) 사하라 사막 이남 아프리카에 있는 대부분의 가능성이 있는 지점들은 아직 개발되지 않았다. 네팔과 같은 나라는 미국에서 이미 개발된 것과 비슷한 양의 포장수력을 지니고 있다. 그렇지만, 네팔은 자국의 포장수력의 겨우 약 4퍼센트만을 개발했다. 그러므로 현재 미국에게 논리적이고 효율적인 해결책으로 보일지도 모르는 것이 아마도 네팔의 여건에는 가장 좋고 가장 적합한 해결책이 되지 못할 것이다.

어휘 recognize 인식하다 economic 경제의
industrialized 산업화된 with the exception of ~을 제외하고
hydropower potential 포장수력, 수력 발전 가능량 logical 논리적인
efficient 효율적인 solution 해결책

09 ②

해설 조합 상징물이 상징적 의미를 가지고 있다는 내용 다음에, 상징적 의미를 가지는 원리를 설명하는 (B)가 이어지고 앞서 설명한 원리가 현대까지 이어지고 있다는 (C)가 그 다음에 온다. 그리고 (C)에서 소개한 Venice Beach에 있는 광고회사를 'this spectacular building'으로 언급하면서 건물 전면의 상징적 의미에 대해 설명하는 (A)가 마지막으로 와야 흐름이 자연스러운 글이 된다.

해석 랜드 마크를 만들기 위한 매우 오래되고 전형적인 유럽의 방식은 조합 상징물이다. 가게 전면에 있는 커다란 열쇠는 '자물쇠 장수가 여기에서 일하고 있다는 것을 알려주는 것이 예사였다. (B) 조합 상징물은 즉각적으로 어떤 장소와 그 장소의 의미, 그리고 거기에서 일어날 것으로 기대되는 활동들에 대한 인지각본을 촉발한다. 그 상징물은 그곳의 전면 뒤쪽에서 무슨 일이 일어나고 있는지에 대한 표시인 것이다. (C) 그 원리는 건물의 상인방의 형태로 오늘날까지 이어지고 있다. 캘리포니아 주의 Venice Beach에 있는 광고회사의 상인방은 실제로 그 자체로 감탄의 대상이 되고 심지어 숭배되는 존재가 되었다. (A) 가게 정면의 대부분을 덮으며, 걸어서 들어갈 수 있을 만큼 큰 쌍안경의 모양을 가진, 인기 건축가 Frank Gehry가 지은 이 당당한 건물은 정면 뒤쪽에서 일어나고 있는 일이 통찰력, 선견지명, 미래에 대한 안목과 관련이 있음을 말해주고 있다.

10 ④

해설 Farm Security Administration(FSA)에 들어가 미국 농촌 지역의 생활 여건을 보도했다(~, she joined the Farm Security Administration (FSA) and reported on living conditions in the rural areas of the USA.)고 했으므로, ④가 글의 내용과 일치하지 않는다.

해석 Dorothea Lange의 모든 작품은 20세기의 사회 기록사진에 가장 감동적이고 헌신적인 공헌을 한 것들 중의 하나로 여겨진다. 그녀는 뉴욕의 컬럼비아 대학교에서 공부한 이후, 샌프란시스코에서 자영하는 인물 사진작가로 활동하기 시작했다. 대공황 중에 일자리를 찾는 노숙자의 수에 충격을 받고서, 그녀는 거리의 사람들의 곤경에 대한 관심을 끌기 위해 그들의 사진을 찍기로 결심했다. 1935년에, 그녀는 Farm Security Administration(FSA)에 들어가 미국 농촌 지역의 생활 여건을 보도했다. 직접적으로 그녀는 이주 노동자들과 그들 가족의 지독한 빈곤을 기록했다. FSA프로젝트에서 가장 유명한 사진 중 하나는 세 명의 자녀를 둔 한 캘리포니아 이주 노동자의 인물 사진인 Migrant Mother이다. 이 고도로 응집된 (사진의) 이미지는 Dorothea Lange를 사회적으로 뚜렷한 의식을 가진 사진 분야의 아이콘으로 만들었다.

제 20 회 하프 모의고사 해설

문제편 p.081

ANSWER

01 ①	02 ④	03 ③	04 ②	05 ②
06 ③	07 ③	08 ④	09 ①	10 ③

01 ①

해설 (A) 문맥상 '또한 ~이 아닌'의 의미이어야 하고, 네모 다음에 <조동사(is) + 주어(it)>의 어순으로 보아 nor가 적절하다.
(B) 동명사의 의미상의 주어인 Some people이 훈련받을 대상을 가리키므로 수동형인 being disciplined가 적절하다.
(C) 술어 동사 is의 보어 역할을 하는 절이 필요하다. 이 절에서 문장의 주요 요소로 빠져있는 것이 없으므로 that이 적절하다.

해석 동료 의식에 의해 움직이는 사람은 집단의 일원으로서 일을 완수할 기회에 의해 동기를 부여받는다. 여기서 핵심 요인은 팀플레이어(단체 작업을 잘하는 사람)가 되는 능력이 아니고, 연대의식 그 자체도 아니다. 그것은 어떤 사람이 자신이 바라는 결과를 얻기 위해 다른 사람들과 함께 일하고 있다는 사실에 의해 일을 완수하고 최고의 결과를 달성하도록 얼마나 많이 동기가 부여되어 있는가이다. 예를 들어 실내 운동용 자전거를 생각해 보라. 어떤 사람들은 체육관에서 훈련받고 그것들을 타는 데 전혀 문제가 없는데, 그 체육관에는 같은 동작을 하는 다른 사람들이 있다. 하지만 그들의 집에 (실내 운동용 자전거) 한 대가 있다면, 그것에는 먼지가 쌓이고 절대 사용되지 않는다. 그 이유는 품성이 모자라거나 규율이 없기 때문이 아니다. 그 이유는 이러한 사람들의 강력한 동료 의식이라는 동기 요인이 집에 혼자 있을 때는 활성화되지 않는다는 것이다.

어휘 companionship 동료 의식 motivate 동기를 부여하다
factor 요인, 요소 capability 능력 follow through 일을 완수하다
achieve 달성하다 exercise bike 실내 운동용 자전거
discipline 훈련[훈육]하다; 규율 character 품성, 인격
activate 활성화하다

02 ④

해설 ④ 'if I had given up'에서 if가 생략되어 had가 앞으로 나간 had I given up ~의 형태는 바르다. 그러나 의미상 이렇게 훌륭한 성과를 얻지 '못했을 것이다'는 부정이므로 조동사 뒤에 not이 와야 한다. 또한 '~하지 못했다'는 가능의 의미에는 의무를 나타내는 should보다는 could가 어울린다.
① 시간의 부사절을 이끄는 접속사 as soon as에서는 미래시제인 will을 사용할 수 없고 현재 시제로 대체해야 한다.
② '~했어야 했다(그런데 안 했다)'는 'should have p.p' 또는 'rought to have p.p'로 표현할 수 있다.
③ 'Because he has been abroad ~'의 문장이 분사구문이 된 것이다. 그가 지난 10년간 해외에 있었던 것이므로 having been abroad의 완료형 분사구문이 바르게 왔다.

03 ③

해석 위험할 땐, 정착민들은 요새에 모였다. 그들은 요새의 강한 통나무 벽 뒤에서 안전하다고 생각했다.

어휘 congregate 모이다(=gather, convene)
coordinate 조정하다, 협력하다

04 ②

해석 고통은 그가 참을 수 있는 것 이상이었다.

어휘 bear 낳다, 품다, 참다 cure 칠하다 tolerate 참다
carry 운반하다 produce 생산하다

05 ②

해설 시간이 얼마나 걸리는가에 대한 물음에 '이번 주말까지'라는 대답은 어색하다. 따라서 ②가 정답이 된다.

해석 ① A: 왜 이 장치는 제대로 작동하지 않지?
B: 우선 전원을 연결해야 해.
② A: 집에서 사무실까지 얼마나 오래 걸리나요?
B: 바라건데, 이번 주말까지면 좋겠네요.
③ A: 휠체어를 어디서 빌릴 수 있는지 아세요?
B: 후문 주변에서 빌려보세요
④ A: 당신은 이번 주말에 직원교육 모임에 참여할 예정이지요?
B: 그건 의무적이지 않나요?

06 ③

해설 야생 생쥐를 잃은 슬픔을 새로운 생쥐를 얻고 잊은 것처럼 사랑하던 고양이가 죽고 난 뒤 새로운 고양이를 들이는 내용으로 보아, 빈칸에는 ③ '대체함'이 적절하다.
① 울음
② 무시함
④ 관찰함

해석 다섯 살 정도였을 때 나는 집 근처 들판에서 야생 생쥐를 발견했다. 분명히 그 생쥐는 아팠는데, 만약 그렇지 않았다면 그 생쥐는 내가 자기를 집어 들고 집으로 데려오도록 내버려 두지 않았을 것이다. 아버지는 그 생쥐에게 우리를 만들어주셨고 나는 풀씨를 먹였다. 다음 날, 내가 새로운 '친구'를 위해 풀을 한 움큼 가지고 학교에서 돌아왔을 때, 그 생쥐는 죽어 있었다. 내가 얼마나 슬펐는지 오늘날까지 나는 기억한다. 이것이 나의 첫 번째 상실이었다. 아버지는 나의 불행함을 참을 수 없어서 나를 안아 올려 주셨다. 우리는 애완동물 가게로 가서 새로운 생쥐를 샀다. 의도적으로 내게 가르쳐주는 사람이 아무도 없어도, 대체함으로 애통함을 피할 수 있다는 것을 나는 배웠다. 14년 정도 후에 사랑을 많이 받던 고양이가 죽었을 때, 나는 고양이 구조 센터에서 역시 흰색인 수컷 고양이를 고르고 있었다. 애통해하는 방법을 배우는 데에는 성인으로서의 많은 세월이 나에게 필요했다.

어휘 obviously 분명히 otherwise 그렇지 않다면[않았다면]
cage 우리, 새장 feed 먹이를 주다 a handful of 한 움큼의, 한 주먹의
bear 참다, 견디다 consciously 의도적으로
grieve 애통하다, 몹시 슬퍼하다 kitten 새끼 고양이

07 ③

해설 주어진 문장의 this가 가리키는 것은 협력 관계를 공고히 해가는 유기체 집단의 경우를 가리킨다. ③ 다음 문장의 They가 가리키는 것은 주어진 문장의 'organisms ~ reciprocate'이다. 그러므로 주어진 문장이 들어갈 적절한 위치는 ③이다.

해석 각 개체가 낯선 자들과 마주칠 때 임의로 협력하거나 그러지 않는 유기체로 구성된 집단을 상상해 보라. 낯선 자들이 만나서 처음에 협력한다면, 그러면 협력이 점점 더 가능해지는 행동 유형을 확립하는 방향으로 더 높고 더 멀리 나아간다. 내가 당신과 협력하는 것은 당신이 나와 협력할 가능성을 더 높게 만들고, 그것은 내가 당신과 협력할 가능성을 더 높게 만들며, 그렇게 계속된다. 이것은 사회 제도를 가능하게 만드는 행동의 하부 구조이다. 보답하는 경향이 없는 유기체들과 이것을 비교해 보라. 그들은 협력이 일어나는 임의의 사례를 경험할 수 있지만, 이런 사례들이 협력의 가능성을 증가시키지 않으므로, 이 유기체들은 지속적인 상호 보강의 협력이 주는 이득을 얻지는 못할 것이다. 당장에 이기적인 방식으로만 행동하는 자들은 훨씬 더 형편없이 할 것이다. 그들은 삶이 '험악하고 야만적이고 짧은' 자연의 상태에 빠져 꼼짝 못할 것이다.

어휘 organism (사람, 동물, 미생물을 포함한) 유기체
tendency 경향 population 집단, 개체군, 인구
confront 마주치다, 직면하다 randomly 임의로, 닥치는 대로
cooperate 협력하다 initially 처음에 establish 확립하다, 설립하다
infrastructure 하부 구조, 기간 시설
social institution 사회 제도, 사회 시설
incident 사례, 일어난 일, 사건

08 ④

해설 (A) 바로 앞 문장에서 개인주의적인 문화에서의 사람들은 흔히 시간을 자원으로 여긴다고 기술한 후, (A)가 있는 문장에서는 미국인의 예를 들고 있으므로 for instance가 가장 적절하다.
(B) 바로 앞에서는 개인주의적인 문화인 미국의 사례를 기술한 후, (B)가 있는 문장에서는 한국처럼 집단주의적인 문화에서는 효율성보다는 사회적 화합을 강조한다고 기술해서 앞부분의 내용과 대조되므로 In contrast가 가장 적절하다.

해석 문화적 메시지는 많은 의사소통상의 행동을 형성하는데, 청취도 예외는 아니다. 특히, 청취 행동은 특정 문화의 사람들이 시간의 중요성에 대해 어떻게 생각하는지에 의해 영향을 받는 것처럼 보인다. 개인주의적인 문화에서 사람들은 흔히 시간을 자원으로 여긴다. 예를 들어 미국인들은 보통 "시간은 돈이다"라고 말하고, 시간을 절약되고, 사용되고 그리고 낭비될 수 있는 상품으로 여긴다. 그런 문화의 사람들은 일반적으로 효율성을 중요시하고, 다른 사람들도 똑같이 할 것을 기대한다. 그들은 직접적이고 솔직한 의사소통을 중시하고, 청자(聽者)는 '본론으로 들어가지' 않는 화자(話者)를 참지 못한다. 그에 반해서 한국처럼 집단주의적인 문화는 효율성보다는 사회적 화합을 강조한다. 이런 문화의 사람들은 자신들의 청취 행동의 한 부분으로 화자의 메시지의 의미를 알아내기 위해 흔히 비언어적인 행동과 전후 사정과 관련된 단서에 세심한 주의를 기울인다.

어휘 shape 형성하다, 모양 짓다 exception 예외, 제외
in particular 특히 affect ~에 영향을 미치다
individualistic 개인[이기]주의적인 resource 자원
commodity 상품, 물품 typically 일반적으로 efficiency 효율(성)
straightforward 솔직한 impatient with ~을 참지 못하는
get to the point 본론으로 들어가다, 요점을 언급하다
emphasize 강조하다 nonverbal 비언어적인, 말에 의하지 않는
contextual 전후 사정[맥락]과 관련된 cue 단서, 암시
determine 알아내다, 밝히다

09 ①

해설 자연에 존재하는 냄새와 인위적으로 합성한 냄새를 구별할 수 있다고 생각한다는 내용의 주어진 글 다음에, '합성 물질'의 사전적 정의와 그에 대한 예시가 나온 (B)가 나온 다음, 자연에 존재하는 냄새와 인위적으로 합성한 냄새를 구별하는 것이 간단하지 않으며 자연에 존재하는 냄새라고 생각하는 가죽 냄새가 화학 작용에 의한 냄새라는 내용의 (A)가 오고, 이어서 인위적으로 합성한 냄새라고 생각하는 향수가 자연에 존재하는 제품에서 나온다는 예시와 함께 자연적인 것과 인위적으로 합성한 것의 경계가 모호하다는 내용의 (C)가 오는 것이 적절하다.

해석 향수와 음식이 아닌 근원지에서 풍겨 나오는 냄새의 경우에 사람들은 근원지의 특성에 따라 '자연에 존재하는' 냄새와 '(인위적으로) 합성한' 냄새를 그들이 직관적으로 구별할 수 있다고 믿었다. (B) '합성 물질'은 옥스퍼드 영어 사전에 '특히 천연물을 모방하기 위해 화학적 합성으로 만들어진 물질'로 정의되어 있다. 예를 들면, 향수는 일반적으로 합성한 것으로 설명된 반면 가죽은 그것 자체의 자연스러운 냄새가 있다고 여겨졌다. (A) 그러나 자연에 존재하는 냄새와 합성한 기원을 가진 냄새 사이의 구별은 보이는 것만큼 그렇게 간단하지 않다. 예를 들면, 가죽의 냄새는 무두질의 결과로 발생하는데, 그것은 그 자체가 화학 작용에 의존하는 과정이다. 또한 가죽의 합성한 냄새는, 이런 냄새가 몇몇 새 차에 뿌려질 때 그러한 것처럼, 가죽이라고 착각하게 하고 품질 및 새로움과 연관성이 생기게 하기 위해 제품 제조 과정에서 자주 사용된다. (C) 게다가 몇몇 향수 냄새는 자연에 존재하는 산물의 결합 또는 추출에 의해 생산된다. 따라서 자연적인 것과 자연적이지 않은 것, 진짜와 합성의 경계는 냄새에 대한 인식이라는 면에서 매우 모호해지는데, 사람 사이에도 다양한 차이가 있다.

10 ③

해설 'spending their lives collecting flower fragrances that they store in special grooves on their hind legs and that may be released to attract females'라는 부분으로 미루어 보아, 난초벌 수컷은 뒷다리의 홈에 향기를 모으므로 ③은 글의 내용과 일치하지 않는다.

해석 난초벌은 자신들이 가루받이를 해 주는 난초만큼 예쁜데, 아주 밝은 금속성의 청색, 초록색, 그리고 자주색이 선명한 색깔로 배열된 형태를 띤다. 이 벌들은 꿀벌처럼 사회적이지 않다. 그들은 분업이 없고 공동체 활동이 거의 없으며 보통 홀로 벌집을 짓는다. 수컷은 태어나자마자 벌집을 떠나 돌아오지 않으며, 꽃의 향을 모으며 일생을 보내는데, 그 향을 뒷다리의 특별한 홈에 저장하고 그 향은 암컷을 유혹하기 위해 방출되기도 한다. 암컷들은 진흙, 수지, 그리고 다른 재료들로 벌집을 만들며 다양한 식물로부터 꿀과 꽃가루를 모은다. 200종의 난초벌은 중앙아메리카와 남아메리카 토종벌이며 많은 난초의 수분에 중요한 역할을 한다. 한 종류만 미국에서 발견될 수 있다. 이 벌, 즉 Euglossa vidrissimia는 멕시코 혹은 중앙아메리카로부터 최근에 들어온 것인데, 아마도 우연히 미국으로 들어왔을 것이다.

제 21 회 하프 모의고사 해설

문제편 p.085

ANSWER

01 ④	02 ④	03 ③	04 ④	05 ④
06 ②	07 ④	08 ①	09 ①	10 ③

01 ④

해설 ④ 타동사 detect가 react to와 and로 연결되어 목적어를 공유하기 위해서는 change가 changing으로 바뀌어 뒤에 오는 events를 수식하면서 명사구 changing events를 이뤄야 한다.

① 관계사 that의 선행사인 the skills and abilities가 촉진하는(encourage) 행위의 대상을 가리키므로 과거분사 encouraged를 사용한 것은 적절하다.

② 동사 improve를 수식하는 것은 부사여야 하므로 significantly의 사용은 적절하다.

③ they(= recent studies) have shown playing video games to increase short-term ~과 같은 능동태 문장이 수동태 문장으로 바뀌면서 playing video games가 주어가 되고 have shown이 has been shown이 된 구조이므로 to increase는 적절하다.

해석 비디오 게임에서 촉진되는(길러지는) 기술과 능력의 일부는 많은 다른 목적을 위해 쓸모가 있다. 무엇보다도, 비디오 게임은 시각적 인식을 계발하는 데 탁월하다. 예를 들어, 최근의 연구는 그것(비디오 게임)이 외과의가 수술할 때 손을 사용하는 기술을 상당히 향상시킬 수 있다는 것을 분명히 보여 준다. 또한, 비디오 게임을 하는 것은 실험 집단 내의 사람들의 단기 기억을 증대시키는 것으로 증명되었다. 이것의 이유는 대부분의 게임이 게임을 하는 사람들에게 변화하는 사건을 감지하여 반응하도록 그들의 주의력을 화면 전체에 빠르게 펼치도록 요구하기 때문이다. 사실, 비디오 게임을 하는 것은 공간주의력에 필수적인 신경 연결 통로를 발달시키는 데 중요한, 이전에 활동하지 않던 유전자를 촉발할 수 있다. 이제 연구는 비디오 게임을 하는 것이 주의 지속 시간을 줄이기보다는 심지어 늘릴 수조차 있다는 것을 보여 주고 있다.

어휘 **excellent** 탁월한 **visual** 시각적인 **awareness** 인식
significantly 상당히 **operation** 수술
short-term memory 단기 기억 **detect** 감지하다, 발견하다
trigger 촉발하다 **previously** 이전에
inactive 활동하지 않는, 활발하지 않은 **spatial** 공간의
span (어떤 일이 지속되는) 시간[기간]

02 ④

해설 ④ 가주어 it, 진주어 to부정사, 의미상의 주어 for가 사용된 올바른 형태이다. 또한 비교급인 much easier에 대해 접속사 than이 올바르게 연결되고 있다.

① 동사 believe의 목적어로 명사절인 that절에서 주어인 the alternatives에 대한 동사는 won't work이므로 명사인 the alternatives의 뒤에는 관계대명사절 또는 분사의 형태로 수식어가 오는 것이 적절하다. 주격 관계대명사는 생략할 수 없으므로 had 앞에 that/which를 넣어주거나 had been을 생략하여 offered가 과거분사로 명사를 수식하는 분사 형태로 고쳐야 한다.

② 가정법 문장으로, if절의 동사가 hadn't invaded로 가정법 과거완료이므로 주절도 가정법 과거완료시제로 일치되어야 한다. 따라서 World War II might not have taken place라고 써야 한다.

③ wait은 자동사로서 the shadow라는 목적어를 취할 수 없다. 문맥상 the shadow는 to부정사인 to reappear의 의미상의 주어로 쓰이는 것이 적절하다.

03 ③

해석 이 일은 그의 성격과 잘 들어맞는다.

어휘 **congruous** 일치하는, 조화를 이루는 (= coherent, consistent)
avaricious 탐욕스러운 **industrious** 근면한
harmonious 조화로운 **luxurious** 사치하는

04 ④

해석 Bazille은 인상주의파들의 친구이자 후원자 동료로서 인상주의 운동의 형성기에 중요한 역할을 했다.

어휘 **benefactor** 후원자 **critic** 비평가 **peer** 동료, 친구
master 장인 **contributor** 기부자

05 ④

해설 ④ A는 자신에게 온 메시지가 있는지 묻고 있는데 이에 대한 대답으로 예약이 꽉 찼다는 답변은 적절하지 않다.

해석 ① A: 무슨 일이세요? 왜 아침부터 우울해하고 있나요?
B: 그렇게 보이시나요? 저는 조금 몸이 안 좋아요.

② A: 이번 여름에 어디로 여행을 가고 싶은지 결정했나요?
B: 글쎄요, 사실 지금 어떤 제안이든 수용할 수 있어요.

③ A: 전 수도꼭지가 다시 샌다는 것을 믿을 수가 없어요.
B: 그 말은 곧 당신이 엄청난 금액을 지불해야 한다는 것인가요?

④ A: 전 351호에 머물고 있습니다. 저에게 온 어떤 메시지가 있나요?
B: 체크해보겠습니다.... 죄송하지만 오늘밤은 모두 예약이 됐습니다.

06 ②

해설 야생 동물의 수가 너무 많아져서 생태계의 건강이나 인간의 안전을 위협할 대 그 종을 사냥하는 데 대한 제한을 없애고, 거주 지역에서의 동물을 관리하기 위해 전문 사냥꾼들을 고용하는 등의 내용에서 빈칸에는 ② '야생 동물 관리 수단'이 적절하다.

① 신체 훈련 프로그램
③ 사교적이고 경쟁적인 행사
④ 남성을 위한 오락 활동

해석 사냥은 때때로 야생 동물 관리 수단으로 사용된다. 육식 동물이 없을 때 사슴과 먹잇감이 되는 다른 종의 수는 서식지가 지탱하는 능력을 때때로 넘어서고, 그 수가 억제되지 않을 때 그것들은 생태계의 건강이나 인간의 안전을 위협한다. 사냥꾼들이 동물의 수를 줄인 결과로 살아남은 것들이 건강한 삶을 살기에 충분한 먹이과 피난처를 가지게 된다. 예를 들어 어떤 기러기 종을 사냥하는 데 대한 제한이 제거되어 왔는데, 그 기러기 종은 수가 너무 많아져서

북극과 북극에 가까운 곳에 있는 많은 종의 번식지를 파괴하고 있는 중이다. 전문 사냥꾼들은 공원에서의 곰 같은 거주 지역에 있는 동물들을 통제하기 위해 때때로 고용된다. 현대 미국의 사냥꾼들은(사냥용으로) 따로 확보해 둔 땅을 구입하거나 사냥감의 보호를 위해 정부에 로비를 함으로써 자신들의 스포츠를 보호하기 위한 (자연) 보호 노력을 지원한다.

어휘 predator 육식 동물 prey species 먹잇감이 되는 종
exceed 넘어서다, 초과하다 habitat 서식지
unchecked 억제되지 않은 ecosystem 생태계 shelter 피난처
goose 기러기, 거위 subarctic 북극에 가까운, 아(亞)북극의
breeding ground 번식지 populated area 거주 지역
set aside 확보해 두다, 한 쪽으로 치워 놓다 lobby 로비를 하다

07 ④

해설 주어진 문장의 these problems는 ①과 ④ 사이에 있는 내용을 가리킨다. ④ 뒤의 문장은 주어진 문장에서 따옴표로 표시된 질문을 했을 때 얻을 수 있는 부가적 효과에 대한 내용이다. 따라서 주어진 문장은 ④에 들어가는 것이 가장 적절하다.

해석 질문을 할 때마다, 왜 그것을 물어보는지 말하라. 질문만 있다면 듣는 이의 머릿속에 "왜 그가 그 질문을 했지?"와 같은 또 다른 질문을 일으킨다. 여러분이 말을 건네는 사람은 가능한 대답을 머릿속에서 생각하기 때문에 여러분에게 귀 기울이는 일을 즉시 멈출 것이다. 그들은 여러분이 그 질문을 하고 있는 이유를 모른다면 짜증날 수 있다. 그들은 여러분의 질문이 여러분에게 정보를 제공하라는 그들에 대한 요구이기 때문에 여러분이 그들을 반대신문하고 있는 것 같은 느낌을 받거나 불안을 느낄지도 모른다. 예를 들어 여러분의 질문에 앞서 "방금 말씀하신 것을 제가 이해하고 있는지 확인하기 위해 질문을 하나 하겠습니다."라는 말을 하면 이런 문제들을 제거할 수 있다. 어떤 사람이 말한 것에 대해 잘못된 속단을 내리는 일을 피하는 것 이외에도, 그 사람이 여러분에게 전하고 있는 것에 대해 여러분은 관심을 보여 주며, 그것은 결국에는 여러분이 할 말에 대해 그들의 청취력을 강화한다.

어휘 eliminate 제거하다 precede ~에 앞서다, 선행하다
instantly 즉시 irritated 짜증난 cross-examine 반대신문하다
jump to the conclusion 속단하다 communicate (생각을) 전하다
in turn 결국에는, 차례차례 sharpen 강화하다, 날카롭게 하다

08 ①

해설 (A) 신문과 잡지 같은 인쇄 매체에서 발행 부수는 실제 배포된 숫자를 가리키지만, 독자 수는 출판물 한 부에 대해 여러 명이 될 수 있기 때문에 발행 부수와 총 독자 수는 다를 수 있다. 따라서 역접을 나타내는 However가 가장 적절하다.
(B) 앞에서 구체적인 예를 들어가며 설명한 발행 부수와 독자 수에 관한 내용을 하나의 문장으로 정리하므로 Thus가 가장 적절하다.

해석 서로 다른 매체는 서로 다른 방식으로 독자를 모은다. 신문과 잡지 같은 인쇄 매체에서 성공의 한 가지 척도는 배포된 출판물의 실제 숫자, 즉 발행 부수이다. 하지만 출판물 한 부를 보통 한 명이 넘는 사람들이 읽는다. 예를 들어 대부분의 신문은 평균적으로 한 부당 두 명의 독자가 있는 반면에, 'People'과 같은 어떤 잡지들은 한 부당 여덟 명이 넘는 독자가 있을 수도 있다. 그래서 총 독자 (수)는 발행 부수 곱하기 한 부당 독자 (수)이다. 따라서 인쇄 매체에서 발행 부수는 인쇄된 부수인 반면에, 독자 (수)는 그런 (인쇄된) 출판물의 부수를 읽은 사람들의 수이다. 여러분은 출판물 한 부당 한 명이 넘는 독자를 끌어들이기를 원하기 때문에 독자 수는 보통 배포 수보다 더 많을 것이다.

어휘 accumulate 모으다 audience (잡지 따위의) 독자(층)
print media 인쇄 매체 measure (판단·측정의) 척도[기준]
actual 실제의 publication 출판(물) distribute 배포하다
circulation 발행 부수, (신문·잡지 등의) 배포
average 평균하여 ~하다[~이 되다] upwards of ~보다 많게
multiply 곱하다, 증가시키다 attract (사람을) 끌어들이다

09 ①

해설 법 사회화와 도덕 사회화의 목표에 대해 설명하는 주어진 글 다음에, 그 둘이 보통 같은 목표를 향해 작용하는 것 같지만 꼭 그런 것은 아니라는 내용의 (B)가 이어져야 한다. (B)의 the two는 주어진 글의 legal socialization과 moral socialization을 가리킨다. 법 사회화와 도덕 사회화가 다르게 작용할 수 있다는 (B)의 마지막 문장 다음에, 법으로 금지하는 행동과 비도덕적 행동이 같은 것은 아니라는 내용의 (A)가 나와야 한다. 비도덕적인 행동을 법으로 금지하는 것을 사람들이 지지하지 않을 수도 있다는 내용의 (A)의 마지막 문장 다음에 사람들이 비도덕적 행동에 대한법적 규제를 설령 지지한다 하더라도 법적 개입의 방식과 정도에 대해서는 의견이 다르다는 내용의 (C)가 나와야 한다.

해석 법 사회화의 목표는 사람들에게 법을 따르고 법적 권위를 수용할 절실한 의무감이나 책임감을 심어주는 것이다. 도덕 사회화의 목표는 사람들에게 규칙과 규범과는 관계없이 적절한 행동의 사회적 기준을 따를 의무감을 심어주는 것이다. (B) 보통의 일상생활에서 사회가 비도덕적이라고 여기는 그런 행동들이 빈번하게 법에 의해 금지된다는 점을 고려하면, 그 둘은 보통 같은 목표를 향해 작용한다. 하지만, 항상 그런 것은 아니다. (A) 어떤 행동을 법으로 금지하는 것은 그것을 비도덕적으로 만드는 것이 아니며, 모든 비도덕적인 행동이 반드시 법으로 금지되는 것도 아니다. 대부분의 사람들은 어떤 행동이 비도덕적이라고 믿지만 사람들이 그것을 하는 것을 막기 위해 그것을 법으로 금지하거나 법의 온전한 힘을 사용하는 것을 자신들이 지지하지 않을 경우를 생각 할 수 있다. (C) 동시에 사람들은 비록 자신들이 비도덕적 행동의 법적 규제를 추상적으로 정말 지지한다고 하더라도, 어떻게 그리고 어느 정도나 법체계가 개입하기를 원하는지에 있어서는 서로 다르다. 그러한 관점들은 사람들이 사회 안에서 법의 위치와 기능을 이해하는 방식에 의해 강하게 형성된다.

10 ③

해설 1964년에 McCarthy는 캘리포니아주에 있는 Stanford University의 교수진에 합류했고, 그 학교의 인공지능 연구소를 설립했다(In 1964 McCarthy joined the faculty of Stanford University in California and founded the school's AI lab.)고 했으므로, ③이 글의 내용과 일치하지 않는다.

해석 1940년대에 John McCarthy가 California Institute of Technology의 학생일 때 그는 헝가리계 미국인 수학자인 John von Neumann의 '자기 복제 자동 장치', 즉 스스로 복제할 수 있는 기계에 대한 강연에 참석했다. (그런 기계는 존재하지 않았다. Von Neumann의 생각은 그저 이론이었다.) 강연 후에 McCarthy는 스스로 복제할 수 있는 기계는 어떤 형태의 지능을 가질 수 있을지도 모른다고 추론했다. 그 생각은 그의 뇌리에 박혀 있었다. 1964년에 McCarthy는 캘리포니아주에 있는 Stanford University의 교수진에 합류했고, 그 학교의 인공지능 연구소를 설립했다. 그 당시에 그는 10년 안에 과학자들이 인공지능 시스템을 만들 수 있을 것이라고 낙관했다. 나중에 McCarthy는 더 현실적인 시각을 가졌다. 2003년에 Journal of the Association for Computing Machinery에 기고하면서 그는 인공지

능을 달성할 가능성이 '앞으로 49년 안에는 0.5의 확률이지만, 지금으로 부터 49년 후에 그 문제가 오늘날과 꼭 같이 복잡할 확률은 0.25'라고 설정했다.

제 22 회 하프 모의고사 해설

문제편 p.089

ANSWER

01 ④	02 ④	03 ②	04 ④	05 ①
06 ①	07 ③	08 ④	09 ④	10 ④

01 ④

해설 (A) Not only가 절의 앞으로 이동하면서 <조동사(can) + 주어(the climate) + 동사원형>의 어순이 되어야 하므로 동사원형인 determine을 사용해야 한다.

(B) 동명사 helping은 동사와 같은 성질(목적어(them)와 목적격보어(to slide off)를 취함)을 가지고 있기 때문에 이를 수식할 때 부사 efficiently를 사용해야 한다.

(C) <with + 명사구(the majority of the structure) + 분사>의 구문이 a greenhouse를 수식하고 있다. the majority of the structure가 덮어 가리는 동작(house)의 대상을 가리키므로 housed를 사용하는 것이 적절하다.

해석 계절에 따라 다른 기상 상태는 늘 온실 원예사들의 관심사이다. 기후는 어떤 형태의 온실을 지어야 할지를 결정할 수 있을 뿐만 아니라, 온실이 지어진 이후에 철에 따라 그것(온실)이 어떻게 기능을 할 것인가를 결정하는 데 있어서 중요한 역할을 할 수도 있다. 예를 들면 눈이 심하게 자주 오는 추운 날씨의 기후에서는, 경사가 큰 지붕이 이상적일 수 있는데, 왜냐하면 그것이 얼음과 눈이 미끄러져 떨어지는 것을 효율적으로 도와줌으로써 그것들이 쌓이는 것을 막을 수 있기 때문이다. 더 적은 강설량을 접하지만 차갑고 강한 바람이 부는 지역에서는, 구조물 대부분이 땅속에 덮여 가려진 온실인, 태양에 의해 가열되는 구덩이 형태의 온실이 제일 나은 선택일 텐데, 왜냐하면 그것이 자연적으로 단열이 되어 가동하는 데 열을 덜 필요로 하기 때문이다. 기후가 더 온화한 지역에서는 이와 똑같은 종류의 지붕이 실용적이지 않을 것이다.

어휘 seasonal 계절에 따라 다른 determine 결정하다
critical 중요한 frequently 자주 snowfall 강설량
high-pitched 경사가 큰 ideal 이상적인 build-up 증가, 축적
location 지역, 장소 structure 구조물
house 덮어 가리다, 넣어 두다, 저장하다 operate 가동[운영]하다
practical 실용적인 temperate (기후가) 온화한

02 ④

해설 ④ '~이 없었다면'의 과거완료는 'If it had not been for ~'라고 쓴다. 주절의 would not be는 가정법 과거이므로 would not have been으로 고쳐야 한다.

① '마치 ~처럼'을 의미하는 as if 뒤에 가정법을 사용할 수 있는데 현재 사실에 대한 가정을 하므로 가라고 쓴 것이 옳다.

② <What if + 주어 + should + 동사원형>은 '~하면 어떻게 하지?'라는 우려와 걱정을 의미하는 표현이다.

③ If로 시작하는 조건절에서 미래의 will은 현재 시제로 대체한다. tomorrow라는 미래 If의 부사가 있지만 will rain 대신에 현재인 rains로 표현한 것이 옳다.

어휘 gravitation 중력

03 ②

해석 그는 마지막 순간까지 의식이 있었다.

어휘 conscious 의식이 있는 severe 혹독한 awake 깨어있는
eternal 영원한 courageous 용기 있는

04 ④

해석 개인은 관대한 통제 아래서 조차도 무력하다

어휘 benevolent 친절한 valuable 가치 있는
plausible 그럴싸한 obscure 애매한 generous 관대한

05 ①

해설 저녁식사가 괜찮았는지를 물어보는 질문에 음식의 장소를 이야기 하고 있다.

해석 ① A: 저녁식사 어땠어?
B: 냉장고를 뒤졌는데 거기에 저녁이 있었어.
② A: 점점 추워지고 있어.
B: 걱정마. 내가 담요를 갖다 줄게.
③ A: 둘 중 어느 것을 선택해야 할지 모르겠어.
B: 점프 볼 상황 같구나.
④ A: 왜 옷깃 밑이 그렇게 닳아 올랐어?
B: 남자 친구와 막 한바탕 했거든.

06 ①

해설 화요일에 주식이 오른 것과 수요일에 주식이 오르는 것은 서로 관계가 없다는 예를 들면서 어제 무슨 일이 일어났는지를 안다고 해서 내일 무슨 일이 일어날지의 가능성을 알 수는 없다고 하는 본문의 내용으로 보아, 빈칸에는 ① '추세에는 경향성이 없었다'가 적절하다.

② 더 많은 시도에 의해 가능성이 증가할 수 있다.
③ 우리는 미래를 예측하고 준비할 수 있다.
④ 사람들은 주식이 올랐을 때 더 적은 위험을 원했다.

해석 특정 주식이 내일 오를 가능성이 50%라고 가정해보라. 이제 화요일에 그 주식이 오른다고 가정해보라. 수요일에 그것이 오를 가능성은 얼마인가? 화요일의 결과와 수요일의 결과가 서로 독립적이라면, 즉 추세가 없다면, 수요일에 그것이 오를 가능성은 화요일의 가능성과 똑같은 50%이다. 화요일에 주식이 올랐다는 사실이 어떤 것도 변화시키지 않았다. 주식이 수요일에 오르는지 아닌지는 화요일에 그것이 올랐는지 아닌지와 상관이 없다. 대부분의 연구와 측정값에서는 추세에는 경향성이 없었다는 것을 발견했다. 여러분이 내일 무슨 일이 일어날지의 가능성을 산정할 때, 어제 무슨 일이 일어났는지를 아는 것은 도움이 되지 않는다.

어휘 suppose 가정하다 chance 가능성 stock 주식
independent 독립적인 trend 추세, 경향
have nothing to do with ~와 상관이 없다 measurement 측정값
assess 산정하다, 평가하다

07 ③

해설 ③ 이전에서는 전진 패스가 합법화되지 않았을 때의 미식축구의 상황을 말하고 있고, ③ 뒤에는 전진 패스가 합법화되고 난 다음의 상황을 말하고 있으므로, 전진 패스를 허용하도록 규칙이 개정되었다는 내용의 주어진 문장은 ③의 위치에 들어가는 것이 가장 적절하다.

해석 1905년에 미식축구는 달리며 공을 차는 점수가 적게 나는 스포츠였다. 가죽 헬멧을 쓴 한 무리의 사람들이 미식축구장에서 줄지어서 3~4 야드 전진을 얻기 위해 상대편을 뒤로 밀칠 수 있는지 가늠하곤 했다. 4야드 전진은 대단한 일이었다. 1906년에 전진 패스가 합법화되었을 때, 손목을 한 번 휙 움직여 더 많은 거리를 전진하는 것이 갑자기 가능하게 되었다. 그 규칙이 바뀐 후 첫 시즌 동안 한 팀을 제외하고 모든 팀들은 여전히 전통적인 달리기 경기에 머물러 있었다. 미식축구가 변화의 시대, 즉 전진 패스의 시대에 들어섰다는 것을 깨닫고서, St. Louis University의 코치들은 (전진) 패스를 이용한 공격적인 게임에 재빨리 적응했다. 그 시즌에 그들은 기꺼이 변화하고자 했기 때문에 상대팀들을 402대 11로 크게 이겼다!

어휘 legalize 합법화하다, 공인하다
flick 휙 움직임; 잽싸게 움직이다 wrist 손목, 팔목 bunch 무리, 묶음
leather 가죽 helmet 헬멧 a big deal 대단한 일
conventional 전통적인 era 시대 adapt to ~에 적응하다
outscore ~보다 많이 득점하다 opponent 상대편

08 ④

해설 (A) 앞에는 몸집이 더 작은 동물들이 더 많은 체열을 잃는다는 점이 언급되었고, 뒤에는 몸집이 매우 작은 생쥐나 벌새가 체온을 꾸준히 유지하기 위해 많은 칼로리를 연소시켜야 한다는 내용이 언급되었으므로 인과관계를 나타내는 As a result가 가장 적절하다.
(B) 앞에는 작은 동물들은 물질대사가 활발하여 체열의 손실이 많다는 요지의 내용이 전개되지만, 뒤에는 큰 동물들은 커다란 몸집 때문에 따뜻한 몸을 가질 수 있다는 대조적인 내용이 나오므로 Conversely가 가장 적절하다.

해석 동물은 표면을 통해 체열을 잃으므로, 더 높은 표면적 대 부피의 비율은 더 큰 체열의 손실이라는 결과를 가져올 것이다. 이는 몸집이 더 작은 동물들이 더 많은 체열을 잃는 이유이다. 그러므로 생쥐나 벌새는 일정한 체온을 유지하기 위해 많은 칼로리를 연소시켜야 한다. 이는 온혈동물들이 몸집이 커짐에 따라 물질대사 비율이 감소하는 주된 이유이다. (몸집이) 작은 포유동물들은 상대적으로 더 많은 체열을 생산하도록 진화하였다. 그것들의 더 빠른 물질대사 비율은 그것들이 그만큼 오래 살지 못한다는 것을 의미한다. (몸집이) 작은 동물들은 (몸집이) 큰 동물들보다 수명이 더 짧은 경향이 있고, 온혈동물은 냉혈동물보다 수명이 더 짧은 경향이 있다. 반대로 (몸집이) 큰 동물들은 따뜻한 몸을 가질 수 있는 데, 단지 그것들이 크기 때문이다. 예를 들면, 대형 공룡들은 아마도 온혈동물이었을 텐데, 단순히 그것들의 낮은 표면적 대 부피의 비율 때문이었다.

어휘 constant 일정한, 꾸준한 decline 감소하다
mammal 포유동물 relatively 상대적으로 warm-blooded 온혈의
cold-blooded 냉혈의 dinosaur 공룡

09 ④

해설 수년 동안 다양한 분야에서 경쟁 관계였던 영국과 프랑스 사이의 사망자 수와 평균 수명에 대한 기록에 대해 언급하고 있는 주어진 글 다음에, 그 기록(this)의 차이를 발생시키는 요인이 엄격함을 중시하는 민족성의 차이에서 기인한다는 영국인들의 생각을 담은 (C)가 이어지고, 또 다른 요인으로 남과 북의 지역차를 거론하는 (B)가 연결되고, 마지막으로 앞서 언급한 남과 북의 차이가 프랑스 국내에서도 발생한다는 (A)가 오는 것이 가장 적절한 글의 순서이다.

해석 오랫동안 영국과 프랑스의 경쟁은 럭비 경기, 정치, 그리고 모욕적 언행을 주고받는 것에서 사망률 통계를 주고받는 것에 이르기까지 확대되었다. 프랑스에서 기록이 정확하게 수집되기 시작한 이래로 기록들은 (프랑스가) 영국보다 심장병으로 인한 사망자 수가 상당히 적고 수명이 더 길다는 것을 알려주었다. (C) 프랑스인들은 이를 자랑스러워하지만, 많은 영국인 동료들은 그 차이의 상당 부분이 죽음을 동일한 '앵글로 색슨의 엄격함'을 가지고 제대로 기록하기를 꺼리는 것에 기인한다고 말한다. (B) 다른 사람들은 (사망자 집계의) 분류 오류는 기껏해야 그 차이의 20퍼센트만을 설명할 수 있다고 주장하면서 이 말에 동의하지 않고 유럽 전역에서 일관되게 나타나는 남북 차이를 거론한다. (A) 심지어 프랑스 자체 내에서도 남과 북 사이에는 큰 차이가 존재하고, 이는 영국과 프랑스의 대부분의 차이가 남부 사람들의 더 건강한 습관 때문이라는 것을 암시한다.

10 ④

해설 2층짜리 목조 건물로 이루어진 학교에 기숙사가 없어서, 석조 건물을 새로 세웠다. 그러므로 ④는 글의 내용과 일치하지 않는다.

해석 Alexander Lucius Twilight은 버몬트 주(州)에서 1795년에 농부의 아들로 태어났다. 1823년에 그는 대학을 졸업한 최초의 미국 흑인이 됨으로써 역사에 남았다. 그는 학교에서 가르치기 시작했으며 뉴욕 주의 Peru와 버몬트 주의 Vergennes에서 설교할 수 있는 설교자로서의 면허를 가지고 있었다. 1829년에, 그는 버몬트 주의 Brownington으로 이주하여, 회중 교회의 목사이자 카운티 중등학교인 Brownington Academy의 교장이 되었다. 버몬트 주가 그의 학교에 계속해서 자금을 제공할 것을 확실히 하기 위해, 그는 버몬트 주 의회 선거에 출마하여 선출되었으며 그런 지위에 선출된 최초의 미국 흑인이 되었다. Twilight이 Brownington Academy의 교장직을 수락했을 때, 그 학교는 2층짜리 목조 건물로 이루어져 있었다. 기숙사가 없어서, 학생들은 인근 지역에 있는 가정에서 함께 지냈다. Twilight은 그런 상황을 바꾸기로 결심했다. 그는 Athenian Hall이라 불리는 크고 견고한 석조 건물의 건축 자금을 제공할 충분한 돈을 간신히 마련했다. 그 석조 건물은 현재 버몬트 주의 Orleans 카운티 역사 협회 본부이다.

ANSWER

01 ③	02 ④	03 ①	04 ②	05 ④
06 ②	07 ③	08 ④	09 ①	10 ③

01 ③

해설 ③ 관계절에는 문장의 요소가 하나 반드시 빠져 있어야 한다. what 다음에 빠져 있는 문장 요소가 없으므로 figure out의 목적어 역할을 하는 절을 이끌 수 있도록 what을 that으로 바꿔야 한다.

① when speaking with a child는 접속사가 명시된 분사구문이다. you가 이 분사구문의 의미상의 주어이고 말하는 행위자이므로 speaking을 사용하는 것은 적절하다.

② it은 the phrase slam the door를 대신한다.

④ 주어인 The chances for a successful response for child의 핵이 chances이므로 술어 동사로 복수형인 increase를 쓰는 것은 적절하다.

해석 아이와 말할 때 여러분이 원하지 않는 것을 강조하기보다는 원하는 것을 표현하는 것을 배워라. 아이들은 자신들이 받는 메시지에 매우 즉각적으로 반응을 보인다. 어른이 "문을 쾅 닫지 마라."라고 말하면, (그 말을) 듣는 아이는 앞에 '하지 마라'라는 단어가 놓인 '문을 쾅 닫다'라는 어구를 듣게 된다. 그 아이는 문을 쾅 닫는 것이 바람직하지 않은 행동이라는 것을 이해해야 하는데, 그것은 특히 어린 아이들에게 이해하기가 어렵다. 아이로부터 성공적인 반응을 끌어낼 가능성은 어른이 "문을 부드럽게 닫아 주렴."이라고 말할 때 극적으로 증가한다. 이제 그 아이는 따라야 하는 시각적 이미지를 가지게 된다. (아이에게) 건네진 말은 그 요청과 잘 들어맞고, 이는 그것("Please close the door gently."라는 말이 요청으로 사용되고 있다는 것)을 이해하기 훨씬 더 쉽게 해 준다.

어휘 put emphasis on ~을 강조하다
responsive 즉각적으로 반응하는 figure out ~을 이해하다
undesirable 바람직하지 않은 comprehend 이해하다
dramatically 극적으로 fit together well 잘 들어맞다

02 ④

해설 ④ '벽돌로'라는 의미를 전달하기 위해 도구, 수단을 의미하는 전치사 with가 적합하다. by는 행위자나 방법을 설명할 때 사용된다.

① so that이 결과의 의미, 즉 '그래서'라는 의미의 부사절 접속사로 바르게 쓰였다.

② more ~ than의 비교급 구문이 바르게 쓰였으며, 비교급인 more boring을 비교급 수식 표현인 far가 수식하고 있다.

③ <It ~ to>의 가주어, 진주어 구문에서 형용사가 사람의 성격을 의미하는 인성형용사일 때, to부정사의 의미상의 주어는 for가 아닌 <of + 목적격>으로 표현하는 것이 옳다. 인성형용사 thoughtful이 쓰여 의미상의 주어 of him이 바르게 쓰였다.

03 ①

해석 의견의 일치가 있었다.

어휘 consensus 일치 approval 승인, 동의 dissent 반대
dispute 논쟁 contradiction 모순, 반박

04 ②

해석 Anthony와 Robert가 그날 아침 호수로 항해를 나갔을 때 날씨는 온화했지만, 정오에는 상황이 급격하게 변했다

어휘 benign 인자한, 온화한(= benevolent) steady 꾸준한
crucial 중대한 temperate 온화한, 절제된 tremendous 거대한

05 ④

해석 ① A: 마감시간까지 이 프로젝트를 끝낼 수 있을 것 같지 않아.
B: 천천히 해. 분명 끝낼 수 있을 거야.

② A: 엄마, 어머니의 날에 무얼 받기를 원하세요?
B: 나는 아무것도 필요 없다. 너 같은 아들을 가진 것만으로도 행복하다.

③ A: 이 케이크에 뭔가 문제가 있어. 전혀 달지가 않아.
B: 니 말이 맞아. 그냥 소금 덩어리 맛이야.

④ A: 이걸 좀 들어 주시겠어요? 제가 손이 충분치 않네요.
B: 물론이죠. 제가 바로 넘겨 드리겠습니다.

06 ②

해설 갑자기 흔들리는 비행기 안의 공포스런 상황에서처럼, 사람들은 소속감과 위안감을 느끼기 위해서도 자신의 감정이나 반응을 타인의 것과 비교할 것이라고 했으므로 빈칸에 가장 적절한 말은 ② '유대'이다.

① 통제
③ 우월
④ 투지

해석 많은 사회 비교 연구는 평가를 야기하는 객관적 특성들에 대해 사람들이 어떻게 자신과 다른 사람들을 비교하는지를 강조해왔다. 일반적으로, 그러한 비교는 대비 효과를 낳는데, 그로 인해 자기 자신의 특성을 다른 사람들과 다르거나 그들에 비해 두드러진다고 여긴다. 하지만 흔히 사람들은 유대감이 생길 수 있는 상황에서 자신의 감정이나 반응을 다른 사람들의 것과 비교한다. 예를 들어, 만약 여러분이 착륙 전에 갑자기 상당히 거칠게 흔들리고 기울기 시작한 비행기에 타고 있다면, 여러분은 아마도 자신의 반응을 근처 승객들의 반응들과 비교할 것이다. 그렇게 해서 여러분이 의도하는 것은 자신의 공포 반응을 평가하기를 바란다기보다 그 경험을 함께 하고 있는 타인들에게서 소속감과 위안감을 느끼기 원하는 것일 것이다.

어휘 comparison 비교 objective 객관적인 invite 야기하다
evaluation 평가 result in ~을 낳다, 초래하다 contrast 대비
attribute 특성, 속성 distinctive 두드러진, 뚜렷이 구별되는
relative to ~에 비하여 wildly 거칠게, 심하게
settle down 착륙하다 in so doing 그렇게 해서

07 ③

해설 주어진 문장에서 휴가 계획을 위해서 평균 기온을 계산할 때에는 극단의 것을 무시하는 것이 좋을 수 있다고 하였고, ③ 뒤에서는 날씨의 물리적 특성을 연구할 때에는 이러한 방법(극단의 것을 제거하는 것)이 효과적이지 않다고 하였으므로 주어진 문장이 들어가기에 가장 적절한 곳은 ③이다. 'But it does not work ~'에서 it은 주어진 문장에 있는 'to take out the extremes'를 가리킨다.

해석 물질적 세계에서 많은 과학자들은 통계를 잘못 해석하면서, 어리석음을 범하기 쉽다. 한 가지 명확한 예는 지구온난화 논쟁에 있다. 많은 과학자들은 기온의 급등이 재발할 것 같지 않다는 소신 하에 표본에서 이것(기온의 급등)을 제거했기 때문에 초기 단계에서 그것(지구온난화)을 알아채지 못했다. 휴가 계획을 위해 평균 기온을 계산할 때에는 극단의 것들을 제거하는 것이 좋은 생각일 수 있다. 그러나 날씨의 물리적 특성을 연구할 때에는, 특히 누적 효과에 대해서 신경을 쓸 때에는 그것이 효과적이지 않다. 이 과학자들은, 드물기는 하지만 이 급등이 누적되는 만년설의 용해를 불균형적으로 증가시키는 영향을 미친다는 사실을 처음에 무시했다. 재정에서와 마찬가지로, 드물지만 큰 결과를 가져오는 사건은 그냥 무시될 수 없다.

어휘 take out 제거하다, 빼다 extreme 극단, 극도
compute 계산하다, 산출하다 physical 물질적인, 물리적인
be subject to ~의 영향을 받기 쉽다, ~당하기 쉽다
foolishness 어리석음 misread 잘못 해석하다 statistics 통계
obvious 명백한 recur 재발하다 property 특성
particularly 특별히 care about ~에 신경을 쓰다 nitially 처음에
add to ~을 증가시키다 disproportionately 불균형하게
melting 용해 ice cap 만년설

08 ④

해설 (A) 어떤 야생 생물들은 보초 종의 역할을 하고 환경적 건강을 추적 관찰하는 데 사용된다는 내용에 이어, 점박이 올빼미가 그 사례로 제시되고 있으므로 For instance가 들어가야 한다.
(B) 점박이 올빼미가 노숙림이 부족해질 경우 가장 먼저 영향을 받는 종들 중 하나라는 내용에 이어, 점박이 올빼미의 건강한 개체 수를 유지해 줄 정도의 충분한 노숙림이 있다면 다른 종들이 필요로 하는 것들을 충족할 정도로 충분한 숲이 있다고 판단할 수 있다는 내용이 나온다. 두 문장 사이에 논리적 인과 관계가 성립되므로 Hence가 들어가야 한다.

해석 야생 생물의 과학적 가치는 그것이 과학의 발전에서 수행하는 역할에 기인한다. 우리가 생태계와 행동에 대해 알고 있는 것의 많은 부분은 야생 생물을 연구하는 것으로부터 나왔다. 어떤 유형의 야생 생물은 보초 종의 역할을 하고 환경의 건강 상태를 추적 관찰하는 데 사용된다. 예를 들어 점박이 올빼미는 우리가 미국의 태평양 연안 북서부에 충분한 노숙림(숲의 나이가 오래된 산림)을 보존해 왔는지를 추적 관찰하기 위해 환경 운동가들에 의해 이용된다. 점박이 올빼미는 넓은 행동 범위를 가지고 있기 때문에 그것들은 노숙림이 부족해질 때 가장 먼저 영향을 받는 종들 중 하나이다. 그러므로 우리는 만약 점박이 올빼미의 건강한 개체수를 지탱해 줄 충분한 노숙림이 있다면, 그러면 다른 종들이 필요로 하는 것들을 충족해 줄 충분한 양의 숲이 있을 것이라고 추론한다.

어휘 wildlife 야생 생물 advancement 발전, 진보
monitor 추적 관찰하다, 감시하다 spotted 점무늬[물방울무늬]가 있는
environmentalist 환경 운동가 preserve 보호하다, 지키다
home range 행동 범위, 활동 범위 scarce 부족한, 드문
sufficient 충분한

09 ①

해설 감자는 수확하고 나면 곰팡이와 부패에 취약해서 보관이 힘들다는 주어진 글 뒤에는 however와 함께 남아메리카 원주민들이 감자를 저장하는 방법을 개발했다는 내용의 문장이 이끄는 글 (B)가 와야 한다. (B) 뒤에는 감자를 저장하는 과정을 묘사하는 (A)가 와야 하고, 그 과정을 통해 만들어진 chuño의 보관법과 조리법이 언급된 (C)가 마지막에 와야 글의 흐름이 자연스럽다.

해석 감자는 일단 수확되면 이상적인 조건에서도 겨우 몇 달간만 신선하게 유지되다가 싹이 나고, 곰팡이와 부패에 취약하다. (B) 하지만 남아메리카 원주민들은 기근에 대비한 안전장치를 제공하기 위해 그것들이 수년간 보관될 수 있도록 그것들을 (썩지 않게) 저장하는 방법을 개발했다. Altiplano(안데스 산맥의 높은 고원)의 춥고 건조한 기후가 이것을 가능하게 했다. (A) 감자는 수확 후에 이슬이 그 위에 내려앉는 것을 막기 위해 덮인 상태로 몹시 추운 기온에 하룻밤 밖에 놓여진다. 그다음 날에 그 감자는 태양에 노출되고, 농가 식구들, 즉 남자, 여자, 아이들이 모두 언 감자를 밟아 으깨어 그 액을 짜냈는데, (이는) 그다음 여러 날 동안 여러 번 반복되는 과정이었다. (C) 그 결과로 생긴 chuño라고 불리는 냉동 건조된 감자는 수년간 신선하게 유지되다가 (상태가) 나빠지게 될 밀폐된 영구 냉동 지하 창고에 보관되었다. chuño는 빻아서 가루로 만들어 구워서 빵으로 만들거나, 수프와 chupe 같은 스튜를 걸쭉하게 하기 위해 물을 넣어 원상으로 되돌려 사용되었는데, 그것(chupe)은 구할 수 있는 고기와 채소로 만들어졌다.

10 ③

해설 세계에서 가장 유명한 마야의 고고학 유적 중 일부가 국토의 북쪽에 있다는 진술이 있으므로 ③이 일치하는 내용이다.

해석 과테말라는 중앙아메리카, 즉 Mesoamerica에, 북쪽으로 멕시코, 남쪽으로 온두라스와 엘살바도르 사이에 있다. 그곳은 태평양과 멕시코 만을 따라 작은 해안 평야만을 가진, 산이 많은 국가이다. 저지대의 열대 기후와 고지대의 더 서늘한 기온을 가진 과테말라는 바나나를 재배하기에 완벽한 장소이다. 스페인 정복 시대 이전에 과테말라는 마야 문화 지역 안에 있었다. 오늘날 세계에서 가장 유명한 마야의 고고학적 유적 중 일부가 이 나라의 북부에서 발견된다. 서기 9~10세기에 그 문명이 붕괴되었을 때도 그 민족은 사라지지 않았다. 대신에 그들은 전국에 산재되어 마을 안에 남아 있었다. 마야어를 사용하는 사람들은 여전히 그곳에, 주로 고지대에 살고 있으며, 그 인구의 약 40퍼센트에 상당한다. 나머지 인구의 대부분은 메스티조, 즉 유럽인과 토착인의 혼합된 유산을 가진 사람들이다.

구문 • Instead, they remained [in villages] scattered across the country.
→ scattered는 remained의 보어로 사용되었다. in villages가 동사와 보어 사이에 삽입되어 있는 구조이다.

ANSWER

01 ②	02 ④	03 ③	04 ①	05 ④
06 ②	07 ④	08 ③	09 ②	10 ③

01 ②

해설 (A) 주격 보어인 Closely related ~ characters가 문두로 옮겨지면서, 어순이 <주격 보어 + be동사 + 주어>가 되었다. 주어인 the question of ~ experience가 단수이므로 is가 사용되어야 한다.

(B) the types of emotions를 선행사로 하고 동사 generate의 목적어로 이해되기 위해서는 관계사 that이 필요하다.

(C) 술어 동사 calls가 이미 나와 있으므로 또 다른 술어 동사 implies를 쓸 수 없다. 문맥상 주절이 기술하는 상황에 부수적으로 이어지는 분사구문이 와야 하므로 이를 이끄는 implying이 적절하다.

해석 독자가 경험하는 감정의 본질이라는 문제는 소설의 등장인물에 관해 독자가 갖는 개념에 대한 논의와 밀접한 관련이 있다. 소설에 대한 유의미한 감정적 반응의 가능성을 감안하는 많은 철학자와 문학 연구가는 소설이 만들어 낼 수 있는 여러 유형의 감정의 본질에 대하여 단서를 달고 의구심을 표하면서 그렇게 한다. 사실 이것은 일부 이론가로 하여금 한편으로는 소설과 소설의 등장인물에 대한 독자의 반응과, 다른 한편으로는 실화와 실제 삶 속의 사람들에 대한 독자의 반응을 분명하게 구별하게 해 주었다. 미국의 철학자 Kendall Walton은 소설로 유도된 감정이 실제 삶에서의 우리의 경험과는 완전히 성격이 다르다는 것을 암시하며, 그것을 '유사 감정'이라고 부른다. 그렇지만 이 구분은 겉으로 보이게 되는 것보다 덜 분명하다.

어휘 debate 논의, 토론 conception 개념, 구상
fictional 소설의, 허구적인 literary 문학의, 문예의
scholar 연구가, 학자 allow for ~을 감안[참작]하다
qualification 단서, 제한, 자격 reservation 의구심, 예약
generate 만들어내다, 발생시키다 imply 암시하다, 의미하다

02 ④

해설 ④ '~ 또한 그러하다'는 의미의 so 뒤에서는 도치가 발생한다. 도치할 때 동사가 일반 동사이면 do동사를 대신 써서 도치해야 한다. 주어가 her son이고 동사가 일반 동사의 과거형인 loved이므로 did를 써야 한다. so did her son이 바르게 도치되었다. 또한 '그러하다'는 표현은 긍정문의 경우는 so를 쓰고 부정문에 대해 '또한 그러하다'를 의미할 때는 <neither + 동사 + 주어>의 표현을 사용한다.

① '~하기를 고대하다' <look forward to -ing>를 써야 한다. 이때 to는 전치사이므로 목적어로 동명사가 와야 하므로 receive를 receiving으로 고쳐야 한다.

② rise는 자동사이므로 목적어를 가질 수 없다. 뒤에 목적어 my salary가 있으므로 타동사인 raise로 고쳐야 한다.

③ '~할 만한 가치가 있다'는 의미의 <be worth -ing>를 써야 한다. 주어인 그의 계획이 고려되는 것으로 수동의 의미이지만 <worth -ing> 형태로 표현해도 수동의 의미를 가질 수 있으므로 수동형으로 쓰지 않는다. 따라서 worth considered을 worth considering으로 고쳐야 한다.

어휘 receive 받다

03 ③

해석 그 사건에 대한 그의 묘사는 경찰이 보고한 것과 일치한다.

어휘 consistent 일치하는, 상응하는(= coherent)
effective 효과적인 viable 실행 가능한 compatible 잘 어울리는
venomous 독이 있는

04 ①

해석 그는 너무 당황해서 그는 뭘 할 줄 몰랐다.

어휘 bewilder 당황하게 하다(= embarrass)
confuse 혼란스럽게 하다 amuse 즐겁게 하다

05 ④

해석 ① A: 이번 주에 저와 함께 저녁 하러 가시겠어요?
B: 좋습니다. 그런데 무슨 일 때문입니까?
② A: 언제 농구하러 가지 않을래?
B: 물론이지. 시간만 말해줘.
③ A: 여가 시간에 뭐 하세요?
B: 그냥 집에서 쉽니다. 가끔은 TV를 봅니다.
④ A: 제가 도와드릴 게 있나요?
B: 네, 저도 그러고 싶습니다. 그렇게 하면 좋을 것 같습니다.

06 ②

해설 농업의 지속 가능성을 위해 토양 비옥도를 무한히 유지하는 기술을 채택하는 것과, 땅을 갈아줌으로써 토양의 영구성을 해치게 되는 것은 서로 상반되는 진술이다. 따라서 빈칸에는 ② '정확히 정반대의 일을 한다'가 가장 적절하다.

① 이득이 되는 것으로 이어진다
③ 잡초와의 전쟁에서 항상 승리한다
④ 실용적인 대안을 시사한다

해석 쟁기는 농업 생산성의 신성한 상징일 수 있지만, 그것은 토양을 망가뜨리며, 우리가 오랫동안 알고 있었듯이, 기본적인 농업적 안녕을 위태롭게 한다. 1943년에 출간한 저서 'The Living Soil'에서 Lady Eve Balfour는 "오랫동안 지속 가능한 농업의 척도는 영구성이라는 한 단어로 요약될 수 있는데 이는 토양 비옥도를 무기한으로 유지하는 기술을 채택하는 것을 의미한다."라고 언명했다. 그러나 잡초를 관리하기 위해 땅을 가는 것은 정확히 정반대의 일을 한다. 그것은 토양을 메마르게 하고 만성적인 침식을 야기하며 그렇게 함으로써 토양을 비영구적으로 만든다. 바로 이 이유에서, 똑같이 1943년에 집필을 하면서, Edward Faulkner는 'Plowman's Folly'에서 "방해를 제외하고는 우리의 토양에는 아무 문제가 없다."라고 언급했다. 그의 책 제목이 시사하는 것처럼, Faulkner에게 방해는 쟁기를 의미했다.

어휘 plow 쟁기 sacred 신성한, 신성시되는

wreck 망가뜨리다, 파괴하다 compromise 위태롭게 하다
declare 언명하다, 분명히 말하다 criterion 척도, 기준
sustainable 오랫동안 지속 가능한 sum up 요약하다
permanence 영구성, 영속성 adopt 채택하다, 취하다
fertility 비옥(의 정도) indefinitely 무기한으로 chronic 만성적인
erosion 침식 interference 방해, 간섭

07 ④

해설 '예를 들어, 어느 소비자가 자신의 체중에 대한 의구심을 가지고 있어서 신사복을 입어보면서 그러한 우려를 표현할지도 모른다.'는 내용의 주어진 문장은 판매사원이 잠재 고객에게 중요하지만 확신이 없는 특성에 관해 아첨을 할 때에 고객이 호의적으로 반응할 것이라는 내용과 판매사원이 할 수 있는 구체적인 말을 제시한 문장들 사이인 ④에 들어가는 것이 가장 적절하다.

해석 아첨은 어떤 사람이 자신에 대해 기분 좋게 느끼도록 만들어 주려고 의도된 과도한 찬사나 칭찬을 포함한다. 아첨은 가식적일 필요는 없다. 사실은, 효과적인 아첨은 사람들이 자신의 능력이나 임무 수행에 대해 확신을 갖지 못하는 중요한 특성을 겨냥해야 한다. 예를 들어, 친구가 최근에 한 어느 중요한 연설에서 자신이 한 것에 대해 불안감을 표현한다면, "천천히 그리고 또박또박 말해 주어서 고마워."와 같은 진심어린 말은 환심을 사려는 사람에게 호의를 얻게 해줄 가능성이 있다. 비슷하게, 판매사원이 잠재 고객에게 중요하지만 확신이 없는 특성에 관해 아첨을 할 때, 고객은 호의적으로 반응할 것이다. 예를 들어, 어느 소비자가 자신의 체중에 대한 의구심을 가지고 있어서 신사복을 입어보면서 그러한 우려를 표현할지도 모른다. 똑똑한 판매사원은 그가 '그의 연령대에 있는 대부분의 남자들보다 몸 상태가 더 좋다'고 언급함으로써 그 고객에게 아첨할 수 있다.

어휘 reservation 의구심, 거리낌 excessive 과도한, 지나친
compliment 찬사 insincere 가식적인, 진실하지 못한
attribute 특성, 속성 anxiety 불안감, 염려 deliver (연설 등을) 하다
earnest 진심어린, 성실한

08 ③

해설 (A) 멘토는 자신이 교육하는 분야에서 경험과 지식을 갖춘 사람이라는 내용이 나오고, 빈칸 (A)를 포함한 문장의 내용이 그러한 경험이 바탕이 되는 예를 들고 있으므로 For instance가 적절하다.
(B) 멘토가 학생에게 제공할 수 있는 혜택에 대한 내용이 앞에 나오고, 빈칸 (B)를 포함한 문장이 그러한 혜택의 추가적인 정보를 제공하므로 Moreover가 적절하다.

해석 멘토는 자신들이 교육하는 분야에서 아주 큰 경험의 폭과 깊이를 가진 사람들이다. 멘토는 자신들이 가르침을 주어야 하는 과목에서 경험과 전문적 교육을 모두 받아왔다. 예를 들어 지도력 멘토는 지도자로서 적합한 경험을 갖추어야 하고 그들 자신도 지도력 교육을 이수했을 것이다. 멘토는 학생에게 정규 교육 시간이 제공하지 못하는 무엇을 제공할까? 우선 멘토는 자신의 학생을 위해 개인적인 경험을 교과로 사용할 수 있다. 더욱이 멘토는 그 분야에서 자신들의 풍부한 지식과 경험 덕택에 변화무쌍한 문제들을 해결하는 능력이 있다. 교육 프로그램으로는 학생이 도저히 예상치 못한 도전에 직면하도록 준비시킬 수 없다. 멘토는 학생의 성격과 멘티가 직면하는 다양한 수준의 복잡성에 따라 자신들의 교육을 다양화할 수 있다.

어휘 mentor 멘토(경험이 없는 사람에게 조언과 도움을 베풀어 주는 유경험자)
vast 막대한 breadth 폭, 너비 adequate 적절한 undergo 겪다
formal 정규적인, 공식적인 resolve 해결하다
dynamic 변화무쌍한, 역동적인 abundant 풍부한
unexpected 예상치 못한 complexity 복잡성
mentee 멘티(멘토에게서 상담이나 조언을 받는 사람)

09 ②

해설 이 글은 가리키는 몸짓이 언어 학습에 어떻게 기여하는가를 설명하고 있다. 내면에 있는 대상에 대해 의사소통할 때에는 그것을 지칭하기 위한 도구가 필요하다는 내용의 주어진 글 다음에 언어가 그런 역할을 하며 가리키는 몸짓이 이에 도움을 준다는 내용의 (B)가 이어지고, 이런 비유적 주장에서 더 나아가 어떤 대상을 가리키는 몸짓이 언어 학습을 위한 기틀을 형성한다고 주장하는 (C)가 이어지며, 마지막으로 이에 대한 예로 부재하는 아빠에 대해 말하기 위해 아빠가 앉았던 의자를 가리키는 아이의 예시를 다루는 (A)로 이어지는 흐름이 자연스럽다. 따라서 글의 순서로 ② (B) - (C) - (A)가 가장 적절하다.

해석 대화를 하는 사람들이 외부 세계에 대해 의사소통할 때, (손으로) 가리키는 것은 지시 대상에서 사람들의 생각이 (서로) 만나게 하기에 충분하다. 하지만 그들이 그들의 내면세계에 있는 지시 대상을 공유할 필요가 있을 때에는 다른 도구가 필요하다. (B) 어느 면에서 언어는 우리의 내면세계에 있는 장소들을 '가리킴'으로써 공동의 주의 집중에 이르게 하는 도구이다. 이 방법은 가리킴, 다른 형태의 몸짓, 그리고 감정 표현으로 달성된다. (C) Susan Goldin-Meadow는 이런 비유적 주장을 넘어서서, 아이들에게 '가리키는 몸짓은 언어적인 의사소통이 기초하는 기반을 형성하며, 따라서 이후의 언어 학습을 위한 기틀을 마련한다.'라고 쓰고 있다. 예를 들어, 12개월 정도 된 언어를 사용하기 전의 아이들은 때때로 부재하는 대상이 최근에 있었거나 보통 위치하는 장소를 가리켜서 그것을 환유적으로 지칭한다. (A) 예를 들어, 유아는 부재하는 아빠를 가리키는 표현으로 아빠의 의자를 가리킬 수 있다. 이런 유형의 지시는 가리킴을 일시적인 의미를 지닌 초기 단계의 지시사로 이용하는 것으로부터, 가리킴을 더 영구적인 의미로 상징적으로 사용하는 것으로의 이행으로 볼 수 있다.

10 ③

해석 수영 강사를 찾습니다
Little Swimmers Program에서 지금 수영 강사를 찾고 있습니다.
- 8~10세의 아이들을 대상으로 하는 여름 방학 수영 프로그램입니다.
- 8월 1일에 시작하는 4주간의 프로그램입니다.
자격 요건
- 나이가 20세가 넘어야 함
- 전에 아이들을 가르친 경험
- 인명 구조원과 응급 처치 자격증
지원자는 지원서 양식을 웹 사이트 www.littleswimmersclub.com에서 내려 받아야 합니다. 지원서를 완성한 후에 그것을 이메일로 lsp@me.com에 늦어도 7월 15일까지 제출하십시오. 추가 문의사항은 123-456-7890으로 연락하시거나 저희 웹 사이트를 방문해 주십시오.
① 프로그램은 8월 1일부터 5주간 계속된다.
② 지원자의 나이 제한이 없다.
③ 지원자는 어린이를 가르친 경험이 있어야 한다.
④ 이메일로 지원서를 제출할 수 없다.

어휘 certification 증명, 증명서 applicant 지원자
submit 제출하다 no later than 늦어도 ~까지는 inquiry 문의, 질문

제 25 회 하프 모의고사 해설

문제편 p.101

ANSWER

01 ②	02 ④	03 ④	04 ①	05 ④
06 ②	07 ③	08 ②	09 ②	10 ③

01 ②

해설 ② 본문의 what절(what he has to shoot)은 상위절에서 어떠한 역할도 하지 못한다. 따라서 문맥상 the situation을 선행사로 취하고 관계절에서 in the situation의 의미로 이해되는 where나 in which로 바꿔야 한다.

① 전치사 in의 목적어 역할과 moral wisdom을 목적어로 취하는 동사의 역할을 동시에 할 수 있는 것은 동명사이므로 describing의 쓰임은 적절하다.

③ such는 <such+ a(n) + 단수 명사> 또는 <such + 복수 명사> 형태로 쓰이며 '그러한'이라는 의미를 가지므로 적절하다.

④ 문맥상 a target을 수식하는 to부정사구가 필요하므로 to aim은 적절하다.

해석 그리스의 철학자인 아리스토텔레스는 도덕적 지혜를 설명할 때 궁수를 자신이 가장 좋아하는 예로 든다. 우선 과녁이 무엇인지를 알고 다음으로 쏴야 하는 상황을 결정하는 모든 환경(수단)을 안다면 궁수는 자신이 해야 할 일을 이해하고 있는 것이다. 그는 바람의 세기와 방향, 화살의 특징과 활의 장력을 잿다. 아리스토텔레스는 지혜로운 사람을 그러한 궁수, 즉 과녁(목표)과 그 목표에 도달하기 위한 수단(경로)에 관한 지식을 가진 사람으로 본다. 궁수는 자신에게 겨냥할 과녁이 있다면 (과녁을) 제대로 맞힐 가능성이 더 높다. 아리스토텔레스는 뛰어나게 하려고 노력하는 것이 중요하지만, 목표에 관한 지식은 그 목표를 달성하고자 하는 노력(작인(作因))이 있어야만 유용하다고 말했다.

어휘 cite (예로) 들다 comprehend 이해하다
circumstance 환경 means 수단 determine 결정하다
assess 재다, 평가하다 direction 방향 characteristic 특징
tension 장력, 팽팽함 pathway 경로
strive for ~을 얻으려고 노력하다 excellence 탁월함
attain 달성하다 agency 작인(作因), 발생의 원인

02 ④

해설 ④ Under no circumstances는 '어떤 상황에서도 ~ 아닌'을 의미하는 부정의 구로서, 강조를 위해 문장의 앞에 위치하면 뒤의 주어와 동사는 도치되어 <동사 + 주어>의 어순을 취한다. 또한 중복된 부정부사인 not을 제거해야 한다. 따라서 'should you leave ~'라고 써야 한다.

① 타동사 regret은 뒤에 동명사 목적어를 취하면 '~한 것을 후회하다'라는 의미로 사용된다. regrets라는 동사가 현재이므로 젊었을 때 열심히 일하지 않았던 과거 사건에 대한 후회를 의미하는 동명사의 완료형 having worked가 올바르게 사용되었다.

② 전치사구인 of ~ 이하가 앞선 명사인 a man을 수식하는 명사 수식의 용법인 형용사적 용법으로 바르게 사용되었다.

③ '건강한'을 의미하는 형용사 healthy가 올바르게 사용되었고 두 개의 형용사가 접속사 and를 통으로 수식하고 있다.

03 ④

해석 그는 전쟁에서 두드러진 용맹성에 대해 십자훈장을 수여받았다.

어휘 conspicuous 두드러진, 현저한(= outstanding) terse 간략한
rational 이성적인 abortive 실패의 noticeable 눈에 띄는

04 ①

해석 그 전문가는 자신의 편견을 알지 못할지 모른다.

어휘 bias 사선, 편견 prejudice 편견 hobby 취미
jeopardy 위험 inability 무능

05 ④

해설 어떻게 계산할거냐는 질문에 자신이 돈을 내서 기쁘다고 하고 있다.

해석 ① M: 초코칩 쿠키 만드는 법을 알려주시겠어요?
W: 그래, 하지만 꽤 복잡해.

② M: 당신은 공포 영화를 좋아하지 않습니까?
W: 그렇지 않아요. 나는 액션 영화를 더 좋아합니다.

③ M: 오늘 언젠가 우리가 이야기를 할 수 있을 것 같습니까?
W: 그러고 싶지만 오늘 일정이 꽤 빡빡해.

④ M: 이것을 어떻게 지불하시겠습니까?
W: 비용을 지불하게 되어 정말 기쁩니다.

06 ②

해설 연못 거북이가 바다를 경험하지 못했기 때문에 바다의 장엄함을 이해하지 못할 거라는 비유를 통해 감정을 경험하지 못하는 것은 그것을 경험하는 것과 큰 차이가 있다는 것을 말하는 글이다. 그러므로 빈칸에 들어갈 말로 가장 적절한 것은 ② '거기에 도달한 후에야 알 수 있다(경험한 후에야 알 수 있다)'이다.

① 우리의 진짜 감정을 숨기는 경향이 있다.

③ 흔히 중요한 행사를 놓친다.

④ 다른 사람들 사이에서 두드러지는 것을 좋아한다.

해석 우리 중 일부는 우리가 무엇을 놓치고 있는지 알지 못한다. 자신의 감정에 접근하지 못하며, 그것이 어떤 느낌인지 또는 어떤 좋은 것이 그것의 결과로 나올 수 있는지 상상할 수 없다. 우리의 감정을 인정하는 것과 그것을 누릴 수 있는 우리의 능력을 차단하는 것 간의 차이는 아이가 4살 때 아는 것과 아이가 17살에 이해하는 것, 또는 데이트하는 것과 사랑에 빠지는 것 간의 차이만큼이나 클 수 있다. 우리는 거기에 도달한 후에야 알 수 있다(경험한 후에야 알 수 있다). 두 마리의 거북이, 즉 연못에서 온 거북이 한 마리와 바다에서 온 거북이 한 마리가 이야기를 나누고 있다고 생각해보라. 연못 거북이는 자신의 연못 환경이 좁기 때문에 바다의 장엄함을 이해할 수 없다. 바다 거북이는 연못 거북이가 직접 봐야지만 진정으로 이해할 거라는 것을 알기 때문에 자신과 함께 바다로 가자고 연못 거북이를 초대한다.

어휘 have access to ~에 접근할 수 있다 come of ~의 결과이다
comprehend 이해하다 magnificence 장엄함, 광대함
limited (공간이) 좁은

07 ③

해설 '그에 반해서 독일인들은 훨씬 더 길고 고단한 항해를 했다.'는 내용의 주어진 문장은 영국인에 관한 내용에서 독일인에 관한 내용으로 넘어가는 위치인 ③에 들어가는 것이 가장 적절하다.

해석 아메리카에 정착한 영국인들과 독일인들은 둘 다 영양 관련 질병을 앓았다. 그럼에도 불구하고 후자가 훨씬 더 높은 사망률을 경험했다. 두 집단이 먹은 음식은 비슷했으나, 영국인들이 더 좋은 건강 상태로 도착했다. 대서양을 가로지르는 그들의 여정이 더 짧았으며, 배 위에서 그들은 만족스러운 음식을 제공받았다. 영양 관련 질병의 증상이 나타날 무렵에 최초의 농작물이 수확되고 있어서, 영국 정착민들 사이에서 심각한 (질병의) 발생을 막아주었다. 그에 반해서 독일인들은 훨씬 더 길고 고단한 항해를 했다. 그들의 음식은 적절하지 못했으며, 배 위에서의 상황이 결코 만족스럽지 못했던 것으로 밝혀졌다. 도착 당시에 더 문제가 많았던 그들의 건강 상태를 고려해 볼 때, 영양 관련 질병의 특징적 증상이 비교적 일찍 나타난 것은 놀라운 일이 아니다. 짧은 기간 내에 47명의 원래의 정착민들 중 18명이 영양 관련 질병이나 2차 감염으로 사망했다.

어휘 tiring 고단한, 피곤한　voyage 항해, 여행
nutritional 영양상의　the latter 후자　mortality rate 사망률
harvest 수확하다　inhibit 막다, 억제하다　outbreak (질병 등의) 발생
span 기간, 시간　secondary infection 2차 감염

08 ②

해설 (A) 아이가 여러 명 있는 경우에 많은 부분이 부모의 주의를 벗어날 수 있다는 단점이 언급되고 난 후에 약간의 불이행이 일어나기 마련이라는 단점이 언급되고 있으므로, 빈칸에는 In addition이 적절하다.
(B) 아이들에게 빈틈없이 계속 관심을 가질 수 없다는 여러 명의 아이를 둔 부모의 단점을 언급하고 나서, 외동아이의 입장에서는 부모의 관심이 집중되는 것에 대해 부담스러워할 수 있다는 내용을 언급하면서 대조하고 있으므로, 빈칸에는 however가 적절하다.

해석 외동아이를 둔 부모의 커다란 장점 중 하나는 부모들이 세부적인 것을 감독하는 것이다. 여러 명의 아이들이 있으면 많은 부분이 부모의 주의를 벗어날 수 있다. 게다가 부모의 어떤 결심은 일관성 있게 적용되지는 못하고, 어떤 좋은 의도는 완전히 이루어지지는 못하며, 어떤 요구는 일률적으로 시행되지는 못하는데, 아주 많은 아이들을 감당하다 보면 약간의 불이행은 일어나기 마련이기 때문이다. 부모가 아이 한 명에게 할 수 있는 것만큼 빈틈없이 아이 세 명에게 계속 관심을 가질 수는 없다. 그러나 흐트러지지 않은 부모의 관심이 집중되면 외동아이는 항상 현미경 아래에 놓여 있다고 느끼고 때로는 가족 내에 부모의 관심을 다른 곳으로 돌려 줄 또 다른 아이가 있었으면 하고 바랄 수 있다. "일부 외동아이들은 관심의 집중을 거의 감당할 수 없다고 생각한다."

어휘 of detail 세심한, 상세한　multiple 다수의, 많은
parental 부모의　notice 주의, 주목　resolve 결심, 결의
consistently 일관성 있게　apply 적용하다, 응용하다
intention 의도, 목적　carry through ~을 달성하다, ~을 완수하다
requirement 요구(물), 필수요건　uniformly 일률적으로
enforce 시행하다, 실시하다
be bound to ~하기 마련이다, 반드시 ~하다
keep up with ~에게 계속 관심을 가지다
undistracted 흐트러지지 않은　constantly 일관성 있게
microscope 현미경　overwhelming 저항[대응]하기 힘든, 압도적인

09 ②

해설 주어진 글에서 지구의 자전축이 23.5도 기울어져 있다고 언급하고 (B)에서 지구의 극이 기울어진 채 태양을 돈다고 이어가고 있다. (C)에서의 These two physical changes는 (B)에서의 태양 직사광 및 낮의 길이 증가를 의미한다. (A)에서의 this burst of plant and insect life는 (C)에서의 식물 및 무척추동물의 급성장을 의미한다. 그러므로 주어진 글 다음 에 이어질 글의 순서로 ② (B) - (C) - (A)가 가장 적절하다.

해석 새들의 봄철 이주는 근본적으로 태양을 도는 지구 궤도의 물리적 특성이 원인이다. 지구의 자전축이 태양을 도는 지구의 연간 궤도와 관련하여 수직으로부터 23.5도 떨어져 기울어져 있기 때문에 봄이 생긴다.
(B) 지구가 태양을 원을 그리며 돌 때, 지구의 극은 기울어진 채 점점 태양 쪽으로 향했다가 그러고 나서 태양으로부터 멀어진다. 지구가 지구 북반구의 동지점에서 춘분점으로 이동할 때, 더 많은 태양 직사광이 북반구의 지표면에 내리쬐고 낮의 길이가 증가한다.
(C) 지구에서 우리의 북부 온대 지역에 생긴 이 두 가지 물리적 변화로 인해 봄의 진행이 일어난다. 낮의 연장과 하루 태양 복사열의 증가는 식물 및 식물을 먹고 사는 무척추동물의 급성장을 촉진한다.
(A) 태양이 계절에 따라 북쪽으로 이동할 때, 식물과 곤충의 이런 폭발적 증가를 따라가려고 새들이 북쪽으로 이주한다. 철새들은 계절적으로 가장 풍요로운 시점에 자신의 번식 서식지에 도착하기 위해 자신의 이동 시기를 맞춘다.

10 ③

해설 Žižek은 슬로베니아로 돌아와서 대학에서 일자리를 잡지 못해 몇 년간 병역을 이행했고 그 후 실업자가 되었다고 했으므로, ③이 글의 내용과 일치하지 않는다.

해석 Slavoj Žižek은 (당시는 공산국가 유고슬로비아의 일부분이었던) 슬로베니아의 Ljubljana에서 1949년에 태어났다. 그의 아버지는 경제 관료였고, 어머니는 국유 기업의 회계사였다. 그는 정신분석학을 공부하러 파리에 가기 전에 Ljubljana 대학교에서 철학 박사 학위를 받았다. 슬로베니아에 돌아와서 Žižek은 대학교에서 일자리를 잡을 수가 없었고, 병역을 이행하는 데 몇 해를 보냈으며, 그 다음에는 실업자였다. 1970년대 후반에 그는 정신분석학자 Jacques Lacan의 작업에 초점이 맞춰진 슬로베니아 지식인 집단의 일원이 되었고, 1980년대에는 Freud, Lacan, 그리고 Althusser의 글을 슬로베니아어로 번역했다. 1980년대 후반에 그는 영화 이론에 관한 책을 출간했고, 대안 잡지인 'Mladina'에 글을 썼으며, 유고슬라비아의 민주주의를 계속적으로 요구하는 활동가였다. 슬로베니아가 1990년에 독립을 했을 때, 그는 성공하지 못한 대통령 후보가 되었다.

구문 • Back in Slovenia, Žižek [was unable to get a university position], [spent several years in national service], and [was then unemployed].
→ 세 개의 [ ]는 and에 의해 연결되어 병렬 구조를 이루고 있다.
• In the late 1970s he was part of a group of Slovenian intellectuals [focused on the work of psychoanalytical philosopher Jacques Lacan], and ~.
→ [ ]는 과거분사구로 a group of Slovenian intellectuals를 수식한다.

MEMO

박노준
PATTERN
영 어